Popular Culture

Popular Culture in Ancient Rome

Jerry Toner

polity

First published in 2009 by Polity Press

Polity Press
65 Bridge Street
Cambridge CB2 1UR, UK

Polity Press
350 Main Street
Malden, MA 02148, USA

ISBN-13: 978-0-7456-4309-0
ISBN-13: 978-0-7456-4310-6(pb)

A catalogue record for this book is available from the British Library.

Typeset in 10.5 on 12 pt Times
by SNP Best-set Typesetter Ltd., Hong Kong
Printed and bound in Great Britain by MPG Books Ltd, Bodmin, Cornwall

For further information on Polity, visit our website: www.politybooks.com

Contents

Illustrations

Acknowledgements

I want to thank a number of people, without whom this book would never have been written: Justin Meggitt and Peter Garnsey for all their help, support and intellectual input over many years; Melanie Wright and Chris Kelly for all their advice and encouragement; and Emma Widdis and Anne Henry, who introduced me to, and taught me much about, the area of sensory history. I also want to thank Jon Gifford, Jason Goddard, Chris Hartley, Peter Harvey and Miranda Perry, who all helped keep me sane while I was carrying out my research. I owe a special debt of gratitude to the President and Fellows of Hughes Hall, Cambridge, for their generous award of a Research Fellowship, which allowed me to carry out my work in such a pleasant and stimulating environment. I also want to thank the staff of the Cambridge University Library and Classics Faculty, who have always been exceptionally helpful. The team at Polity did their usual excellent job in producing the book and my thanks go to Andrea Drugan in particular. The anonymous readers for Polity provided many astute comments and helpful criticisms, for which I am very grateful.

My mother worked for many years in Cambridge as a college servant, as they were known in those days, to support her three children and disabled husband. Watching her showed me how hard it can be for ordinary people to make ends meet and deal with a socially distant and sometimes difficult elite (thankfully the Governing Body of her college did not possess the powers of the Roman judiciary). Thankfully also she believed in education, which allowed me to 'move upstairs' and indulge in the luxury of Roman history. This book is dedicated to her in gratitude for that.

Introduction: Elite and Popular Cultures

This is a book about popular culture in the Roman world. Popular culture is probably best defined in a negative way as the culture of the non-elite.[1] The non-elite (I shall also call them simply 'the people') comprised a whole host of different social groups – peasants, craftsmen and artisans, labourers, healers, fortune-tellers, storytellers and entertainers, shopkeepers and traders – but also consisted of their women, their children, and the have-nots of Roman society: slaves and those who had fallen into destitution and beggary. The culture these groups shared was very much the unofficial and subordinate culture of Roman society.

In total, we are talking about tens of millions of people inhabiting a region stretching from the damp lowlands of Scotland to the baking-hot banks of the river Nile. Dozens of local languages, most of which we have little or no trace of, jostled alongside the official Latin and Greek. It will never be possible to re-create the richness of each of these local cultures. We are also looking at a period spanning hundreds of years, from roughly 100 BCE to 500 CE. The evidence is so scanty that we cannot examine the popular culture of any one point in time. Regrettable though this is, it need not present an insurmountable obstacle. The argument of this book is that the popular culture can best be understood as a whole. Popular culture represented a set of attitudes, which in many ways can be seen as responses to the broadly similar social, economic and environmental conditions that the majority of the population of the Roman Empire faced throughout its history. I will be trying to look at the themes that characterized and dominated the lives of these largely voiceless people.

The non-elite were too great a hotchpotch of differing groups to be united by a single, monolithic culture. They inhabited a complex world of different geographies, wealth and status levels that meant that no uniform way of life could ever exist. One of the main internal divisions was between slaves and the free. Most Roman citizens saw themselves as anything but servile. But the poorest of the free could easily find themselves in a far worse material condition than most of the slave population. An increasing number of them drew their ancestry from the slave body. That might explain their vigorous protests against the execution in 61 CE of Pedanius Secundus's entire household of 400 slaves, after his murder by one of them.[2] The fervent desire for freedom that we encounter among many slaves argues for a shared outlook with the free. Both free and slave valued the same privileges. They took their pleasures in the same boisterous way. They faced the same social pressures, albeit in varying degrees. Both had to cope with a system of hierarchy that placed them at the whim of the powerful, even more so as the value of citizenship declined under the empire. The people had their own marginals too: beggars, bandits, the mad. There was never just a simple division between free and slave.

The non-elite were not unified by class interests: few if any elements of class consciousness can be sensed in the surviving record. Most of them saw their neighbours as competitors not comrades in the harsh struggle for scarce resources. To have nothing was to be nothing in the Roman world. Theirs was a culture where people strove to look down on their neighbours with something of the same disdain that the elite looked down on them. For the most part, these were people who were far too busy getting on in the world, or just striving to maintain what little they had, than to worry about whether anything fundamental was wrong with the system itself.

Not a class but a culture none the less. A mosaic of popular subcultures united by broadly similar interests, facing the same day-to-day problems of making a living, and equipped with the same tried-and-tested ways of trying to get things done in a tough, hierarchical world run by the elite for the elite. Popular culture was far more than a collection of circus entertainers and half-remembered songs from the theatre.[3] Popular culture was how people survived.

The non-elite comprised about 99 per cent of the empire's population of about 50 or 60 million. The elite consisted of the senators, the equestrian class and the local governing class. The elite numbered perhaps 200,000. The army numbered another half a million or so. The status of the army is a moot point given that they represented a group with a strong subculture of its own and, for reasons of space, I have largely omitted them from the discussion.[4] Of the non-elite about 80–85 per cent lived in the country, mostly eking a living from the land either as small-holders, tenants or labourers, or indirectly as slaves. Of the 15 per cent of the total population who comprised the urban non-elite, about 30–40 per cent represented Hoggart's 'respectable' sorts – tradesmen, craftsmen and the like. And 50–60 per cent worked as labourers.[5] Rome was one of history's great slave-owning societies and slaves accounted for about 10–15 per cent of the total non-elite population, but perhaps 15–25 per cent in Italy, and are double-counted since they worked mostly as labourers or for craftsmen. A substantial portion of the population, which will have varied hugely depending on local factors, lived at little more than subsistence levels of income. About a tenth of the population were destitute, scraping by on begging and thieving, but this represented only a base figure, which could balloon in periods of economic crisis to as much as two-thirds of the population.[6]

The elite for the most part set themselves sharply apart from this mass of Roman society. A huge wealth gap served to distance them from the majority. The richest of the rich possessed fortunes exceeding 100 million sesterces, which can be expressed as about 25,000 times an annual subsistence income (though this is actually a lower ratio than exists today). More importantly, the elite felt themselves bound together by a common upper-class culture of learning (*paideia*).[7] This educated, literary outlook represented the shared world-view of the ruling class. Recondite, academic and stylistic, *paideia* served as a hard-won badge of class membership. It excluded the majority by relying on what it saw as taste and discernment, but also on what can be seen as deliberate obfuscation. So, in the court of the later emperors in Constantinople, a mode of handwriting was developed known as *litterae caelestes*, 'heavenly writing', which was the preserve of palace administrators.[8] Similarly, the legal profession developed a sophisticated jargon. All of this must have been complete gobbledygook to the non-elite. They were expected to look on in awe at elite culture: 'whatever is highly placed must be prevented from becoming low and common in order to preserve due reverence'.[9]

It is this element of social conflict that makes it dangerous to think about the non-elite in terms of having a folk culture. 'Folk' suggests a common culture that all members of Roman society shared equally, regardless of social position. It tends to ignore issues of politics, ideology and conflict so as to emphasize the communal. There is no doubt that there was much culture that the elite and the non-elite did hold in common. The risk is that 'the folk' become the harmless characters from an H. E. Bates novel, sitting in their farmyards drinking mead and discussing olive oil; and folklore comes to represent a romanticized, rosy view of Roman life, with the non-elite content to be under the wise rule of their betters. Roman society cannot simply be seen as a culture characterized by social consensus. This is to deny its conflictual elements. The vast and widening gaps in wealth that the acquisition of empire had created meant that social contrasts were stark. There was little direct, personal contact between the elite and most of the populace, particularly in the city of Rome where its colossal size meant that traditional face-to-face social mechanics had broken down. Most of the non-elite, as a simple matter of arithmetic, were not hooked into the network of patrons and clients. The city's population was full of slaves, perhaps as many as a third, who cannot safely be assumed to have been happy with their lot.[10] Herodian blames the melting-pot of Rome, which had resulted from mass immigration, for the intensity of urban violence.[11] Outside Rome, we know that some at least of the oppressed passionately resented their imperial oppressors. Everywhere, the people lived in a power structure that dealt out a steady stream of degrading treatment. Such humiliation was never humdrum. It hurt.

All of these people confronted a daily reality of a steeply stratified society in which power was concentrated firmly at the top. Discussions about the exact meanings of Latin terms such as *populus, plebs, turba, multitudo* or *vulgus* are in danger of missing the point. It is hardly surprising that the elite failed to express themselves more clearly when talking about the the non-elite because, to put it crudely, they didn't give a damn about them. So, to be clear, this is not a book about the narrow role or otherwise of the Roman plebs in the world of largely elite Roman politics, an approach which risks implying that the people only mattered to the extent that they existed as an adjunct to power. Rome was a complex society and as such requires a more complex model of social relations. That is why the modern term 'popular culture' is so useful: the term recognizes the plurality of Roman culture and the difference, division and contestation between the non-elite and the elite. Real differences existed between many of their values, beliefs and behaviours. The non-elite represented a variety of social groups distinguished from society's economically, politically and culturally powerful groups. Potentially, these groups could be united and so represented a potent threat to the elite, one that needed to be carefully observed, policed and, where possible, reformed.

We must not fall into the trap of being melodramatic here. The flip side of seeing the people as members of a folk culture is to reduce them to the status of mere victims, romanticizing their suffering in the process. It is easy to exaggerate the overall level of poverty when judged against the standards of the time (the people were undoubtedly all poor in comparison to modern, Western standards of living). Nor was this a crude class struggle between elite and subordinate. The popular culture definitely did include elements of resistance against the dominant groups in society, but even then much of this took the form of minor skirmishes along the borders of class relations; more friction than warfare. There were also obviously significant 'grey areas' along the division between the popular and elite cultures. Social mobility did allow some lucky few to break through the glass ceiling of servile, plebeian or provincial status into the upper echelons of Roman society, even though the elite do 'have a way of looking the same over the centuries'.[12] This book does not, though, concentrate on these areas of overlap. Obviously there are many points where I will discuss the differences or otherwise between the popular and elite cultures, but to make that the primary focus of the book would be to make the mistake of seeing the non-elite as of interest only in terms of the way that they related to the elite. This is an attempt to describe and analyse the popular culture on its own terms, on a stand-alone basis. This is, after all, how elite culture has traditionally been viewed: as something as worthy of study in its own right and not simply as an adjunct to the popular culture.

Great and little traditions coexisted. The great tradition – classical learning, knowledge of Greek, philosophy, rhetoric – contrasted sharply with the little tradition: folk tales, proverbs, festivals, songs and oracles. The great tradition sometimes participated in the little, in for example sermons or speeches given at meetings before the plebs in Rome. The elite sometimes joined in the fun at festivals, and they gambled, and quoted well-known proverbs. But the great tradition was harder for the people to penetrate, requiring as it did years of rigorous learning and large amounts of cash. Harder but not impossible. One of the themes of this book is that the two traditions were interdependent and frequently affected each other. Cultural influence flowed both ways and served to create new traditions. It did not just trickle down from above to a people below who were grateful for the opportunity to have something to imitate.

Nor were the people simply passive consumers of Roman culture, in the 'bread and circuses' style. It suited the elite to think of the people as apathetically apolitical because it helped justify their own tight grip on the exercise of power. Instead, the people actively interpreted the cultural images that the ruling elite put before them. In some cases they took them at face value. In some cases they sought to reinterpret these symbols in a way that clearly aped the elite way of doing things but for a non-elite purpose, as in the organization of their associations. In others, such as apocalyptic literature, they actively subverted them to create a message that entirely contradicted the original meaning and purpose. The non-elite cannot simply be seen as receptacles for the values that their social betters deigned to send their way. Popular culture was more creative than that. People were always able to adopt, adapt and reject as they saw fit.

The non-elite frequently bore the charge of being indiscriminate and gullible. Popular religious ideas in particular earned the pejorative label of being mere superstitions, foisted on a credulous public by a mercenary and cynical class of diviners, oracle interpreters and magicians. This does too little justice to the active use to which people put these religious ideas so as to understand, influence and control their social environment. Similarly, elite condemnation of the crowd in the games focused on their seemingly mindless and wanton obsession with trivial horse races and gladiatorial combats. In fact, the games were a place where the non-elite took an active role in consuming the images that elite benefactors placed before them. The detailed expertise that many of the crowd exhibited acted both to establish social identities and as a training in the key life skills that a member of the non-elite needed to survive and thrive in Roman society.

In an article on using less conventional sources for gleaning evidence concerning daily life in the Roman world, Millar rightly notes that 'in a perfectly literal sense', ancient historians 'do not know what we are talking about'.[13] The problems of discovering lay attitudes from elite sources can seem to be insurmountable. No ready made body of source material exists. Evidence is fragmentary, with the sources sometimes obscure and usually far from comprehensive. I make use of elite literary texts, popular texts such as oracles and joke books, papyri, graffiti, magical spells and curses, as well as inscriptions, law codes and archaeological artefacts.[14] Precision is impossible in this situation and may in any case be inappropriate for a subject area that requires a high level of generalization. Most of these generalizations will be subject to major exceptions given that we are dealing with evidence drawn from very different times and places. It definitely involves some speculation if only to put forward the most likely and plausible solutions. Overall the argument proceeds by piling up fragments that give a reasonable impression of what it was like to be one of the people in Rome. Nor can a book of this size hope to be comprehensive – I have, as already mentioned, omitted the army, but also do not cover the status of lower class women's culture adequately, nor do I enter into the dense debate concerning the degree of non-elite literacy, which in any case risks seeing the people as mattering only to the extent that they could participate in elite culture. I have focused on specific areas of religious practice, such as oracles, festivals and exorcism, where I believe these to be critical to understanding the popular culture, but there were many other rites, such as household worship, mystery cults and disposal of the dead, which do not receive the coverage they deserve. The regions are under-represented, with Rome, as usual, hogging the limelight. I am also guilty of using the term 'elite' somewhat indiscriminately to cover all the wealthy and powerful in Roman society. In reality, of course, elite culture was every bit as diverse as I am arguing the non-elite culture to have been. Elite literature cannot therefore be read simply as an unmediated presentation of elite attitudes. But in the context of a book about the people, the term 'elite' will have to do as a historical generalization to stop the argument from grinding to a halt in a quagmire of qualifications.

Roman popular culture changed. Rome was a society in constant, albeit steady, transition and non-elite culture changed with it. It is very easy to slip into a view that sees popular life as an unchanging cycle of recurrent life events, a permanent now of seasons and festivals. This is an exaggeration. The creation of a large empire, the growth of a huge capital city to match, and the changes in the leadership structure of Roman society all gave great impetus to the popular culture to adapt itself to these unsettling new realities. In the later empire, new popular heroes and religious movements testified to the continued dynamism and ingenuity that characterized the non-elite's attempts to protect their interests and get something out of the system. Maintaining access to some form of power through patronage, whether secular or spiritual, and having to adapt when social realities changed: the people were no different to the elite in that respect.

The first chapter concentrates on the ways in which the non-elite dealt with the significant array of problems that beset their lives. If the elite had their *paideia*, the people had communal experience found in such things as fables and proverbs: a knowledge and practical wisdom won from the daily battles they engaged in to survive. In the eyes of the elite this was knowledge that was simply not worth having; the people were ignorant of everything that really mattered. But this archive of collective wit and repertoire of communal action mattered in the popular world. The people shared a range of tactics that enabled them better to cope with living with Roman inequality. One element of this was the active management of social superiors, not so much wealth-management but management of the wealthy. Another was that the non-elite had a strong sense of social justice that operated as, in Thompson's famous phrase, a 'moral economy' to ensure that the elite fulfilled their social obligations to the people. The popular world was one full of physical insecurity, with both physiological and psychological distress. Fear was pervasive, both real (wild animals, illness, thieves, bandits, authorities) and imagined (demons, premonitory dreams, portents). The people acquired by themselves a set of creative, if sometimes contradictory, means to stay alive in this threatening, risky environment. Mutually exclusive practices coexisted within the non-elite view, but such occasional contradictions served to help the people adapt to changing circumstances. They supplied a range of options on which to draw according to the requirements of the particular situation.

In case the popular culture should appear as calmly rational, I move on to examine the mental health of the non-elite. A huge amount of profitable work, pioneered by Garnsey, has been done on the level of physical health that the Romans had.[15] Here I look at what degree of mental health we can reasonably expect to have existed given what we know about the various kinds of social stressors that most people faced. Hierarchy and violence cause human beings high levels of stress and stress-related disorders, and both factors were in plentiful supply in Roman society. Mental health should not be confused with madness. Rather mental health represents a spectrum, ranging from severely debilitating illnesses such as schizophrenia to a range of less serious problems such as depression and personality disorders. Modern comparative evidence would lead us to expect as poor a level of mental health among the overall Roman population as was the case with their physical health. The evidence would also strongly suggest that incidence of mental disorders will have correlated negatively with social status. The world of aberrant mental phenomena was therefore a core issue for the popular culture to deal with.

If one thing characterizes popular culture for most people, though, it is its informality, fun and irreverence. The third chapter looks at the festivals that the people enjoyed to alleviate the stresses of their everyday lives by turning their hierarchical world bottom up. Using Bakhtin's notion of carnival, I look at the themes of the inversion of the normal hierarchy, the popular focus on the body and its functions to bring everyone down to the same level, and the use of humour to mock and ridicule all forms of authority. This spirit of carnival, however, spilled over into all forms of non-elite fun. It was not just contained in an annual jamboree. The elite found this unsettling in that many of their members chose to participate in these popular pleasures. In the collapse of the republic and the crisis of leadership it engendered, it became clear that a new way of integrating the government and the people had to be found. I argue that the imperial games can be seen as a way of incorporating some of the carnival spirit so as to entice the people into a new social contract. Popular culture fed upwards into new forms of elite behaviour.

The elite and the people inhabited different sensory worlds. Whether it was in their use of delicate perfumes, fine art, or writing itself, the elite strove to define itself in terms of sensory refinement and taste. The non-elite, by contrast, lived in narrow, noisy, stinking places of overweening proximity. The elite adopted certain practices precisely because they were in contradiction with popular behaviour, but they then used this invented sense of their own good taste to condemn the non-elite as immoral and worthless: the city's filth and scum. The city was seen as particularly threatening because the senses were thought to affect the individual's physical and moral self directly. You were what you smelled. The new imperial settlement sought to re-order the sensory universe by giving the non-elite access to taste, thereby bringing it under the calming and morally improving influence of the refinements that the elite had previously sought to keep for themselves. The splendour of imperial largesse overwhelmed the senses. Luxury became a point of communal consensus, even if this did create tensions with the traditional elite.[16] Most analysis has focused on the architecture, art and the use of urban space to convey powerful imperial images and ideological messages. Here I look at how the emperors used the whole world of the senses to create and manage a new context for the coming together of ruler and ruled. The literary texts which form the basis for this chapter are themselves expressive of a new sensuousness in Roman literature, which reflected a wider cultural shift in that direction. The overblown tales of imperial largesse, while not fully believable as records of historical fact, show that luxury became the normal context for the meeting between the emperor and his people, whatever misgivings the literary elite might still have had about that fact.

Many slaves hated their masters. Many free men loathed their patrons. Many provincials despised Rome. Any analysis of the popular which did not look at how these people expressed the resentments born of their subordination would be seeing Roman culture too much from the elite point of view. Resistance, however, is a broad term that can cover a whole array of acts, ranging from the dramatic revolts of Spartacus to the daily acts of dissent and deceit that a slave might save for his master. I suggest that popular culture, as the culture of the subordinate classes, will always try and carve out for itself a free space in which it has greater room for self-expression and manoeuvre. In Rome, this was achieved primarily though the use of new, imported religions. The dominant culture will largely be indifferent to such spaces so long as they do not publicly threaten the status quo, at which point they will come down with full state coercive power. But the powerful will also try and incorporate elements of the oppositional subculture into a new mode of government, as the Romans did with Constantine's conversion to Christianity.

Rome did not possess a monolithic, homogeneous culture. The concept of popular culture brings in difference, diversity and resistance to how we see the Roman world. This in itself raises questions about the degree to which people actually believed the emperors' ideological claims to good governance. Focusing on the production of images in imperial art and architecture runs the risk of ignoring their reception. Once we recognize that the people could actively reinterpret and undermine any image that was put before them, it becomes impossible to be so confident about how those images were perceived. Popular culture in ancient Rome was not just about folklore; it was about how people sometimes mocked, subverted and insulted their superiors; how they manipulated the elite to get something of their own way; and how they saw through the ideologies by which the powerful sought to dominate them.

1

Problem-solving

Problems and risk

This chapter deals with the attitudes, tactics and beliefs that helped the overwhelming majority of the non-elite make a relatively reasonable living in all but the most exacting periods of crisis. I have characterized this approach as one of problem-solving because it seems to me that life for most people represented a series of difficulties to be overcome, of a varying nature and size. Most of these problems had arisen before and were already addressed by cultural attitudes that people had learned at their mother's or father's knee. The non-elite therefore came ready prepared to address most of the troubles that were likely to come their way.

Difficult problems tend to share certain characteristics. First, they lack clarity in that it is often unclear exactly what the problem is, what has caused it or what will be the outcome of doing nothing. Difficult problems also tend to force people to confront multiple goals that they might have and to decide between them by selecting a least-bad option. Above all, difficult problems are complex – they include a variety of interrelated factors and often involve the pressure of time constraints too. Modern management textbooks tell us that the resolution of tough problems like these requires each factor to be tackled in turn. The problem for the average Roman was they had only very limited knowledge on which to base their decisions. They did not have the luxury of modern analysis. I would argue that, in such an uncertain environment,[1] the popular approach to problems was generally characterized by one or more of the following: keeping to simple, clearly defined solutions; focusing on one primary aim; relying on trusted techniques; sticking firmly to their own areas of expertise; referring to backward-looking precedents; trusting individual cunning first and turning to mutualism only occasionally; and finally trying to kick the problem upstairs to those with more resources to cope with the situation.

Exactly what constitutes a problem is often socially constructed. It is not just a rational balancing act between a fixed set of dilemmas. Certain priorities are probably fairly universal – food, marriage plans, threats to safety – but others vary considerably in the degree of importance which people attach to them. As is so often the case in Roman society, status concerns loomed large. A significant portion of the oracles and spells of the Roman world concerned the removal of perceived and actual threats to status, opportunities for status advancement, and gaining revenge for actions by social competitors that had resulted in a loss of face.

The main variable that confronted any member of the non-elite when facing a problem was that of risk. Risk means facing an uncertain future and in a world where the average person considered themselves 'vulnerable to impoverishment',[2] and even middling sorts 'lived under a permanent threat of impoverishment',[3] levels of uncertainty were high. Put simply, the man *in* the street was never far from becoming the man *on* the street. Gallant has shown that when faced with a 'capricious natural environment and armed with a rudimentary technology, Greek peasants developed an extensive but delicate web of risk-management strategies' to help them cope.[4] Recently, Eidinow has provided us with a remarkable study of how the ancient Greeks used oracles and curses to control risk, finding that 'those who used oracles were uncertain and wanted to be sure they were making the right choice; those who turned to curses were usually already in a situation of danger and wanted to limit the damage their enemies might inflict'.[5] In addition to this, I suggest that risk can usefully be thought of as representing volatility, as it does in modern portfolio management theory.[6] The problem with the term 'risk' is that it tends to highlight the downside. Volatility is a more neutral term that reflects the fact that risk can produce equally good and bad results. Risk in itself, therefore, is not the problem. It is the vulnerability of the risk-taker to negative events that will dictate their appetite for taking risk.

Risk perceptions changed according to social status. The rich were able to tolerate high degrees of volatility of returns and so were happy to invest in speculative ventures such as shipping. Those close to subsistence level were much more vulnerable to volatility and so focused on controlling their downside risks, even if this came at the expense of giving up some upside possibility. Broadly speaking, risk tolerance was inversely related to social status. Compare the extravagantly reckless speculation of the nouveau riche Trimalchio in the *Satyricon*, where his fortunes oscillate to the tune of tens of millions per day, with the natural conservatism of the rustic in the *Aesop Romance*, riding an ass, loaded with wood, to which he says, 'The sooner we get there and get the wood sold for a dozen farthings, the sooner you'll get two of them for fodder. I'll take two for myself, and we'll keep the eight against bad times, for fear we'll get sick or some bad weather will come along unexpectedly and keep us from getting out.'[7] Trimalchio is mocked because his behaviour is a caricature of rich freedmen aping the risk-taking attitudes of the elite to an absurd degree. By contrast, the peasant living on little more than subsistence income levels has to employ basic risk-management techniques – ensure a sale, save for a rainy day – to keep himself from falling into starvation. He has prioritized his aims and adopted a clear, tried-and-tested strategy, revolving around the utilization of his own area of expertise, which, in this case, is selling firewood. Interestingly, Tacitus notes that both the utterly poor and the vastly rich could be shamelessly reckless.[8] In fact, recklessness was associated with the needy.[9] Perhaps by the time an individual sank into destitution their risk appetite increased again; either they had nothing further to lose or they needed to take substantial risks in order to make any meaningful difference to their lives.

An additional issue concerning risk that affected people's handling of it was that harvests in the Roman world varied considerably from year to year. Agricultural volatility can be exceptionally high in the Mediterranean region, with average variations in interannual wheat yields in excess of 60 per cent in Tunisia.[10] Egypt at 12 per cent has the lowest annual variation in yield, which helps account for the reliance emperors had on it for generating tax revenues and surplus grain supplies. The distribution of the crop returns will not therefore have exhibited the bell-shaped, normal distribution curve that statistics tell us to expect from a particular set of outcomes. In practice, the curve for Roman harvests will have exhibited kurtosis, meaning that it had 'fat tails'. Whereas a normal curve tells us to expect two thirds of outcomes to be within one standard deviation of the norm, with only an occasional extreme event, the reality was that extreme, four or five standard deviation events happened far more frequently than would statistically be expected. Bumper harvests could easily be followed by years of dearth. Unless reserves had been put aside, the impact of these shocks could be devastating. The effect of these two additional factors was to place even more emphasis on risk control. The overriding aim of the vulnerably poor, those close to the threshold of subsistence, was to secure stability of income at or above subsistence and try and put something by for a rainy day. Those with greater assets at their disposal could afford to take a more liberal attitude to risk-taking. For all, life involved constant calculation, weighing up the risk and likely outcomes based on what had happened in the past.

As well as employing risk-control techniques, the non-elite sought to spread their risk and so limit their potential downside by diversification. Peasants sowed a variety of crops, lest one should be hit by disease. Younger family members might be sent out to work as apprentices to provide a valuable additional income from a source less correlated with agricultural returns. It was an attitude that spread to whatever they were doing, so that when faced with illness it seemed natural to use a variety of resources in order to find a cure, be they magical incantations, folk remedies or Greek medicine. Patrons needed to be cultivated so that they might help out in times of dearth. Networks of friends, kin and neighbours also had to be established as an insurance policy against hard times. The mantra of 'spread risk, diversify sources of income' informed much of non-elite life.

In many ways the popular attitude to volatility was derived from their idea of the 'limited good'.[11] The non-elite saw everything as a zero-sum game. They did well only to the extent that another did badly. Moreover, 'limited good' means that another's good fortune is a direct threat to your own. In fact, one's own misfortune comes to be seen as the direct result of another's gain. This was a sensible position to adopt in a society where economic growth was close to zero. If the size of the pie stayed the same then someone having a good feed was having it at another's expense. This is why putting curses on social competitors was not just the result of 'envy, fuelled by gossip' that might lead to supernatural attack;[12] it was a desperate attempt by people to stop someone else taking what little they had, leaving them stranded on the wrong side of the subsistence threshold.

Likewise a belief in the power of luck, which the non-elite almost uniformly seem to have shared, can be seen as a belief in the power of averaging (in that over the long term luck will even out). This is itself just another restatement of the limited-good hypothesis. If a person were having more than their fair share of luck, it meant by definition he or she must either be cheating or relying on the manipulation of magical powers to sustain it. The only rational response to such a situation was to launch a counter-attack to try and rebalance the position, through means such as curses. This was a mindset born of a society that fostered fear, envy and intense rivalry among its members. People fought not just for basic subsistence but for what might be termed 'subsistence status'. The non-elite were prepared to act vigorously to maintain their limited interests and standing in the world if they perceived it to be under attack from another.

Did it work? Did the popular approach to solving the problems they faced make them happy and fulfilled human beings? That is too much to answer. But what happiness economics can tell us is that their approach was a good one for maximizing their overall levels of satisfaction given the low level of resources available to them. The Easterlin paradox observes that at low levels of income happiness increases quickly for only minor additional increases in income, but not beyond. People's aspirations increase along with their income and, after their basic needs have been met, most find satisfaction only in being relatively better off than others. The wealthy, it seems, are like dogs chasing the tail of their own happiness, only ever content if they are richer than their neighbour.[13] Rome was a world where even small changes in income or luck could have a major impact on the quality of life of the average person. It could also have significant concomitant effects on their relative standing within the community, which in itself would likely have an additional impact on their quality of life. Their focus, naturally therefore, was on doing everything in their power to ensure that they secured those small additional boosts to their income that would push them up the status ladder, while avoiding those gut-wrenching hits to the downside. As Augustine said, the labourers in the fields 'sing with transports of joy' at times of abundant harvest.[14] Or, as they traditionally say in Iceland when they win the jackpot, 'Beached whale!'.

Family management

The popular culture had a different attitude towards time. High mortality rates themselves affected people's attitudes, given that average life expectancy at birth was probably only twenty-five years. The elite prided themselves on being able to look to the long term, with the family acting as the focus of this social investment. The elite caricatured the poor as being fixated with daily issues such as bread and circuses. In fact some of the poor may also have aspired to longer-term dynastic ambitions, as is seen in some gravestones of freedmen marking their success for perpetuity. But, for most of the lower orders, long-term thinking was a luxury they could ill afford. More pressing problems crowded in on them closer to home: finding the rent, which sometimes was paid by the day, buying the daily bread, getting work. In difficult times this could require drastic measures: feeding the women or weaker children less food to keep up the strength of the male wage-earners; moving down the food chain to eat the acorns which usually fed the pigs, along with other crops not usually considered good for human consumption;[15] and in some circumstances selling one or more of the children into slavery, or to a begging gang who would mutilate them by twisting their limbs and cutting out their tongues, to increase their begging-power.[16]

These actions provided immediate solutions to current problems and it would be wrong to see them as short-termist. Most people's lives had a hand-to-mouth aspect, a day-to-day outlook. They had no alternative but to focus on keeping their heads above water, even if that meant a tradesman selling off the tools of the trade that supplied his living. Lucian has a fictional tale about the widow of a smith slipping into poverty after his death, selling his tools for cash, then spinning wool to help raise their child, who she plans to prostitute eventually to support them both.[17] From such a perspective, time becomes an extremely relative concept. Longer-term planning had to take a back seat. Just hanging on in there for a few more days until the boats carrying the corn arrived, or they started hiring for the new public-building works, could seem like an eternity. The alternative, after all, was death and that was only a solution in the most negative of ways.

Problem-solving within the context of the family group was paramount. Family management was vital if the domestic unit was to maximize its resistance to shocks and smooth the volatility of its income and expenditure. Otherwise life would be as it was fated for the man born when Mars or Saturn stood in aspect to Jupiter in the second house, and 'his life will be constantly changing, at one time abounding in riches, at another oppressed by poverty'.[18] Family, kinship and social roles defined social identity, and the family unit represented the primary buffer against risk. As the Aesop fable says, family life is like a bundle of sticks – so stick together.[19] Risk was highest when most of a family group's income came from the same source. For this reason women were exceptionally vulnerable to the death of their husband, who for most was the main breadwinner. Many widows fell into dreadful poverty.[20] In crisis situations such as this, the solution to the problem was clear: cut costs where they are easiest to make by reducing the number of mouths to feed: 'My husband died and I was left to toil and suffer for my daughter by him ... and now I no longer have the means to feed her ... I have requested that you receive her from me as your daughter.'[21] If children found themselves orphaned and so unattached to any family unit, it was vital for them to try and re-attach themselves to another as soon as possible, primarily by looking to the wider kinship structure.

The mother of Tare, an Egyptian girl, died while they were in Syria. Tare wrote as follows to her aunt back home: 'Please be informed, dear aunt, that my mother, your sister, has been dead since Easter. While my mother was with me, she was my whole family; since her death, I have remained here alone in a strange land with no one to help.'[22]

If the family unit was intact, increasing income, preferably from diversified sources, enhanced security. Again, the younger members of the non-elite family played an important role here. The orator and writer Lucian, originally from a modest background, describes how at about the age of thirteen he was sent out to work as an apprentice to a sculptor: 'in a short time I would even delight my father by regularly bringing him an income'.[23] Thirteen is likely to have been a late age to be put to productive use, probably reflecting Lucian's somewhat wealthier family background. Something between age five and ten seems to have been the most common age for a non-elite child to be sent to work.[24] One gravestone is inscribed: 'In memory of Viccentia, a very nice girl, a gold-worker. She lived for nine years.'[25] For most parents, children acted as income generator, insurance scheme and pension provider, all rolled into one. As Augustine says, the man with many children and grandchildren thinks that he is 'assured against the dangers of death'.[26]

But children were a cost base too, an expensive commodity to maintain for the years before they could generate a positive return. For that reason, the head of the family had to take care to manage the overall size of the unit, ensuring that the structure of the family was regulated to spread costs evenly: 'sometimes when parents have begotten one, two, or three children, they fear to give birth to any more lest they reduce the others to beggary'.[27] In Egypt, at about the time of the birth of Jesus, one absent father, Hilarion, wrote to his expectant wife: 'I beg you and entreat you to take care of the child and, if I receive my pay soon, I will send it up to you. If you have the baby before I return, if it is a boy, let it live; if it is a girl, expose it.'[28] Exposure horrifies modern sentiments, but it is important to see it in the context of the good of the overall family unit. It was also not the worst option for the baby: exposure was an alternative to simple infanticide.[29] Seneca describes how some fathers threw out weak and deformed babies rather than expose them.[30] Nor was exposure always an economic measure: some were cast out simply because they had been born under an unlucky star or their father 'favours his expulsion' and has 'a belief in misfortune'.[31] Sometimes it was fated by the stars that a child, 'will be nourished for a few days before being thrown into water',[32] or 'will either be exposed or not nurtured'[33] (in other words, not fed), or 'be suffocated at birth'.[34] Exposed babies might be picked up by slave dealers or those families looking to increase their size, with the dump on the edge of town functioning like a market to match surplus children with demand: a Roman eBaby. But we should not imagine that it always worked out so neatly. The astrologer, Firmicus Maternus, notes frequently on the charts of exposed infants simply that they 'will be devoured by dogs'.[35]

Becoming a dog's dinner was not a fate reserved for the unwanted children of the poor. Musonius Rufus describes how it was not just the poor who exposed infants, 'but those who have an abundance of things', removing an additional cost in order that 'those previously born might be more prosperous'.[36] Such a zero-sum strategy held other risks, given that death could come terrifyingly quickly in the form of disease, leaving the parents bereft of heirs. Inheritance concerns are also reflected in some jokes: a punchline from the Philogelos, a Roman joke book, has a son complaining to his father: 'Can't you see what a rotten trick you played on me? Why, if you hadn't been born, I would have been my grandfather's heir!'[37]

Making money

Maintaining income through paid employment or a craft was a vital concern for the urban non-elite. As the dream interpreter, Artemidorus, says, to dream of lying on one's back signifies unemployment, 'For we speak of those who are unemployed as being "flat on their backs".'[38] The people could not afford to while away their days in leisure like many of the rich; they expected to work hard. In recommending a young man to a friend, the younger Pliny notes that, 'he loves hard work as much as poor people usually do'.[39] 'What do not merchants endure?'[40] asks Augustine – seas, winds, storms, being away from home. Having a trade was vital to create a steady income that could provide a livelihood, which in turn was a central pillar in establishing identity and status within the local community.[41] A trade epitomized the kind of 'poor-paideia', the expertise of the poor, that we mentioned earlier: a practical expertise and accrued experience that was handed down from generation to generation. Whereas a labourer would always be at the whim of foremen and building projects, by specializing in a niche activity the craftsman went a long way to reducing the volatility of his income. People would always need potters and weavers and bakers. Even then, trades such as these were 'hard work and could scarcely provide just enough'.[42] And, once acquired, it was important to stick to one's area of expertise: a butcher shouldn't try to be a flute player, or else he would end up being eaten alive like a crab on land.[43]

A letter attributed to Hadrian gives us some idea of the degree of competitive industry that the whole urban population of Alexandria showed in their pursuit of making a living:

> They are a most seditious, deceitful and injurious people; but their city is prosperous, rich, and fruitful, and in it no one is idle. Some are glass-blowers, others paper-makers, all at least are linen-weavers or seem to belong to one craft or another; the lame have their occupations, the eunuchs have theirs, the blind have theirs, and not even those whose hands are crippled are idle. Their only god is money, and this the Christians, the Jews, and, in fact, everyone adores.[44]

It is probably fair to say that income and status were broadly aligned in the world of the freeborn non-elite (the fact that freedmen often seem to have striven so hard to establish status suggests they always had to fight against a residual prejudice about their servile origins). You were what you earned. We can therefore get some basic idea about the relative rankings of non-elite occupations by seeing what they earned. The following list shows some examples taken from Diocletian's Edict on Maximum Prices, issued in 301 CE, priced in denarii per day and including maintenance.

General labourers

farm labourer	25
mule driver	25
sewer cleaner	25
shepherd	25
all other general labour	25

Skilled labourers

carpenter	50
stone mason	50
wall mosaics worker	60
wall painter	75
figure painter	150

These figures can only be taken as a guide, but the financial advantage of learning a trade is obvious. And the greater the level of expertise and perceived value, the more people could earn. If the wealthy were happy to pay up for murals and mosaics then so much the better.

These figures can also give us some indication of the breadline existence of the majority of the non-elite who comprised the labouring class. The Edict also tells us that a measure of wheat costs 100 denarii. If we estimate that a family of four requires annually about 1,000 kg of wheat equivalent to maintain minimum subsistence, then we can calculate the degree to which a manual worker's wage met that need.[45] If the adult male of the household worked for 250 days at 25 denarii his annual income would equal 6,250. Maintenance is provided for him on the days he works, so we can reduce the wheat requirement by that amount (250/365 × 250 (one person's share of the family of four's 1,000 kg) = 171 kg). As the adult male, though, he would have taken more than an equal quarter of the food, so we can round that up to 250 kg. The family is left to buy 750 kg, which equates to 75 military modii. At 100 denarii per modius, the total family food requirement comes to 7,500 denarii. The male income leaves a short-fall of 1,250 denarii. In other words, the family could not simply rely on the male breadwinner. Other sources of income had to be found. Remember also that this does not take into account living costs such as rent or clothing, let alone desirable items such as meat, oil or wine. In Rome, the corn dole gave each male citizen approximately 3.3 military modii per month, which equates to an annual cash equivalent of almost 4,000 denarii.[46] Even allowing for the higher cost of living in Rome, this obviously made a significant difference to the quality of life of the average citizen family. But for the vast majority who lived away from the capital and received no automatic subsidy, the need to make the entire family productive is clear.

Non-elite women were central to the household economy. The average Roman woman would have needed to produce at least five live births simply to maintain the population at a stable level.[47] This made fertility and childrearing a primary occupation to ensure a steady stream of new workers for the family. A funerary inscription from Panonia gives some idea of what life was like for most women:

1. Relief showing the inside of a butcher's shop

'Here I lie, a woman named Veturia. My father was Veturius, my husband was Fortunatus. I lived for twenty-seven years, and I was married for sixteen years to the same man. After I gave birth to six children, only one of whom is still alive, I died. Titus Julius Fortunatus, a soldier of the Second Legion, provided this memorial for his wife, who was incomparable and showed outstanding devotion to him.'[48] Women also focused on manufacturing household goods and cloth and the production and preservation of food, as well as cleaning, mending, washing and satisfying their husbands' desires. They also played an active role in improving the household income stream. Treggiari has looked at evidence for lower-class women at work and found evidence of their being employed in thirty-five different occupations. That the range of work available to women was still limited can be seen from the fact that men are found occupying 225 different functions. Women found work mainly in the service sector: spinning wool, making jewellery, serving in taverns, hairdressing, making and mending clothes.[49]

Women's work also consisted of performing the 'softer' household labour. By keeping contact with neighbours and relatives, ensuring that the proper observances were carried out at funerals and in periods of mourning, and functioning as household social workers, the household's women served to maintain the social networks that could prove vital in times of crisis. Popular culture, especially in the country, consisted mainly of an overlapping network of extended families and maintaining those links was important work. Girls were involved early in helping out with bringing up their younger siblings, which may have helped them generate a greater sense of independence and self-esteem than their brothers. Self-induction in the labour process was an aspect of the regeneration of popular culture in general, and girls picked up the traditions of the maternal craft by watching their mothers, aunts and older sisters in action. Women's natural place was held to be in the home, but that supposed 'naturalness' did not prevent men from constantly reminding their womenfolk of that social fact and educating them for it. The subordinate position of women meant that one of the most vital tasks for any young woman, no doubt with her mother's help if she was still alive, was to secure herself a suitable husband who could provide for her needs. One tablet describes a young woman compelling a divine spirit to bring her the man she wants to marry: 'bring him to Domitiana, full of love, raging with jealousy and without sleep over his love and passion for her, and make him ask her to return to his house as wife'.[50] The loss of a male breadwinner was the worst thing that could happen for most non-elite women, since it deprived them of their security and income. Widows became almost synonymous with beggary.

Illness features high on the list of non-elite concerns. Numerous oracles and curses deal with health issues, and hundreds of votive offerings either give thanks to the gods, or plead for an individual's recovery. One reason for the fear of illness was that it made work impossible and so severely dented the family income. The people were also very vulnerable to rising food price inflation as it constituted such a large part of their weekly spend. Sometimes, though, work just dried up and the non-elite had one principal response to such a problem: move. Large parts of the urban population had to be prepared to migrate as and when circumstances dictated: as the moral to one of Aesop's fable says, 'the poor, being unencumbered, easily move from city to city'.[51]

The people had to be practical. The benefits of keeping one's eyes aimed firmly down to earth were made plain in the story of the astronomer out walking at night, who, his head pointing up to the clouds, fell down into a well.[52] This was a mend-and-make-do culture where small acts, like patching and darning clothes,[53] could accumulate to make a big difference to the household budget. 'Poverty is the sister to good sense', as the proverb said. Above all, it was a world where people had to have an eye for making a profit. It is no surprise that the one state cult in Rome dedicated to Mercury – the god of trade, profit and mobility, the god of getting rich – was sited in the plebeian Aventine district. Nor that statuettes of him, money bag in hand, were commonly owned as good-luck charms.[54] The elite sneered at what they saw as brazen deceit: buying something at one price, then selling it to another at a higher one.[55] In the later empire, Libanius complains that traditional patronage relationships have broken down, and that people are trading influence for payment like 'meat and vegetables'; but then this is the kind of behaviour to be expected from officials whose fathers had at best been 'fullers, bath attendants, and sausage makers'.[56] The non-elite could not afford to be so high-minded. Juvenal describes a father advising his son on how to make a living: 'You should make some goods which you can sell at more than 50 per cent profit', which meant not turning one's nose up at jobs like fulling or tanning, which stank so much they were relegated to the other side of the Tiber: 'profit smells sweet' wherever it comes from.[57]

Subprime loans

The problem of debt loomed large in non-elite thinking. If, despite all their efforts to increase and diversify income and minimize outgoings, people found themselves in a situation where extra money was required, then the easiest solution was to borrow it. Credit functioned to smooth fluctuations in income and so reduced volatility. The varying demands of the family, high annual variation in crop size and the frequent imposition of sudden taxes 'all reinforced a pattern of borrowing and dependence'.[58] Given the precariousness of the position that many of the non-elite would find themselves in during a crisis, we could well ask why the wealthier members of society were prepared to lend at all. One reason was that it was simply easier to lend money than to hoard it. There was only a rudimentary banking system, so surplus wealth often had to be housed in a protective storeroom within the household. This did not make for sound sleep. Gregory of Nyssa describes one usurer who 'kept his money in cracks in the wall and plastered over them with mud to hide it'.[59] Lending also had a social side, with loans at low rates acting as a mark of friendship or patronage. But, not surprisingly, the main reason for the thriving debt market was that it was profitable. One of the laws describes commercial moneylenders 'rejoicing in the accession of money which increases day by day'.[60] Their joy could be understood given that usual interest rates stood at 12 per cent, or 1 per cent per calendar month. These rates will obviously have fluctuated according to market conditions; as the Digest says, 'in some places money can be raised easily and at low interest, while in others only with more difficulty and at a high rate of interest'.[61] But 12 per cent is by far the most commonly found rate, so can reasonably be taken as a long-term average for the non-elite as a whole.[62] Loans backed by prime Italian land could be raised at 6 per cent but the non-elite did not possess collateral of that kind. Unsecured, short-term consumer loans could cost as much as 50 per cent.[63] At 6 per cent, as MacMullen says, money doubled in a dozen years,[64] although this would not be in real terms, taking into account the loss in purchasing power that inflation would cause, or when adjusted for any defaults that the lender might suffer. The business was clearly profitable enough that some creditors tried to delay repayment of the principal to keep the monthly interest flowing in.[65]

In the event of default, creditors held considerable legal powers and could sell all the debtor's possessions. A fourth-century papyrus from Egypt describes how a wine dealer has borrowed a great sum of money and, 'being summoned to repay it and failing to meet his liabilities, he was compelled by his creditors to sell all his possessions down to the very garments that cloaked his shame; and even when these were sold, barely half the money could he scrape together for his creditors who . . . carried off all his children although they were mere infants'.[66] Not for nothing did the proverb hold that, 'a debtor does not love his creditor's threshold'.[67] The life of a debtor became a 'sleepless daze of anxious uncertainty'.[68] An Aesop fable describes how a bat borrows some money to go into business with a bramble and a coot, but when their ship sinks the bat is so afraid of her creditors that, 'she won't show herself during the day but only goes out at night for food'.[69] Defaulting could also bring divine retribution: one woman was punished by the gods with an illness in her right breast after failing to repay a loan with interest.[70]

But the worry was not all one way. Lending money was itself a risky business and the lender himself worried greatly over his outstanding loans. As Gregory of Nyssa says, 'If the usurer has loaned to a sailor, he sits on the shore, worrying about the wind's movement . . . and awaiting the report of a wreck or some other misfortune. His soul is disquieted whenever he sees the sea angered.' If the loan had been to someone in the locality, the lender took steps to make sure that he was fully appraised of his debtor's position: 'The moneylender is inquisitive with regard to the activities of the person in his debt as well as his personal travels, activities, movements, and livelihood,' and if he 'hears a bad report about anyone who has fallen among thieves or whose good fortune has changed to destitution, the moneylender sits with folded hands, groans continuously, and weeps much'. It became, Gregory complains, 'an obsession'.[71]

Our hearts bleed, no doubt. For the poor, however, the situation was far worse, such that 'so many are ensnared through usury they cast themselves headlong into torrential rivers'.[72] Christian hyperbole aside, we can get some idea of how bad the general situation was for the non-elite by looking at the default rate implied by the market interest rates they were charged. For the usurers worried with good reason. Many of the non-elite were in no position to pay back loans. Implied default rates will tell us the probability of a borrower not being able to repay his loan. This will tell us roughly what percentage of the non-elite in debt were reduced to penury each year and how important a problem this was for them.

The market interest rate represents the risk-free rate (in the modern world this would be the interest rate on loans to a central bank) plus a risk premium to compensate the lender for the defaults that will be incurred in lending to less secure borrowers. As a fair approximation we can take the 6 per cent rate for loans backed by premium Italian real estate as the equivalent of the risk-free rate. We need to discount this by one year's interest at 6 per cent because the present value of receiving 6 in one year's time is not 6, but is about 5.7 (in other words, the amount of money you would need to invest at 6 per cent today to get a cash flow of 6 in one year's time). We then need to make an assumption about the recovery rate. The recovery rate is the amount of money the creditor manages to salvage from his debtor's assets in the event of default. The market standard for lower-grade corporate debt in the modern world is about 40 per cent, that is to say, in the event of default the company's assets would be sold and would raise about 40 per cent of the value of the outstanding debt. Obviously modern-day companies bear little resemblance to the Roman non-elite. But the example given from Egypt above tells us that the debtor was forced by his creditors to sell 'all his possessions down to the very garments that cloaked his shame; and even when these were sold, barely half of the money could he scrape together for his creditors'. In other words there was a recovery rate of about 50 per cent. In this example, the creditors went on to sell his children. I shall not take this into account as this seems an exceptional part of this account. The default rate will represent the percentage that will equalize the risk-free rate with the market rate. So, for rates of 12 per cent and 50 per cent, the norm and the extreme of the rates charged to non-elite loans, the calculations are as shown in table 1.1.

The market interest rates that Romans charged each other tells us that between 10 per cent and 44 per cent of non-elite borrowers could be expected to go bankrupt each year, depending on the interest rate they were paying. In reality this will represent maximum levels because they do not account for the possibility of selling off family members into slavery to increase the recovery rate. Also, they do not incorporate the excess profit, the risk premium, that lenders will have built into their rates to overcompensate for likely defaults. In theory, though, these excess profit levels cannot be too high because other lenders would then enter the market to provide more competitive rates. It is likely that the lenders will also have experienced the kind of kurtotic returns that we looked at earlier: they would make a healthy profit for most of the time, but any crisis would see default rates rocket as more and more people were unable to cover their

Table 1.1

Year	Cash flow	Survival rate	Default rate
1	112	90	10

Year	Cash flow	Survival rate	Default rate
1	150	56	44

Where price = risk-free rate × [cash flow × survival rate + recovery rate × default rate]
Cash flow = the repayment of principal + interest
Assuming: a recovery rate of 50 per cent, a risk-free rate of 6 per cent (discounted to 5.7), and a price of 100

payments. Moreover, during such crisis periods, recovery rates would collapse as there would be a sudden influx of repossessed goods on to the market at a time of fewer buyers. Subprime loans have always been a risky business.

Given that debt featured so prominently in non-elite attempts to smooth their income flows, a high percentage of the non-elite will at any time have been in debt. The rates they were being charged implies that a significant percentage were failing to meet interest payments and thereby defaulting. This would likely have resulted in destitution and, as in the case of the Egyptian wine dealer, slavery for himself or members of his family or debt bondage. It was no wonder that calls for debt cancellation, *tabulae novae*, featured so prominently in non-elite demands for a new political settlement in the late republic, in provincial uprisings such as the first Jewish revolt, and in the regular tax-remissions that emperors were forced to grant.[73]

Social relations

It was perhaps the constant tensions created by the need to make money which helped make the non-elite less communal than one might otherwise expect. The fables and proverbs warn frequently about the problems of fighting with neighbours and the inconsistency of friends. Envy, need or both could lead to robbery with violence. A petition to the local governor, Andromachus, from a native of Tebtunis in 131 CE complains that, 'Orsenouphis and Poueris, sons of Mieus ... made a bold attack upon my house in the village' and they 'belaboured me with blows on every limb of my body'. Their loot? A white tunic and robe, a cloak, a pair of scissors, some beer and a quantity of salt.[74] Even brothers have 'the same meaning as enemies, for they do not contribute to a person's welfare but rather his detriment' by dividing any inheritance.[75] Or perhaps it was the stresses caused by living in high-density accommodation in Rome itself, where there was little chance to escape from enemies. Whatever the underlying cause, the symptoms revealed themselves as outpourings of local bitterness and bad blood. One lead curse tablet from near Carthage gives a flavour of the competitive, mocking, envious society the non-elite inhabited: 'I, Maslih, make Emashtart melt, the place where he lives and all his belongings, because he has rejoiced at my expense about the money that I have completely lost. May everyone who rejoices at my expense about the loss of my money become like this lead which is now being melted.'[76]

Ridicule like this hurt. So did gossip. In the *Aesop Romance*, the philosopher Xanthus complains that, 'one of those people who go round upsetting decent households with their slander' has prejudiced Aesop by saying that Xanthus mistreats his slaves or beats them, or is a drunk or irritable.[77] But chitchat did not only reflect an envious society; it revealed one where people took it upon themselves to police their own norms of behaviour. It was not the authorities that were the people's primary oppressors – it was the people themselves. Gossip served to keep people in their place, at bay and conforming to what was expected of them. The real law rarely burst in on the non-elite's lives, and for the most part justice was a local, DIY affair.[78] Accusations of immoral behaviour were part of the armoury of sanctions that could be employed to force people to obey the unwritten rules of local behaviour. Graffiti such as 'Ampliatus Pedania is a thief', 'Atimetus got me pregnant', and 'Restitutus has deceived many girls many times', served as scripts for public shaming, regardless of whether the target could read.[79] Consulting a magician was a way of letting it be known that another's actions had created social tensions in the community. And, if all else failed, stonings served as the ultimate in popular justice.[80]

Talk was central to non-elite female society. Very few lower-class women will have been able to read or write, which made theirs a particularly oral culture. Their communal conversations acted as a survival manual of practical advice, a resource to turn to when problems emerged. Conversation also provided the core of their relaxation and entertainment, in such forms as the songs they sang while spinning and washing. In such an environment, gossip was vital for creating and controlling community relations. It served to maintain status and reputation, to network, and to provide essential news about what was going on in the locality. The pressures of non-elite life meant that women could, and were probably expected to, act in a vindictive and bitchy way when they needed to defend their own or their family's interests (which amounted to the same thing). Backbiting, character assassination, rude nicknames, gestures, contemptuous silence and making things known in the neighbourhood were all ways that gossip could police the community. Of course, there was nothing that was inherently female about such activities. They largely reflect the stereotypical gender roles that Roman women were expected to perform. The fact that the archetypal female villain in Roman society was active, malicious and untrustworthy suggests that some men had concerns that this was a gender role that could get out of hand. Some women certainly seem to have made themselves unpopular: one inscription on an altar in Rome reads, 'Here for all time has been set down in writing the shameful record of the freedwoman Acte, of poisoned mind, and treacherous, cunning, and hard-hearted. Oh for a nail and a hempen rope to hang her with, and flaming pitch to burn up her wicked heart.'[81] As ever in Roman society, the unwritten moral assumption seems to have been that women are to be rewarded for modesty and virtue, but that any forwardness or ambition will be vigorously punished. Women who transgressed society's norms could find themselves on the receiving end of rough, local justice. In Apuleius's *Golden Ass*, a woman is accused of poisoning her husband to conceal a love affair, and the crowd call for her to be burned, stoned or lynched.[82]

This was not an environment where mutualism could be expected to flourish. But that is not to say that it did not exist. *Manus manum lavat*, the hand washes the hand, as the saying went.[83] Mutualism was a smoothing strategy that could be tried out if things got bad, particularly among the wider horizontal family and social networks. Alciphron, in the second century CE, wrote an imaginary appeal from one farmer to another:

> A violent hailstorm has sheared off our standing grain, and there is nothing left to keep us from famine. We cannot buy imported wheat because we have no money. But I hear that you have something left over from last year's good harvest. So please lend me twenty bushels, to give me the means to save my own life and the lives of my wife and children. And when a year of good harvest comes along, we will repay you, as they say 'the same measure or better', if our crops are bountiful. Please do not let good neighbours go to ruin in bad times such as these.[84]

From the recipient's point of view, this letter would have provoked a thorough-going risk assessment before any wheat would be sent. Could the wheat be spared? Was the relationship strong enough to warrant it? Could they repay? Would they repay? It is tempting, though, to see this letter as an expression of a more aristocratic notion of reciprocity that was some way removed from the realities of non-elite life. One group that were definitely perceived as being in cahoots were slaves. An anonymous early fifth-century comedy in the style of Plautus, called *The Complainer*, contains the following eulogy of life as a slave: 'The chief element of our happiness is that among ourselves we are not resentful. We all commit thefts, yet no one suffers loss because it is all done mutually. We monitor the masters and exclude them, for among the male and female slaves there is a collective kinship.'[85] This, though, reflects nothing but the stereotypical elite view of slaves: all equally thieving, unreliable and shameless.

If mutualism provided a lesser weapon in the arsenal of strategies the non-elite could employ to overcome problems, individual cunning

2. Relief of a farmer driving to market

was one of the big guns. The Aesop fables provided a store of stories, gathered over the centuries, to be told as a means of showing how the world worked and how the peasant could cope with it. Success in this world does not depend on good behaviour. Instead, Aesop has to rely on his natural wit to outsmart the strong. He is a small, agile trickster who can use his intelligence to wriggle out of almost any predicament. His setbacks in the *Aesop Romance* (the book-length version of his exploits), happen when he acts rashly or is foolish enough to trust the powerful. These are just tales, of course, but they capture the personal characteristics that the non-elite told themselves were good traits for their hero to have and, presumably, good to emulate.

In reality, cunning of this kind could not always be expressed with such Robin Hood-like simplicity, primarily because the people spent most of their time dealing with other members of the non-elite. In that situation, one man's cunning quickly becomes another's cheating. In fact, traders were notorious for it. Aesop tells the story of how Zeus once directed Hermes to give falsehood to all craftsmen and the extra leftover to tanners, and therefore 'craftsmen have all been liars ever since and tanners most of all'.[86] One piece of graffiti complains, 'Damn you innkeeper, you drink the pure stuff yourself and sell us water.'[87] And, as Augustine asked of his flock, have they not lied in business 'that I paid such a sum for this merchandise' although they had not really; and that 'You wish to deceive and carry out fraudulent transactions. How do you accomplish this? You use false scales.'[88] Nobody could be trusted: not a neighbour, who might, like the ant, keep a jealous eye on his neighbours' farms and steal some of their produce.[89] Not fellow spectators, who tried to get more than their share when tokens for food were handed round at the games.[90]

Not even beggars, who used faking strategies to enhance their pite-ousness, such as feigning broken legs or blindness.[91] The *Life of Daniel the Stylite* contains a woman with a twelve-year-old son who has been dumb from birth, but 'the brethren suspected that the stress of poverty had made the mother suggest to him that he should pretend to be dumb'.[92] It was enough to make anyone a sceptic: 'you doubt concern-ing this poor man whom you have received into your house, your mind doubts and hesitates as to whether he is a sincere man' or 'a deceitful man, a pretender, a hypocrite'.[93]

Theft was always a problem in the ancient world, but the perpetra-tors were often close to their victims. The astrologer, Dorotheus of Sidon, gives detailed physical descriptions of thieves who are either from the household or have visited the house and 'its people know him':[94] he is 'thick in the hair on his hand', or else he will be 'fat-cheeked, narrow in the forehead'.[95] The burglars gain entry after weakening or digging out the wall of the house, or they break the lock, or use their inside knowledge to acquire copies of the key.[96] All this, despite the fact that 'there is friendship between him and the people of the house and their trust is in this man'.

Some people boasted as a way of trying to enhance their status unfairly. People retaliated by telling jokes about these types: a boast-ful type is in the marketplace and cries to his slave boy, 'How are all my sheep doing?'; 'Oh,' comes the reply, 'one is asleep, the other is standing up.'[97] Or they could employ the old proverb that says boast-ing made 'an elephant out of a mouse'. Other people went to extreme lengths to avoid their duties: one law prescribes that whoever tries to avoid military service by amputating a finger shall be branded.[98] Nor did people stop at cheating the emperors. People even tried it on with the gods: an inscription from Phrygia and Lydia in modern Turkey reads: 'To Zeus. Diogenes had made a vow for the ox, but he did not fulfil it; for that reason his daughter Tatiane was punished in her eyes.'[99]

Diogenes was a man who had taken a risk and seen it backfire badly. But this was the kind of calculation the non-elite constantly relied upon in their efforts to gain the little extra that could make all the difference to their lives. One of the main leisure activities of the non-elite was gambling.[100] Gambling provided them with an educa-tion in the life skills they would need in their milieu. Gambling was all about assessing risk and solving problems under both pressure and tough time constraints. It involved bluffing and cheating, if it could be done without anyone noticing. It involved frequent arguments and disputes in order to protect one's position. The section in the *Digest* that covers the laws on gamblers repeatedly refers to the use of force, theft, robbery and assault.[101] The historian, Ammianus Marcellinus, writes in the fourth century about the Roman non-elite's endless discussions about the 'smallest details of the good and bad points of charioteers and horses'.[102] This was not just trivial gossip; it reflected the kind of detailed niche expertise that people required in their working lives to do well. It reflected a belief that the world did not lie entirely at the mercy of Fate. Luck meant that anything could happen if one played the dice right. And luck could be encouraged to show favour. A spell from Egypt tells how to win at dice: say the formula 'Let not even one of these playing with me be equal, and I am going to throw what I want.'[103] The prize for the gambler was not simply financial. Local prestige and even fame could result.[104] Ammianus also notes that the gamblers seem to have a genuine camaraderie, a mutual respect, perhaps, that resulted from playing the game well.[105] Gambling was all about the individual coping with risk within a group context, making calculated guesses under pressure, and dealing with the volatility of returns that winning or losing brought. As such, gambling neatly re-enacted the social skills needed to survive in the non-elite world.

Power, politics and the moral economy

We can learn something about how the non-elite would have liked to have seen themselves from the qualities they looked for in their candidates at elections. Not surprisingly, politicians did not emphasize their cunning and ability to cheat. The election slogans we find scrawled up all over the walls of Pompeii are full of such terms as 'good', 'honest', 'excellent', 'most worthy citizen', 'lives modestly', with commendations for having 'done many things generously'. One claims simply that 'he has good bread'.[106] Those that probably capture the spirit of the electorate more closely are the ones that promise 'he will do something for you'. Whatever the reality of these politicians' personal characteristics, people wanted their representatives to be, or at least appear to be, plain and honest. Funerary inscriptions suggest that this was also how many of the non-elite would have liked to have thought of themselves: 'modest, honest and trustworthy';[107] and they looked for the same qualities in their wives: Martinianus describes his dead wife, Sofroniola, as, 'pure, loyal, affectionate, dutiful, yielding', everything a non-elite Roman could want in a wife.[108]

But on the whole the non-elite seem to have distrusted the powerful and those in authority. Cicero says that people hated moneylenders and tax-collectors.[109] 'There are as many tyrants as there are local officials', complains Salvian.[110] The non-elite had plenty of reason to treat the authorities with suspicion. The procurator in Gaul, Licinus, inserted two extra months into the calendar and so increased his takings by over 16 per cent.[111] Nor were the authorities to be relied upon to deliver justice, as Luke warns: 'When you go with your accuser before a magistrate, on the way make an effort to settle the case, or you will be dragged before the judge, and the judge will hand you over to the officer, and the officer throw you in prison. I tell you, you will never get out until you have paid every last penny.'[112] The reality was spelled out to the hedgehog, whose bones had been broken by a woman, by the man it had asked to act as witness: 'You would be more sensible,' he advised, 'if you forgot about the lawsuit and bought yourself a bandage.'[113]

Faced with what they perceived as arbitrary and sometimes despotic government, the non-elite had to exercise great care in their dealings with the powerful. Like the clay pot who asked the copper pot to get away from him for fear of being broken if he so much as touched him, the non-elite avoided the elite wherever possible: as the moral of the proverb states, 'life is uncertain for a poor man when a grasping man of power lives close by'.[114] Or, as the ass who hunted with the lion is told, 'do not form an alliance nor go into any kind of partnership with a man more powerful than yourself'.[115] But avoidance tactics could only go so far. Patronage was an important source of benefits for the non-elite, even if it could be variable, localized, and did not always come via the traditional patron/client route but through such conduits as the provision of games. Patrons would have to be dealt with and the non-elite needed a strategy to ensure they got as much as possible out of the encounter without exposing themselves to undue risks.

They adopted what can be described as a system of patron-management (or master- and husband-management for slaves and women), which was designed to avoid the perilous dangers that contact, let alone confrontation, with the powerful could bring. In effect dual modes of conduct were in operation: one for friends and other ordinary people; another for patrons and superiors. Apuleius notes the deference of the poor for the rich.[116] They assumed the hesitating, risk-averse habits of the slave, always watching attentively for any tell-tale signs of mood-change in their master and shaping their language to conceal any personal opinions that might conflict with his interests. An astrologer describes two of the attributes of the feminine star sign, Pisces, as 'silent and mutable'.[117] Women had to watch what they said and adapt their verbal postures according to the mood of the man they were talking to. It is common in other cultures that 'members of dominated groups or lower strata express deference to dominant members by bumbling ... and language of slow-wittedness or buffoonery'.[118] Such fawning humility in the presence of superiors was a necessary posture for them to adopt. They needed to show that they knew their place because that is what the elite expected of them. It was normal behaviour for social inferiors. By keeping the elite sweet, the non-elite had a far better chance of getting something out of the meeting. The rich, after all, were the winners in Roman society and it was important to be aligned with them. But the fact that the non-elite maintained such a posture in public does not mean we should believe it represents what they actually felt. Just as patrons cared for their clients only to the extent that they brought them the social benefit of enhanced status, so the people's concern with the elite ran only to the material benefits that could be extracted from the relationship.

Competition and hierarchy meant that the need to be two-faced pervaded Roman society. After the death of Augustus, 'the more respectable the person, the more deceptive and eager he was. They arranged their expressions so as not to seem too happy at his death or too upset at the new beginning, combining tears with joy, lamentation with flattery.'[119] If a person lost his status he was no longer worth knowing: 'But now I have become poor I am cut dead and don't even get a glance from those who previously bowed and cringed to me and hung on my nod.'[120] The fact that inheritance provided the easiest route to making a fortune in Roman society, and high mortality rates always kept it as a lively possibility, meant that legacy-hunting became a focus for deception. Artemidorus interprets a dream where a man eats his own excrement on a piece of bread as signifying that he will get an inheritance through illegal means, but will not be above suspicion and will remain full of disgrace.[121] We should remember that there were benefits in the game of legacy-hunting for the will-makers too: it kept people running around after them and attentive to their needs. It was a mark of his perspicacity that when Aesop was asked, 'What circumstance will produce great consternation among men?', he answered, 'If the dead were to arise and demand back their property.'[122]

The elite used wealth to extract deference, but the people also actively managed the elite by showing their appreciation. The elite needed popular approval to help produce public legitimacy for their powerful position. By reacting positively to certain acts of patronage, the non-elite were able not just to encourage donors to continue to give but to give in particular ways. An example of this can be seen in the congiaries, or bonuses, that emperors occasionally paid to Roman citizens. Julius Caesar and Augustus both gave large gifts to the urban plebs, but this established a precedent which the plebs themselves were able to exploit. So when Marcus Aurelius returned to Rome in 177 CE after some years away campaigning in Germany, the plebs sensed an opportunity. They greeted him with shouts of 'Eight' and held up eight fingers to represent the eight gold coins they thought they should each receive. This was a larger sum than any previous emperor had given. Sure enough, Marcus gave in and they got their bonus.[123] In this way, a section of the non-elite were able to exploit precedent and a communal sense of history against an emperor. It was a trick the non-elite generally were always keen to play: trying to transform discretionary gifts into permanent rights. The elite, by contrast, always sought to emphasize the discretionary nature of their gifts so as to maximize both their control and the appearance of generosity.

At the other end of the non-elite social scale, beggars used the same tactics to try and get alms. They worked on a shared sense of pity to encourage people to give them a few coppers. Pity, in that sense, can be thought of as a 'form of insurance against an uncertain future'.[124] It made people think about what would happen to them in that situation, which, given the economic vulnerability of a large part of the population, was not so unimaginable.

3. A wall painting from Pompeii showing bread being doled out to the poor

The elite were not stupid. They knew the game the people were playing. Seneca warns that the wise man is not 'seduced by the flattery of a beggar'.[125] But from the elite point of view, being flattered and treated deferentially was a mark of status. As Artemidorus says, flattery is good for those 'accustomed to flatter, but it indicates humiliations for other men'.[126] The non-elite did not naturally enjoy sucking up to wealthy patrons. It was something they had to do to make a material difference to their lives.

What happened when flattery failed? In certain situations, food crises for example, the non-elite's massaging of elite egos did not produce the desired results. At this point the non-elite could escalate the matter by starting to voice complaints. During problems with the grain supply in Rome, protests broke out in the theatre that 'were more outspoken than usual'. Moreover, 'the complaints were not just kept quiet', as obviously usually happened, and people went so far as to actually manhandle Claudius.[127] The non-elite can be seen as trying to create a moral imperative for the elite to help by gossiping, moaning and generally making it clear that pubic opinion was against the rulers. This was despite the fact that confrontation bought other economic risks: 'Most of the innkeepers desire peace. Their livelihood depends on their custom, which involves calm; every time they are closed, they lose money.'[128]

Politics in the narrow sense were of little use to the non-elite, even for those who did possess political rights. Only a tiny fraction of the Roman people were able to exercise their voting rights during the republic and these also were removed under the empire.[129] We have seen that the non-elite were ambivalent about authority. But when it came to crises, the people showed that they expected their rulers to sort out their problems. In part, this stemmed from the general belief that the elite were to blame for food crises in the first place. It was commonly held that elite middlemen were causing shortages and ramping up prices by hoarding supplies. During a food shortage in Antioch, the shout in the theatre was, 'Nothing is scarce, but nothing is cheap.' The emperor Julian's response was to tell the city's elite to 'reject unjust profits and to benefit the citizens'.[130] In a famous article, Thompson argued that a strong sense of popular morality could be discerned in protests of this kind.[131] The people believed in a fair price for bread and they held a strong expectation that the authorities were obliged to police the market so that it operated fairly. As such, the people believed in a moral economy. Food protests reflected a traditional view of social reciprocity between the rulers and the ruled, and popular anger erupted when this established social contract was broken.

Protest was a way of bringing popular complaints into the public domain, without risking full-scale confrontation. The usual code of deference, combined with elite indifference, meant that otherwise the people could not be sure that the elite were even aware that a problem existed. The people, in part at least, based these complaints on the same paternalistic standard that the elite held. But protest can also be seen as a strategy to try and kick the problem upstairs. And kicking the problem upstairs can be seen as an act of flattery. As Cameron has noted, demonstrations allowed the emperor to display his leadership qualities by solving the problem. It became a golden opportunity to show that he had the 'popular touch'.[132] Nor, as we shall see later, can all riots be seen as driven by moral or economic concerns. Some were about 'trivial matters',[133] such as when the people of Ephesus almost stoned the governor in Ephesus because of the coolness of the water in the public baths.[134]

Popular resources for problem-solving

I want to finish this chapter by looking at some of the different resources which most members of the non-elite could draw upon if they found themselves with a complex problem to solve. So far we have examined the different attitudes and approaches that the people could bring to problems. Here, we will see how far those attitudes were reflected in certain communal texts and whether they can shed any further light on how the non-elite world operated. I start by looking at proverbs and fables, then discuss popular religion and magic in general, before focusing on dice oracles, and the Oracles of Astrampsychus.

1. Proverbs and fables

Proverbs provided all Romans with a collection of compact, memorable pieces of practical advice, covering a whole range of issues.[135] The majority clustered around the basic features of life – birth, marriage, children, death – as well as providing practical strategies for dealing with authority and the powerful. They drew on their tradition for their authority and used their lack of context to be applicable to almost any specific situation. They were widely used and clearly embodied popular attitudes, many of which were shared with the elite. To that extent, they can be thought of as representing the folk or common culture of Rome. Their popularity can be gauged from the fact that good sayings could arouse applause in the theatres.[136]

Taken together, fables and proverbs provided a discourse on traditional rural life. It is a physical world of general conservatism; things are as they are and are unlikely to change. There is little by way of idealism to be found, with the focus more on practical hints at daily survival and coping with the myriad problems that life could send. Self-reliance is seen as praiseworthy, as is a belief in words not deeds. The 'limited good' assumption is hard at work almost everywhere, making the world a place where the best one can probably do is to maintain what one has in the face of strong competition from others. Poverty and destitution are only ever a stone's throw away, but such socio-economic inequality is seen as perfectly natural. Often they are hostile to women: 'don't trust a woman till she's dead' being an extreme example.[137] They are suspicious of power, seeing authorities as people who can only have a negative impact on the peasant's quality of life. They do their best to warn the powerful off: 'there is anger even in the ant'. But overall, as Morgan says, 'Fables paint a picture of a society dominated by inequality, hostility and fear.'[138]

Sayings and stories such as these were useful in stressful situations, in that they provided people with a simple fall-back system on which to rely for advice. It is true that they can occasionally be contradictory and inconsistent, but these contradictions draw attention to the underlying difficulty involved in taking the decision. Proverbs were, after all, things to be deployed in difficult situations. They provided tools to think with. But in doing so they highlighted the fact that traditional sayings still needed active interpretation by the user. Imagination could fashion the fables to produce new and creative meanings. They still left plenty of room for active decision-taking.

Morgan argues that taken together fables, proverbs and sayings provided a 'viable ethical system for the Roman Empire'.[139] Similarly, Veyne suggests that a distinct plebeian morality can be glimpsed in the Sayings of Cato, a discourse forged in daily experience and founded on common sense, far removed from the concerns of the elite world.[140] This is undoubtedly at least partly true. The speech of the freedmen in the *Satyricon* is peppered with such phrases and they clearly reflected something of the traditional popular culture. But such traditional tools had in many ways been superseded by more sophisticated, urban approaches to risk control and patron-management. By the time of the empire, the non-elite had had to learn how to deal with a far more sophisticated society and economy. Simple, peasant tales were never going to be enough to provide an ethical system that could cope with all the nuances of a refined social hierarchy and power structure.

2. *Popular religion and magic*

The non-elite had access to a range of religious ideas to help them overcome difficulties they encountered throughout life. There was, to use Eidinow's phrase, a 'vast market in supernatural services'.[141] These included diviners, prophets and magicians. There were even door-to-door dream soothsayers.[142] Not everyone necessarily regarded all these practices equally. The dream interpreter, Artemidorus, lists a hierarchy of soothsaying: he believes in the interpretation of dreams, animal entrails, the flight of birds, and the constellations, but doubts horoscopes and despises divination drawn from the interpretation of the face, the shape of the hand, dice, dishes, sieves, cheese and necromancers as 'false and misleading'.[143] Some of the elite branded all such popular beliefs as superstition. One writer describes coming across some miracle books and how he was 'seized with disgust for such worthless writings, which contribute nothing to the enrichment or profit of life'.[144] The authorities had always been suspicious of religious practices that had their origin outside of traditional Roman religion. Bacchus worship, for example, with its mixed-sex, nocturnal celebrations, was targeted early for suppression and in 186 BCE was dissolved and the ringleaders executed. Later there were periodic expulsions of astrologers and suppression of groups such as the Druids, who were believed to perform human sacrifice, and Christians.

Popular religion was embedded in every area of non-elite life. People kissed their hands to the gods as they passed sacred places and statues, 'as is the custom of the superstitious common people'.[145] They would often carry a small effigy of their favourite god on their person and would travel far to avoid places of ill-omen. The elder Pliny noted that many Romans only cut their nails on market days, in silence, beginning with the forefinger.[146] Visiting a shrine was common and we can get a sense of the experience from the description of Maximus of Tyre: 'Not far from the lake of Avernus was an oracular cave, which took its name from the calling up of the dead. Those who came to consult the oracle, after repeating the sacred formula and offering libations and slaying victims, called upon the spirit of the friend or relation they wished to consult. Then it appeared, an insubstantial shade, difficult both to see and to recognize, yet endowed with a human voice and skilled in its prophecy. When it had answered the questions put to it, it vanished.'[147]

Popular religion constituted too great an array of practices to be neatly defined and explained. Devotional acts served both private and public functions. Popular associations (*collegia*), for example, were formed as burial clubs, dedicated to particular gods that were appropriate for the club's membership, and provided a communal focus for religious acts relating to funerary rites. Votive offerings were the staple expression of individual religiosity, and articulated popular fears concerning an enormous range of afflictions and illnesses. Hundreds of these clay images have been found in the River Tiber, where it runs through Rome, often depicting such things as internal organs, frequently the uterus. These offerings were also used in healing cults like that of Asclepius on the Tiber island.[148] Offerings such as these, like sacrifices, served to establish a gift-giving relationship between the donor and the recipient. The expectation was that the gods would be obliged to return the favour in some way, hopefully the specific way for which they had been asked. By giving to the gods, the donor also opened up lines of communication with the divine. The individual's relationship with the gods, therefore, established a model for all his or her dealings with the powerful on earth. Rituals such as sacrifice reproduced and openly accepted the existing hierarchy of power. Establishing a relationship, offering fulsome praise, and pandering to their desires by giving them small gifts, all served to try and hook the powerful into a reciprocal relationship that would benefit the individual in times of need.

Typical Roman needs can be seen in the subjects about which people asked for divine help and advice. For example, some of the headings of the astrologer Dorotheus of Sidon's work run as follows: runaways, asking from rulers, freeing slaves, buying land or slaves, building, demolishing, hiring, pregnancy, partnerships, marriage, buying animals, buying and selling, wills, illness, surgery, medicine, spirits, when to start something, arguments, property, travel, the sick, bondage and chains, letters, building ships, debt and eyes. The cult of Diana at Aricia was popular with women and reflected their concerns about such matters as childbirth, death, education, love and healing.[149]

Magic provided another religious method for dealing with divine power. In the popular view, the spiritual world teemed with demons and spirits of the dead, above all those of people who had met a violent death. No clear division of the natural and supernatural world existed, and as a result manifestations of the demonic could happen anywhere and at any time in the real world. Yet these mysterious forces could also be partly controlled if approached in the right way. Since these forces were so strong, it was a matter of vital concern for the individual to find a way of accessing this power. Supernatural powers could help ward off evil spirits, prevent attack or attack others. Illness was not seen as a physiological process but as an invasion of the body by demonic forces, so amulets and apotropaic phalluses helped repel these forces. In fact, the magician's crisis management, 'became a necessity to the lives of ordinary people', and the magician a 'problem solver who had remedies for a thousand petty troubles', from migraines to bedbugs, from love to money.[150]

Lucian mocks the complicated formulas that magicians prescribed: 'If you pick up from the ground in your left hand the tooth of a shrew which has been killed as I have described, wrap it in the skin of a lion which has recently been flayed, and tie it round your legs, the pain stops at once.' 'Not a lion,' someone objects, 'but that of a young female deer, still unmated.'[151] Similarly, in the *Alexander Romance*, the magician, Nektanebos, calculating the courses of the heavenly bodies, urges Olympias to restrain herself from giving birth: 'Hold yourself back ... if you give birth now, you will produce a servile prisoner or a monster.'[152] But there was broad cross-social belief in the power of magic. The orator, Libanius, was cured of health problems after he found a dead chameleon in his classroom, which was in a significant pose: with its head under its hind legs, one foot missing and the other closing its mouth, it was clear that this was the work of a rival carrying out magic against him. Removing the cause of his ailment removed the illness.[153] As Eidinow says, this was 'a society riddled with rumour, beset by envy, suspicion, and rivalry', where risk was 'other people'.[154] Curse tablets provided a means of pre-emptive strike against such perceived risk. Curses also provided a means for those who felt they were under threat to alleviate the danger. Yet there was surely also a sense that other people had to be respected because they too had access to magical powers. In this way magic, or the threat of magic lurking in the background, could act to calm tensions and rein in disputes that might otherwise have got out of hand.

The non-elite are often accused of being naively credulous about religious activities such as magical curses. People, says Betz, 'want to believe so they simply ignore their suspicions that magic may all be deception and fraud'.[155] Yavetz notes that credulity 'is undoubtedly one of the fundamental characteristics of all masses, including the Roman'.[156] The ancient elite also mocked the general belief in fake prophets and healers: in Lucian's *The False Prophet*, Alexander feigns fits of madness with foaming at the mouth, and the sight of the foam filled the people with superstitious awe.[157] Likewise, Paul of Aegina describes how some doctors 'pretend to be able to cure epilepsy, and having made a cross-shaped incision in the back of the head, they extract from the wound something they have hidden in their hands, and thereby impress people'.[158] But the people were far more wary of being conned than they are given credit for. An Aesop fable describes a sorceress, who makes no small profit, being brought to trial and condemned to death as she does not even have the power to persuade her fellow man let alone powerful demons. Another talks of a prophet who fails to foretell the burglary of his own house. Beware fake religious types is the clear message.[159] At the very least, this scepticism forced religious interpreters to come up with creative explanations for failure: 'A man who was to receive an incision around his scrotum prayed to Serapis for the success of the operation. He dreamt that the god said to him, "Undergo the operation with confidence. You will regain your health through surgery." The man died. For, as if he had been cured, he was destined to suffer no pain. It was quite natural that this should be the case, since the god is not an Olympian or celestial deity but rather a god of the underworld.'[160]

Popular scepticism can also be found in the jokes of the Philogelos: an astrologer casts the horoscope of a sick boy, promises his mother he will live a long time and then demands his fee. She says that she will give it to him tomorrow. 'But what happens if he dies in the night?' he replies. Or the one where someone on a trip asks a charlatan prophet how his family are back home. Being told they are all well, especially his father, he says, 'But my father's been dead for ten years!' 'Ah,' the prophet replies, 'clearly you do not know who your real father is.'[161] Nor were people only sceptical about those selling religious services. In the fable of the sick man and the doctor, a man is told by a doctor that sweating, shivering and diarrhoea are all good symptoms. 'Then I'm dying of good symptoms', says the man.[162] As Trimalchio says, 'A man who is always ready to believe what he is told will never do well, in business especially.'[163] The people were too wary of being conned in their daily lives and too watchful of each others' motivations to be blindly credulous of every pedlar of popular religion that came their way. The people shared with the elite a belief in powerful supernatural forces and the possibility of their manipulation, but that did not prevent them from being sceptical about individual practitioners. Nor did an occasional charlatan shake their belief in how the supernatural worked, in the same way that seeing a bad doctor today would not make most people lose faith in the entire medical system.

What characterized all these popular religious notions was that they provided easy access to all; they were widely used; they were believed to work; and they were non-exclusive, in that making use of the services of one did not preclude the use of another so as to minimize the possibility of one solution not working. Seeking divine support from a variety of religious sources was fully in keeping with the non-elite approach of diversifying to reduce risk. One of the reasons the Christians were so easily scapegoated was that the

4. Votive offering of a blind girl hoping for divine help

rejection of pagan gods seemed to be a needless risk to take. As Tertullian complains, 'If the Tiber overflows or the Nile doesn't, if there is a drought or an earthquake, a famine or a pestilence, at once the cry goes up, "Throw the Christians to the Lions!"'[164]

Popular religiosity was to some extent characterized by a commitment to the present. Charms were worn to ensure luck, or gain power over a rival or obtain a cure, not in the distant future but in the here-and-now. There was no general belief that the gods cared for or would reward human virtue in the future. Yet popular ideas about the afterlife did exist. The popular eschatology was, however, as varied as their other religious notions. Again, to some degree the afterlife was seen as an extension to the present life, not as a preliminary to a future state. Heaven became a vision of the household, with the tomb a kind of permanent home: 'here is my home forever; here is a rest from toil', as one epitaph has it.[165] Funerary inscriptions can give us some idea about how those of the non-elite who were wealthy enough to afford such things felt about life beyond the grave. Even if these phrases are often formulaic, the formula did still have to be selected by the customer and so in some way reflects his or her views. Of course, the very fact that many of the non-elite thought it was worth paying so much for a tombstone and an inscription, and belonging to burial clubs that would ensure the correct care of their corpse, shows that many put a high emphasis on giving their remains a proper send-off from this world. Despite this expense, some epitaphs were resolutely nihilist: 'Into nothing from nothing how quickly we go';[166] while *non fui, fui, non sum, non curo* (I was not, I was, I am not, I don't care) was so common that it was often abbreviated to simply *nffnsnc*. Others were unrepentant: 'the god of wine never let me down'. An end to back-breaking work is a common theme: as one woman's tombstone says, 'Where have you gone, dear soul, seeking rest from troubles, for what else but trouble did you have all your life?'[167]

Other tombs have more grandiose ideas and feature personal deification. Several hundred examples of mainly freedmen show them representing themselves on their tombstones as gods, with their portrait being combined with a familiar divine iconographic type and the god's attributes. Appropriately, the gods most commonly chosen were Mercury and Hercules, the gods of merchants, craftsmen and profit.[168] Perhaps the ultimate non-elite tomb is the fictional creation of the wealthy freedman, Trimalchio. He wants it to be decorated with images of himself as a magistrate, doling out money to the people, with statues of his wife, slaves, pets and favourite boy, and a sundial so that anyone who wants to know the time will have to read his name, as well as an epitaph, the last line of which will read, 'he never listened to philosophers'. But he has no illusions about it being treated with respect and plans to employ guards from his own retinue of freedmen to stop people defecating on it.[169] In the eyes of the mocking elite, the wealthy freedman wanted to be remembered for becoming one of the elite, but his choices reveal his true servile status. To what extent this accurately reflects what the real non-elite wanted is impossible to say. The people seem to have had an extremely varied set of beliefs about what happened to them after death. But the fact that the people had an inconsistent and vague eschatology did not mean they had no beliefs concerning the afterlife at all. Rather it reflected the fact that popular religion found a diversity of ways to express itself and did not have the doctrinal focus that later Christian thought was to possess.

3. *Alphabet and dice oracles*

In the centre of the west side of the forum at Kremna, a town in central Pisidia (an area in modern Turkey), in a conspicuous and central position, opposite the forum entrance, stood a tall rectangular marble pillar, on which rested a statue of Mercury, god of trade, profit and travel, and carved on to all four sides of this column, in hexameter verse, were the fifty-six replies of the god to the fifty-six combinations that can be thrown with five knucklebones.[170] So, for example, the throw is 11143; the answer reads 'don't perform the activity which you are now undertaking'. Clear and firm advice. Other pillars such as this, almost exactly the same, have been discovered elsewhere in the region. Similarly, almost a dozen alphabet oracles have also been discovered in this small region alone. Oracles of this kind were extremely popular and widely consulted throughout the empire. Dodds thought that 'No doubt much of the increasing demand for oracles simply reflects the increasing insecurity of the times.'[171] I cannot answer so general a question. Instead I want to look at what these oracles can tell us about the non-elite world.

Many of the knucklebone replies relate to Mercury's specialities. This suggests that the pillar was consulted by small businessmen and traders embarking on travel. It seems that we are dealing with the upper end of the local non-elite rather than the destitute. The replies are mostly quite conservative, with a strong emphasis on timing: 'Why do you hurry? Stay calm, for the time is not yet ripe ... but if you relax a little, you will achieve success.' This conservatism is reflected in a keenness to avoid confrontation: 'by avoiding hostility and ill-feeling you will eventually reach the prizes'. There is the usual popular mistrust of the law: 'it is terrible to enter into a quarrel and a judicial lawsuit'. But when strife does occur, we see a fierce determination to crush any adversary: 'you will punish your adversary and have him under your control'.

These decisions clearly caused the enquirers significant amounts of stress. The replies are scattered with phrases such as 'do not distress yourself', 'stay calm', 'don't be afraid'. The stress that the struggle to make a decision has caused is also reflected in the imagery within the text: 'you are struggling against the waves that oppose you', 'you are looking for a fish in the ocean', 'don't strive in vain like the bitch that gave birth to a blind whelp'. The same traditional, rural, down-to-earth images appear in the phrases used to describe the perils that lie in wait for the questioner's venture: 'do not move every stone in case you find a scorpion', 'do not place your hand in the mouth of a wolf', 'a great fiery lion wanders about', 'stay at home lest a deadly beast and tormentor come near'. In Aesop's fables, by comparison, we find, according to Morgan, thirty-seven lions and twenty-nine wolves. These were the kinds of animal that loomed terrifyingly large in the popular imagination, and traditional imagery such as this personified the risks facing an individual into forms they could more easily comprehend.

When individuals consulted a pillar such as the one in Kremna, they were clearly under pressure. Eidinow argues that people used oracles to reinforce predetermined choices, but I do not think that does justice to the stress they were under to make the right decision. What they needed was guidance and reassurance. Or, as one of the alphabet oracles states, 'There are sweaty times ahead, but you will survive them all.' Of the twenty-four lines in the alphabet oracle in Kibyra,[172] sixteen give clear guidance about timing and several others could easily be interpreted this way, as for example the line just quoted. Of those sixteen answers, seven say 'go ahead', five say 'wait' and four say 'don't'. These do not sound like the replies to give to someone who has already made up their mind. They are for people who are still wrestling with major decisions, which could have a meaningful impact on their lives, and who need some divine help to take them.

The replies to the dice oracle in Kibyra and Kremna give us a rough idea of the likelihood of a 'sweaty time' turning into a nightmare. Totalling up the outcomes, we find the following percentages:[173]

Favourable: 38 out of 56 = 68 per cent
(includes 7 after waiting)
Unfavourable: 10 = 18 per cent
Wait: 8 = 14 per cent

Interestingly, the interest rate charged on maritime loans was generally in the order of 20 per cent because of the high level of risk associated with shipping. Using the same assumptions as for subprime loans, with the crucial exception that the Recovery Rate would be zero because when a ship sinks everything is lost, then we can calculate that a 20 per cent rate implies a failure rate of 12 per cent. So we can say that the 18 per cent failure rate implied in the dice oracle reflects a slightly more conservative expectation than contained in market interest rates, but not one that is of an altogether different order. This points to the fundamental reason the dice oracles were so popular: it was because they broadly reflected the reality of small businessmen's lives and so gave good advice to those who needed it.

The dice and alphabet oracles expressed the popular belief in chance, but also that divine favour could be won to influence the outcomes of chance. But the chance that is found in the oracles is not the kind that could produce a world of limitless, random possibilities. It was a chance that can only ever result in a limited range of outcomes. It was a world where no new outcomes were possible.

4. *The Oracles of Astrampsychus*

The Oracles of Astrampsychus date from the second century and consist of a list of ninety-two questions that it was possible for the questioner to put to the gods through an intermediary. The oracles were extremely popular for centuries, with ten copies being found in the rubbish dumps of Egypt alone.[174] A later Christianized version was also produced, which outlived the Roman Empire. The Christian changes include some that reflect the changing moral atmosphere, so that the question 'Will I get back with my girlfriend?' became 'Will I become a bishop?' Unlike the dice and alphabet oracles, these are very confusing to use, in fact deliberately so in order to enhance the reputation of the diviner who was being consulted. Each question has ten different responses. There are also eleven dummy decades of responses to questions that do not exist so as to make matters more confusing. They are, as Hansen says, 'easy to use but difficult to fathom'.[175] The topics cover the now familiar range: love, money, travel, health, work, business, inheritance, public and private life. Many imply a male questioner, none a female one. They are cross-social, ranging from questions from slaves, 'Am I going to be sold?', to the ambitious, 'Will I be a senator?' They are unsentimental and practical. As Klingshirn says of the later *Sortes Sangallenses*, 'for the most part, it warns clients to look out for their own good fortune, to make decisions on the basis of aggressive self-interest'.[176] Given the list is quite comprehensive, with ninety-two questions, it is tempting to ask what topics were not covered. The two that spring to mind are: violent crime, which might suggest that perhaps non-elite life was not quite so pervasively violent as is sometimes suggested (including by myself); and patronage, which again suggests that perhaps patrons did not figure largely in the popular consciousness. This may reinforce the impression given by Tacitus that patronage only reached down to the respectable poor.[177] I can add, incidentally, that in order to convince myself that these oracles were nonsense and to work out how to use them I tested them by asking a question where I was confident that I knew the answer: 'Will I become a bishop?' Having made various small calculations and leafed through the decades of responses, the reply was 'Yes, you will become a bishop, after a while.' So now I don't know what to think.

For each question, the ten possible answers are spread throughout the text with what appears to be 'a balance between positive and negative responses'.[178] But on closer inspection that is not always the case. Let us look at Question 30, 'Will I rear the baby?' This is clearly a question that reveals the risk concerned with child rearing in Roman society. Of the ten possible answers they divide into the following groups:

3 'survive'
3 'survive with toil'
2 'die'
1 'not reared'
1 'thrives'

This is not a 50–50 split. It shows the various different outcomes that an infant faced in the first days of its life. It also implies probabilities about each of these events happening. So we can say that there was only a 10 per cent chance that the baby would thrive but a 20 per cent chance that it would die. One in ten were not reared, presumably either through infanticide or exposure.

Similarly, when Q64 asks, 'Am I going to see a death?', no less than seven responses say yes, and one that you will see two deaths. Partly this is because death was so common, but presuming that the question refers to a specific incidence of illness, it reflects the fact that the questioner would only be asking if the sick person was already seriously ill, and in the ancient world serious illness was usually fatal; 70 per cent of the time according to the oracles. The response to one of these deaths is that 'you'll rejoice', which underlines the competitive nature of this social world. Q42 asks, 'Will I survive the sickness?', and the answers are weighted the other way round, with 70 per cent recovering, although 20 per cent only 'in time'. But the fact that someone who is well enough to ask still has a 30 per cent chance of dying (still better than the 70 per cent of Q64 when someone else was posing the question), emphasizes the terrifying reality of illness in antiquity.

Is there a way we can we test these implied probabilities against the reality? One easy way is by looking at the percentages for rearing the child in Q30. Comparative evidence suggests that about 30 per cent of all Roman children would have died in their first year.[179] This compares with 20 per cent in the implied figures, which also suggests that 30 per cent only survive 'with toil'. This suggests that the probabilities are not significantly different to the social reality that the non-elite faced. The diviner may also have rigged his answers according to what he could sense from the client about the likely outcome.

This would be easily done, especially if the client were illiterate, and probably not hard anyway given the complexity of the whole procedure. It could be argued that the answers are random. But imagine if the father of an average baby today went to a doctor and on asking him the chances of its immediate survival was told they were only 70 per cent; he would think the doctor were crazy. The Oracles of Astrampsychus worked and were so popular over such a long period of time because they broadly reflected the realities of non-elite life and their experience of how it worked. Clearly any one individual questioner will get a one-in-ten answer, but over the centuries all those answers will have averaged out and people as a whole will have formed the conclusion that the oracles were useful because they reflected life as it was. It told them what they collectively expected to hear. The oracles were not, therefore, just good to think with, they were good to figure with. Because the answers broadly reflected the likelihood of any one particular outcome, it was a way of playing the odds. It focused energies on the probable, not the possible.

What do the other questions tell us on this basis? On travel, Q12 'Will I sail safely?', tells us to expect a 50 per cent chance of delays and a 20 per cent chance of grave danger, including shipwreck. Interestingly, that 20 per cent chance again ties in with the kind of probabilities we found in the dice oracles and interest rates. Q80 'Is the traveller alive?', tells us that there is a 60 per cent chance of him being fine – 'don't be distressed' – but a 30 per cent likelihood of his being dead (one of the deaths is caused by poisoning). These poor odds underline the dangers of travel, particularly for the non-elite who could mostly not afford to employ protection.

On theft, Q40 asks, 'Will I find what I have lost?', and 70 per cent of the time the answer was no, with only 20 per cent positive and 10 per cent saying 'in time'. The lack of police or other means to trace petty criminals meant that the recovery of stolen property was unlikely. What counted in the victim's favour was that often, as Dorotheus warned us above, it was people within, or known to, the household who had perpetrated the theft and so were more likely to be found out.

Debt is a common theme. Q25, 'Will I be able to borrow money?', has a mixed collection of responses: four are outright negative, which underlines that the risks involved in the subprime market meant that the non-elite did not always find it easy to access credit. Of the four positive replies, one says only with collateral, one that the questioner will suffer as a result, another that he will profit and another that he will spend it. The two remaining replies are interesting in that they emphasize what a face-to-face, personal transaction borrowing money could be: 'You will eventually borrow money from the person you wish to' and 'not yet' as 'someone doesn't trust you'. Lenders had to be cultivated in the same way as other wealthy patrons. In Q26 a worried questioner asks, 'Will I pay back what I owe?' This gives a 70 per cent positive set of responses, although two only pay back in time, implying a minimum 30 per cent default rate not taking into account the cost of the two delays, slightly above the middle of the range that implied default rates had earlier suggested. Again, perhaps it is because the questioner is already sufficiently worried about his or her financial position to be asking that makes for a fairly negative outlook in the responses. The replies also include two statements to positive responses which underline the stress that being in debt could create: 'you'll be happy', 'you'll rejoice'. And, as we saw earlier, lending money could be a stressful activity too. Q58 asks, 'If I lend money will I not lose it?' The phrasing of the question is itself indicative of a risk-averse, conservative attitude, but then that was what was probably required to be a successful moneylender. The trouble that the non-elite had in repaying their loans can can be seen in the range of responses: three say lend but only with collateral; four say that the money will be recovered but 'slowly', 'eventually after a fight', 'slowly' again, and 'you'll gratefully recover it' suggesting a few sweaty times for the lender. Three advise strongly against lending: 'don't lend anything', 'don't because you'll lose it', and, in a statement that emphasizes the scepticism that was required, 'Don't be trusting lest you have regrets.' It is interesting to note that the 30 per cent default rate implied by these responses is also close to the centre of the 10–44 per cent range that we inferred from interest rates earlier.

Typical slave concerns are seen in their two questions, Q74, 'Am I going to be sold?', and Q32, 'Will I be freed from servitude?' The first question gives a 60–40 response in favour of sale, which in itself suggests either quite a high turnover of slaves, or that a slave would only ask the question if he suspected something was afoot and so the answers were skewed to meet this expectation. The answers to the second question are interesting because freedom seems to be pushed off into the distance: five say 'not yet', two say 'after some time', another 'once you've paid', which could be any time. One gives an outright 'no' and advises the slave to 'be silent'. Only one is optimistic: they will be freed 'with a good bequest'. This was the life of permanently hoping for a better future that many slaves lived. If they felt unable to wait and fled, the master could seek a response to Q36, 'Will I find the fugitive?' It is heartening to find that, as with stolen goods, the odds favour the runaway: 60 per cent will not be found, 30 per cent will be and 10 per cent only after a time.

As with the dice oracles, business concerns feature heavily. Q31 asks, 'Will I be harmed in the business affair?' The responses are an even split of positive and negative, but are notable for the frequent phrases of reassurance: 'don't worry', 'don't be distressed', 'take heart', 'don't be afraid'. The risk involved in Roman business ventures clearly generated considerable quantities of anxiety for its businessmen. Q18, 'Is it to my advantage to enter into an agreement?', leans strongly in favour of the positive: 40 per cent give an advantage, 30 per cent a great advantage and only 30 per cent negative. Perhaps this suggests that mutualism was more widely favoured than other sources, such as magical curses, suggest. Business agreements would certainly have helped spread the risks of investment undertakings.

Eleven questions deal with official posts, ranging from becoming a clerk in the marketplace to becoming a senator. These are clearly not aimed at the destitute. It is noteworthy that the better off were so concerned as to whether they would acquire a particular position. Official posts were a source of status and greater financial security, and people were understandably keen to know if they were going to get the job. Several questions deal with legal matters, but are all toss-ups between positive and negative replies. This is not surprising given that the law would always divide equally between winners and losers.

The largest number of questions concerns family matters and relationships. Family management was key to placing one's life on a steady footing, which made taking oracular advice a sensible thing to do. The choice of spouse was a critical decision, but choosing a suitable partner was as tricky a business as ever. Q21 asks, 'Will I marry and will it be to my advantage?' This was not simply a matter of romance but a time for cool calculation. I list the main points of all ten responses below:

'not now'
'not now'
'yes if you hurry'
'yes but you'll dissolve it'
'yes but you'll dissolve it'
'you'll marry and then be sorry because you have gained nothing'
'you'll suddenly marry a woman who you know and want'
'you'll marry a woman from your daily acquaintance'
'yes and you'll be filled with regret'
'you'll be harmed in your first marriage; persevere'

Of the ten responses, 80 per cent say the marriage will proceed. Perhaps by the time the questioner has got as far as asking the oracle, matters will have progressed too far to be easily stopped. Note that it suggests that it was unusual to marry a woman who 'you know and want'. A quarter of the marriages end in divorce. Five of the eight can be termed unhappy arrangements. This is a pessimistic message to give a questioner who is considering marriage. It seems that the social pressure to marry pushed people into marriage even though they obviously had doubts. The responses suggest that most people may well have gone into marriage with low expectations of personal happiness resulting from it. It was business as much as pleasure.

Which leads on to Q100: 'Will I be caught as an adulterer?' Note the emphasis of the concern is not being an adulterer but being caught. From the answers, 60 per cent will not be caught, 30 per cent will be, and one unlucky questioner is told that it is his wife that 'loves another man'. Having an affair made people anxious and reassuring phrases such as 'don't be distressed' and 'don't be afraid' are found. As it says, being an adulterer is a 'putrid lot'.

In the event of an unhappy marriage, men sought to know whether they would separate from their wives. Q90 asks, 'Will I be estranged from my wife?', Q97, 'Will my wife stay with me?' Interestingly, the responses to the first question are more positive: 40 per cent will be estranged, 60 per cent will not. 'Persevere' and 'relax' they are told, even though some will 'be reconciled and be sorry'. But the outcome to the second question is that 90 per cent will be left by their wives. This could suggest that these particular questions have a random set of responses that tell us nothing, but it seems unlikely that nine out of ten replies would happen randomly to be the same. The compiler would have noticed and created a more even spread if an even split of answers was required. More likely is the fact that whereas the first question speaks of a mutual estrangement, the second question speaks in a plaintive, passive voice. It is the voice of an anxious husband who can tell that something is not right. Remember that the questioner selected the question. Hence, by the time someone is asking this particular question it can be assumed that marital relations have already deteriorated significantly and the responses are weighted accordingly. Three of the responses tell the husband that his wife is 'committing adultery'.

Inheritance concerns rank high in importance, concerning potential bequests from parents, mothers, fathers, wives, friends and a vague 'someone'. This reflects the fact that inheritance was the main source of wealth in Roman society. A sign of the high mortality rates in the Roman world is that 30 per cent of the replies responding to Q48, 'Will I inherit from my parents?' are 'no, they'll bury you'. Q62 asks generally, 'Will I have an inheritance from someone?', and 80 per cent of the replies are positive. But the importance of inheritances means that it was never quite that simple: 'you won't be sole heir', 'you won't receive all of it', 'you'll suffer a great financial loss', 'with another trial'. One even states, 'yes and you'll die soon'. Perhaps it was the stress of it all.

'Will I be successful?' asks Q19 and the main points of the ten replies, listed below, sum up the experience of trying to get on in the non-elite world;

'no'
'at last'
'eventually'
'soon'
'from your own labours'
'from your own labours'
'from your own labours'
'from inheritance'
'in everything'
'at last and be master of the household'

Getting on required hard work, patience and luck. And if it all came good, you too could be the 'master of the household'.

Conclusion

An inscription from Forlì in Italy recounts the life story of a man nicknamed 'farmer', who had indeed been a success and, through years of effort, had risen from the ranks of the slave gangs to being the master of his own household. 'Take all this as true advice,' he tells us, 'whoever wants to live really well and freely: first, show respect where it is due; next, want what's best for your master; honour your parents; earn others' trust; don't speak or listen to slander. If you don't harm or betray anyone you will lead a pleasant life, uprightly and happily, giving no offence.'[180] This was the kind of conservative, hard-working tenacity that was needed to succeed in the world of the Roman non-elite.

The problem for most people was that poverty was almost impossible to shake off – 'she has countless hooks growing all over her body'.[181] They had to resort to more cunning tricks to ensure their survival, whether it was working the wealthy to ensure they kept giving or gossiping about the neighbours to keep them in their place. Creativity was needed in the long grind of daily existence. This was a society where the concept of the 'limited good' seems to have operated and the perception was that those who prospered did so at another's expense. Such an outlook warranted the adoption of more aggressive, beggar-thy-neighbour tactics. There is perhaps less mutualism than we might have expected, or wished, to find.

The people tried to control the riskiness of their environment by managing the core institution of their life, the family. By keeping the balance of their primary social group in equilibrium they could better hope to survive the frequent shocks that came their way. A bit extra had a huge impact in groups so vulnerable to impoverishment. Constant calculation was required to make do with limited resources, and indeed to acquire them in the first place. Gambling helped train the non-elite in the necessary life skills. The main aim was always to secure subsistence, but for the freeborn that aim was also linked to a notion of their having a minimum level of status that required the elite to help them in times of shortage.

They believed themselves surrounded by many unseen forces, some of which were malevolent or potentially malevolent, and they sought protection by all means available to them. Their wealth, health and security all faced constant threat by spiritual forces. Some of their problems were the work of fate; others chance; others still of people enlisting evil spirits. They had a tendency to adopt a belt-and-braces approach. Given such an uncertain environment, why use just one resource when several would do? But we should not then see them as credulous simpletons. The people had to be discerning to survive. They did not just believe in anything; they believed in what worked.

An Aesop fable describes how Eros was born of Poverty and Resourcefulness. As a consequence he inherited the characteristics of both: he is 'rough and unkempt, has no shoes or house, sleeps on the road ... and is always a companion of need'. But like his father, he is 'courageous, bold, impetuous, a stout hunter, always contriving some scheme ... a powerful beguiler, trickster, and sophist'.[182] These were the traits the non-elite needed to show, if they were to survive the predictably irregular problems that life in the Roman Empire would throw their way.

2

Mental Health

Consider the following case study:

> A young man of nineteen from a moderately wealthy background. He
> was always very close to his parents and never fitted in at school, where
> he had no friends. His parents both died suddenly. Shortly afterwards
> he started hearing voices. He gave away his substantial inheritance and
> left the family home to live in a graveyard on the edge of town, where
> he has remained alone for twenty years. He consistently rejects author-
> ity. He never washes. He suffers repeated visions and shuns all social
> contact.

I showed these notes to a medical doctor and his reaction was an
instantaneous 'schizophrenia'. But the young man in question was not
from the modern world.[1] He was from a small Egyptian village in the
third century, his name was Anthony, and he became famous for his
exploits as one of the first monks. In the late Roman world, he was
not considered to have a mental disorder; he came to be considered
holy almost beyond measure. The aim of this chapter is certainly not
to give retrospective diagnoses of the dead. Nor is it to suggest that
the Romans were living in what Dodds called an 'age of anxiety', an
'endogenous neurosis' caused by 'intense and widespread guilt feelings'.[2] It is to see what modern mental health research can tell us
about the non-elite in Roman society; it is to examine the very different ways in which the Romans thought about mental disorder; and
it is to understand how mental phenomena had a major impact on
popular perceptions of their world.

What is mental illness?

Most people have an image of the mentally ill as suffering from severe forms of insanity. But mental illness covers a wide range of mental disorders: anxiety disorders, depression, schizophrenia, personality disorders and dementia, to name but some of the more widely known. The fourth edition of the *Diagnostic and Statistical Manual of Mental Disorders*, known as DSM IV, is the 'bible' of modern psychiatry.[3] Its 1,000 pages contain detailed descriptions of the symptoms of all recognized mental disorders. To give an idea of the range of illnesses that it covers, the following are the classificatory headings that it employs and the major conditions that each area includes:

1. Disorders of infancy, childhood or adolescence: mental retardation, learning disorders, motor skills.
2. Delirium, dementia, amnestic and other cognitive disorders.
3. Disorder due to general medical condition (i.e., poor physical health).
4. Substance-related disorders, including alcoholism and drug addiction.
5. Schizophrenia and other psychotic disorders (the primary symptoms of schizophrenia include: talking in a seemingly illogical, unconnected way, hallucinations or hearing voices, illusions of grandeur or persecution, being unresponsive to the social environment).
6. Mood disorders: depression (characterized by a loss of interest in nearly all activities, suicidal thoughts, social withdrawal, anxiety and loss of energy), manic episodes such as euphoria.
7. Anxiety disorders: panic attacks, agoraphobia, phobias, OCD, post-traumatic stress disorder caused by military service or an extremely stressful event such as robbery, rape, torture or disaster.
8. Somatoform disorders: disorders for which there is no medical explanation such as hysteria and hypochondria.
9. Factitious disorders: invented disorders such as malingering.
10. Dissociative disorders: disruption in consciousness, memory or perception, such as amnesia.
11. Sexual and gender identity disorders: various paraphilias including fetishism, frotteurism, paedophilia and sado-masochism.
12. Eating disorders: anorexia nervosa, bulimia nervosa.
13. Sleep disorders.

14. Impulse control disorders: kleptomania, pyromania.
15. Adjustment disorders: significant emotional or behavioural symptoms after a psychological stressor.
16. Personality disorders: an enduring pattern of inner experience and behaviour that deviates markedly from the expectation of the individual culture, such as schizoid personality disorder, involving restricted emotional expression and detachment from social relationships; histrionic personality disorder, involving excessive emotionality and attention-seeking behaviour; antisocial personality disorder, involving the disregard and violation of others' rights.

In America, there is a 48 per cent lifetime prevalence rate for psychiatric disorders, meaning that almost half of all people suffer from a recognizable mental disorder at some point in their lives. The prevalence rate over one year is as high as 30 per cent, which is about the same as in the UK. Of the 48 per cent, 56 per cent had two or more disorders. The disorders that accounted for the largest number of cases were major depression (17.1 per cent), alcoholism (14.1 per cent), social phobia (13.3 per cent) and simple phobia (11.3 per cent). Mental illness, therefore, can be thought of as a broad generic term for a range of illnesses that usually include affective or emotional instability, behavioural dysfunction and cognitive dysfunction or impairment.[4]

Mental health is a concept that refers to a person's emotional and psychological well-being. Good mental health reflects a state where people are able to use their emotional and cognitive capabilities, function in society and meet the ordinary demands of everyday life. Mental health describes how effectively people cope with stress and relationships, and how well they bounce back from tough situations. Factors that are good for an individual's mental health include high self-esteem, social inclusion and having access to social support networks. Mental health is a continuum and should not be seen as necessarily the opposite of mental illness. Mental health covers the whole range of mental states, from severe forms of illness such as schizophrenia to relatively minor anxiety disorders, which are often not that impairing, to an absence of any notable mental dysfunction.

Despite the impression that I have given so far, though, no precise definition exists concerning mental illness that is universally applicable. In fact, there is considerable disagreement over what constitutes a mental disorder. No overall explanation of the cause of mental disorder is known. Nor is there any recognized cure. There are four models for conceptualizing the causes of mental illness, which are briefly outlined below.

1. The medical model

The medical model treats mental illness as a disease with a physio-logical cause that can be treated by medical means. Some genetic links have been established for certain conditions, but for the vast majority of mental disorders no organic pathology has been estab-lished. The brains of the mentally ill almost always look exactly the same as those of the sane. Modern mental health care treats the symptoms of mental illness without having much awareness of any underlying cause. Prescriptive drugs simply control the symptoms, without having any curative effect. It seems clear, though, that some people seem to be genetically primed for certain mental disorders and that these can be triggered by certain environmental factors.

2. The psychological model

The psychological model treats mental disorders as being caused by internal crises, powerful instinctive forces and drives, and the repres-sion of these forces. Treatment consists in enabling people to under-stand the factors involved in the repression of these forces. This model sees all people in all cultures and all times as driven by the same internal forces. Some of the mental disorders that result from the repression of these forces were named after characters in Greek tragedy, such as Oedipus. To many critics, this is a modern myth based on an ancient one.

3. The anti-psychiatry model

By complete contrast, some, most famously Foucault, have seen mental disorder as a work of societal fiction.[5] Madness is seen as a social construction that reflects the enforcement of arbitrary norms within a particular society. For example, one definition of mental illness is that it is a 'significant deviation from standards of behaviour generally regarded as normal by the majority of people in a society'.[6] This is a social definition, based on behaviour that disrupts and dis-regards taken-for-granted norms within a society, but would seem to cover any form of eccentric behaviour. Mental illness then becomes a justification and method for society to confine those who it sees as unacceptable. The labelling of certain activities or attitudes as men-tally deviant depends on those who have power to enforce norms. There is no underlying mental pathology, apart from in incidents of actual trauma to the brain, to justify such treatment; it is simply a cultural act that reflects all the inequalities and tensions that a particular culture displays.

From this point of view, even severe disorders such as schizophrenia can be seen as a sane response to a mad world. Madness is a way for individuals to dissociate themselves from the oppressive environment in which they find themselves. The psychiatric profession becomes a self-sustaining industry that enforces a normalizing, repressive ideology by medicalizing deviant behaviour. Psychiatrists are nothing less than instruments of the power structure. Objections to this view focus on the fact that most severe mental illnesses are found to be very similar across all societies, with very similar patterns of behaviour, and are recognized as problematic by their societies.

4. The social stress model

The social stress model is something of a combination of the other three views. It recognizes that mental illness should not be thought of purely as an attribute of the individual and their particular brain pathology, because it is also a social experience. It starts from the elementary observation that 'Disorder is not uniformly distributed throughout society, but occurs more densely within some social strata than others.'[7] Generally, there is an inverse association with socioeconomic status. Different social groups are exposed to different social conditions according to their gender, status, age and wealth level, and these conditions have a meaningful effect on their overall level of mental health. This is not to deny that biological factors are often the main influence in an individual's mental illness. Instead, these personal factors are put to one side to account for individual rather than group differences. Abnormality is seen as a by-product of all societies but will especially result from one which favours certain groups over others, as this stratification results in the intensification of social stressors on the individual in lower groups. These social stressors can impair or overwhelm an individual's coping mechanisms and result in poor mental health and mental disorders. Societal responses to these mental disorders can vary considerably and include such processes as stigma, definition or confinement. The consequences of mental disorder for the individual can be very different from one society to another.

Can we apply any of these models to the Roman world? Are mental disorders objective states that can be analysed according to universal criteria even when comparing groups from different cultures, or is mental illness socially constructed? It is clear that social, economic and cultural forces all impact on how mental disorder is defined. Changes from DSM I to IV reflect this, most notoriously in the original classification of homosexuality as a mental disorder.[8] The prevalence rates quoted earlier are highly variable, depending on factors such as ethnicity or nationality. For example, the lifetime prevalence rate for major depression, which is 17.1 per cent in America, stands at only 2.9 per cent in South Korea. The lifetime prevalence for any mental disorder of 48 per cent in America compares with only 25 per cent in Lebanon and 13 per cent in urban China.[9] Moreover, developments within psychiatry have meant that the classificatory system has become far more sophisticated. Original terms have been replaced with more scientific-sounding labels, so the charming-sounding *folie à deux*, describing the collective delusion of crowds, has become 'shared psychotic disorder'. Yet other terms have been kept: malingering is still malingering, where it seems that the requirement of a work-centred society like America is to employ a word with moral force. Why not 'work avoidance disorder'; or just 'skiving'? There has also been a proliferation of disorders, from only about a dozen at the start of the twentieth century, to 106 in DSM I published in 1952, to 297 in DSM IV. I am happy to take a bet with anyone that when DSM V is published that number will not have fallen. Some of this can be attributed to better diagnosis. Psychiatrists know much more about the factors involved in mental health after decades of research. Perhaps there is more, and more varied kinds of, stress in the world, which has resulted in new forms of mental disorder. But there is also a sense of professionalization: a professional body now has a vested interest in legitimizing their status, which can result in over-medicalization.[10] Every eccentricity of behaviour can now be analysed as a mental disorder. I think I suffer from 'disorder of written expression' (bad handwriting) and most children I have ever met could be labelled as displaying 'oppositional defiant disorder', described as defiant acts by children such as temper tantrums, being annoying, angry or spiteful.[11]

When the *Titanic* sank into the freezing waters off Newfoundland, 2,200 people were left either dead, dying of hypothermia or sitting safely in lifeboats. Almost 70 per cent of the passengers died. The 'women and children first' ethic meant that proportionally more women survived. But 45 per cent of third-class female passengers died. And just 16 per cent died in second class, but a mere 3 per cent in first class.[12] The point of this is to show that social and economic status often has significant implications for personal well-being. Almost all societies have been found to have positive associations between wealth and physical health. The same is also true of mental health. As long ago as 1820, Burrows noticed an association between admission rates to the mental asylums of Bristol and crop failures. Jarvis, in 1885, found a relationship between poverty and insanity in America.[13] There is now a strong body of evidence that has found an inverse link between social and economic status and levels of mental illness.[14] Societal ordering exposes some groups to a much higher level of stress at the same time as limiting their access to ameliorating factors. Schizophrenia levels, for example, are highest among the lower classes who have the highest pressures and lowest resources to cope with them. There may be an element of double-counting at work here, in that the lower social groups also contain those who have drifted down the social scale because of poor mental health in the first place. Certain groups can find particular situations exceptionally stressful. Scheper-Hughes studied how pathogenic the harsh, bleak life of rural Ireland could be for young bachelors.[15] Mental disorders are also concentrated in major urban centres and in the less educated and poor: 'Regardless of the time and place, study after study confirms this general pattern.'[16] Different status groups also tend to suffer from different types of mental disorder. The poor have schizophrenia and personality disorders; the wealthy display more anxiety disorders. The weak tend to have a fatalistic belief that they are at the mercy of external forces, mistrust outsiders and see their lives as being beyond their control. People who feel they lack control in their lives tend to exhibit much higher rates of depression.

Social roles have a major impact on mental health and stresses are often expressed differently. While gender seems to have little impact on overall rates of mental illness, men and women suffer from very different types of disorder. Women tend to show higher incidence of mood disorders such as depression and anxiety, whereas men exhibit higher levels of abuse disorders and personality defects. There is a strong correlation between poor marital quality and poor mental health, especially for women. Employment factors are strongly related to mental illness in men. All of these gender tendencies obviously reflect the economic and social concerns of our modern, work-oriented society and cannot be expected to have been the same in Rome. But it suggests that in a status-obsessed society, status concerns will have had a major impact on Roman mental health.

Acute life events – shocks such as rape, military combat and violent assault – and exposure to chronic stress both result in significantly higher levels of mental illness. There are, however, buffers which can ameliorate the effect of these factors on the individual: high self-esteem, strong relationships and the perception of being in control. Equally, there are amplifiers: anger, hopelessness, repression, traumatic family events in early childhood, shame, death, violence and alcohol, all of which worsen the impact of acute and chronic stressors. Substantial co-morbidity exists between mental health and physical health. The poorer an individual's physical state, the less well he or she is able to cope with stressful situations. As DSM IV notes, the term 'mental' implies a distinction with 'physical' that is a 'reduction-istic anachronism of mind/body dualism'.[17] There is much that is physical in mental illness.

What exactly is meant by stress? The imagery is from engineering and relates to an external force acting upon a resistant body. In a social context, stress can be thought of as the result of conditions that threaten the individual, or as the effect that results from difficult socio-economic situations which tax the individual's capacity to cope. There is no agreement on what constitutes a stressor, particularly with regard to chronic stressors and the degree of severity they need to exhibit to be classified as such. It is not just dramatic events that cause mental health problems; often it is the repetition of the mundane that corrodes the individual's ability to cope. Acute event stressors require major adaptation by the individual to deal with the event. But not everyone reacts in the same way: some people seem almost immune to shocks, whereas others are highly sensitive. Susceptibility to mental illness is not just affected by social factors; it also depends on an individual's constitution and personal resources.

The lower down the social scale an individual sits, the higher the frequency and size of the stressors he or she is likely to face. Not only that, but the individual will have access to fewer of the resources which can act as buffers. Both these factors can be expected to result in significantly higher rates of mental disorder. The social aspects to poor mental health are complex and involve many factors. People react differently to the same set of stressors. Often, it is the speed of change as well as the undesirability of a major event that can over-whelm the ability to manage the situation. Widowhood is seen as especially stressful for this reason. The Social Readjustment Rating Scale was derived from survey evidence to see how people perceived certain stressful events. Death of a spouse was ranked highest at 100. Others include: divorce 73, death of a close family member 63, injury or illness 53, dismissal from work 47, change in financial situation 38, trouble with in-laws 29, and a family holiday 13. As individuals are faced by different stressors of this kind, the total score and the pres-sure mounts, and eventually people crack depending on their own personal resources and their access to support networks.

If mental illness is entirely a cultural construction, there is then no basis for using a social stress model to look at Rome. There is, how-ever, strong evidence that socio-economic inequalities significantly worsen group mental-health levels. I suggest that social stressors in the Roman world would have severely corroded the mental health of the overall population. Moreover, the degree of these stressors increased substantially for lower-status groups as a consequence of the steep stratification of Roman society. We can therefore reasonably expect that the non-elite suffered from a very poor level of mental health, in the same way that low-quality dietary inputs meant that they suffered from poor physical health.

Stressors in Roman society

Rome was 'a society that was more helplessly exposed to death than is even the most afflicted underdeveloped country in the modern world'.[18] We have seen that high infant mortality meant that perhaps a third of children died before reaching their first birthday, and a half before their fifth. People of all classes were exposed to death from an early age. An average Roman could expect to see perhaps two siblings, one or both parents, various uncles and aunts, as well as numerous cousins and friends all die in the course of their life. This will not only have produced frequent acutely stressful experiences, but it will have robbed many of the family support networks that might otherwise have acted as buffers. We should not assume that just because death was more frequent it was therefore less affecting, although it may well be the case that Romans developed better coping mechanisms to alleviate the stress.

One such mechanism for women may have been to limit emotional attachment to infants until they had passed the critical one-month stage, during which they were particularly vulnerable to disease and infection, or until they knew their husbands had decided the babies were to be kept and not exposed. This is a strategy that Scheper-Hughes found was employed in the slums of Brazil, where a kind of lifeboat ethics operated.[19] This may be alluded to in a legal opinion stating that 'children over six years of age can be mourned for a year, children under six for a month'.[20] There was at least a societal expectation that people should not grieve over young children of the high-risk age in the same way as for older children. The existence of exposure and infanticide as commonly used tactics for managing family size and structure may also reflect an emotional detachment from new-born infants. Firmicus Maternus analyses one star chart as showing that it tells of children who will 'either die on the threshold of life, or vital nourishment is denied them at their first steps, or they are exposed by an obstinate mother'.[21] Is the mother obstinate

because she is emotionally attached to her baby? Or is it her obsti-
nacy that is making her expose the child? Seneca talks of a mother
pitying a beggar as she wonders whether it could be her exposed son,
which does not suggest a throwaway mentality.[22] Some mothers felt
relatively little for their offspring: one son's mother 'did not feel for
her son that intense longing and affection for their children which
like a fire consumes some mothers'.[23] Others were almost engulfed
by anxiety. An Egyptian woman called Isidora wrote to her brother
and husband, as was common Egyptian practice, begging him to come
home to his sick child, the mother's anguish revealed in the change
in syntax and the staccato phrases: 'Do anything, postpone everything, and come, preferably tomorrow. The baby is ill. It has become
thin. It is already 200 days since you went away. I fear it will die in
your absence. Know for sure: if it dies in your absence, be prepared
that you might find me hanged.'[24] Fathers, at any rate, seem to
have been perfectly able to make life-or-death decisions about their
newborn offspring, so presumably were better able to cope with their
death. One strategy was to use black humour as a way of distancing
death. The *Philogelos* tells a joke about an egghead who, having just
buried his son, happened to meet the boy's teacher. 'I am sorry my
son was absent from school,' he apologizes, 'You see, he is dead.'[25]

Non-elite life took a heavy toll on the body. Skeletal analysis of
lesser-status individuals from Roman Tarraco in Spain 'suggested a
high infant mortality rate, that most of these "modest" individuals
were involved in strenuous physical activity, and that few reached old
age'.[26] They were the 'wretched paupers, their bodies burdened with
daily toil' that Firmicus Maternus forecast.[27] Elite bodies, by contrast,
were characterized by their not having to do manual labour.[28] Famine,
food crises, episodic malnutrition and endemic undernourishment all
intensified the physical stress on the non-elite.[29] These all had the
effect of weakening individuals' already precarious ability to cope
with mental stressors. Starvation itself had psychological effects by
creating depressions, light-headedness, irritability and mood swings.
Co-morbidity means we would expect to find poor mental health
where we find poor physical health and vice versa: even bishop
Synesius of Cyrene complained how 'bodily weakness has followed
in the wake of mental suffering. The remembrance of my departed
children is consuming my forces, little by little.'[30]

Economic stressors were in plentiful supply and intensified for
those most vulnerable to impoverishment. The oracles showed us the
kind of issues that the non-elite found sufficiently stressful to require
guidance and reassurance: debt, business ventures and agreements.
But it was falling into destitution that provoked the greatest anxiety.
Death and poverty overlapped here because it was often the loss of

the breadwinner that plunged the dependants into penury and also of itself weakened the support structure that the family was able to provide. Paupers were 'destitute of all necessities, without means of daily life. They beg for a living . . . Their bodies are sickly. They suffer from infected wounds or malignant humours under the skin which attack their joints.'[31] Slipping down the wealth ladder was frightening enough: the astrologer Dorotheus forecasts how a harmful decrease in livelihood will bring 'afflictions and agony'.[32] The stress caused by loss of income 'often stirs up revolutions among the people . . . They voice stupid hostilities, are unreasonable, with a temper which almost amounts to insanity.'[33] But collapse into poverty was a truly terrifying experience: 'He will abound in calamity, misfortunes in his property will reach him until everything he possesses disappears, and he will be frightened, perplexed, obsessed with delusions.'[34] Poverty launched an all-out assault on people's physical and mental health, such that, 'oppressed by weight of poverty so that throughout their whole life they will be almost naked and dressed in rags', 'from torment of body and mind they do not live out their allotted life span'.[35]

Both rural and urban life will have had a psychological impact on the non-elite. The city left people exposed to crime and living in overcrowded conditions, although it did offer compensations in greater variety and opportunities for work. One example has sixteen people living in one room.[36] Overcrowding can be regarded as both a subjective and objective experience. Non-elite Romans may well have had lower space and privacy expectations, so could have been less affected by living in high-density housing. Modern research suggests that both subjective and objective overcrowding relate strongly to poor mental health, primarily because of the poor-quality relationships and poor childcare which cramped conditions promote. Moreover, those who lack space tend to lack everything. They therefore have fewer resources to draw on in the event of acutely stressful situations. By contrast, life in rural areas tends to leave people feeling isolated and stuck in a routinized existence, but provides them with better support in the form of a more integrated social group. Such conservative societies can be stifling, though. Rome also had a high number of economic migrants. Immigrants tend to have poorer mental health because of weaker social support networks, traumatic experiences while migrating or that caused migration in the first place (such as being forcibly evicted from land), low-status occupations, problems integrating in their new home and problems of feeling homesick for the place they have left behind.[37]

Military service can be exceptionally traumatic, particularly if it involves exposure to life-threatening situations, injuries or extreme combat situations. Hopkins estimated that in the early second century

BCE over 50 per cent of all male Roman citizens served in the army for an average of about seven years. Under Augustus, perhaps one sixth of all male Italian citizens performed military service for twenty years.[38] The endless series of bloody wars that the Romans fought in the republic in order to acquire their empire is well known. Significant percentages of the male populace will therefore have been exposed to highly traumatic events such as hand-to-hand combat. The camaraderie of military life can be a significant ameliorating factor for soldiers while on active service. Unfortunately, this also makes it very difficult for them to adjust to civilian life and many end up with alcohol and addiction problems, or homeless, or both. The Romans may of course have been collectively a tougher bunch than most, but exposure to high levels of combat stress were likely to have resulted in significant mental health problems for many who did not have the resources to cope. In the later empire, indeed, some were prepared to go to the lengths of self-mutilation to avoid military service.[39]

Military activities could also be particularly stressful for the provincials on the receiving end. Procopius evokes the dreadful suffering of the poor in war, where they became the innocent victims in power politics, eating grass and loaves made from acorns, starving till their skin shrivelled and turned black, their faces fixed with a 'dreadful sort of insane stare'.[40] Rebellions were crushed with heartless brutality. Fear was always a fundamental part of Roman rule, and the military acted like mini-lords.[41] An inscription from North Africa records a petition to the emperor Commodus from tenants on an imperial estate, who have been 'beaten with rods and cudgels', even though citizens, and forced to work by the local military.[42] They were the lucky ones in that their petition was successful. Others who became entangled in the Roman legal system ended up being flogged, like St Paul, or facing the threat of torture. Seneca evokes the terror that threat of torture created.[43] In Mark's Gospel,[44] the story of the Gerasene Demoniac tells of a 'man with an unclean spirit', who 'lived among the tombs and no one could restrain him any more, even with a chain ... Night and day among the tombs and on the mountains he was always howling and bruising himself with stones.' And when Jesus came to throw out the demon that was troubling him, what was its name? Legion. Judaea at the time was a new and rebellious province, and it seemed natural to equate the Roman legions, which were causing them so much collective suffering, with an individual's own mental anguish.[45]

Natural disasters were as difficult to deal with then as they are today. Concern for his health was a constant factor in the orator Libanius's life, after having been struck twice by thunderbolts.[46] The

5. A detail of the Arch of Marcus Aurelius, showing the anguish on a captured barbarian boy's face

shock of the deaths of his friend, uncle and mother in an earthquake at Nicomedia turned his hair white.[47] Famines were periods of collective stress and anxiety that activated deep-seated animosities, especially between the people and local elites. The worst effect of disasters, as far as the non-elite were concerned, was that the poorest were often hardest hit for the longest period of time. Disasters like famine could mean they had to use all their reserves, sell everything and move, all of which would then take them time to recover from. Environmental stresses also came in less dramatic forms: small accidents were common in the building trade, as were fire, assault and robbery in daily life. Illness created considerable anxiety for all members of society, to judge from the content of oracles and *ex voto* offerings to the gods in gratitude for recovery.

The oracles and curses also tell us, as we saw in the last chapter, about the intense rivalry, competition and envy that Roman society could engender. Status concerns ranked high and the fact that people felt the need to take divine counsel concerning matters such as inheritance, marital relations and neighbours shows what stresses they caused. High status differentials across society also obliged the non-elite to show deference and suppress their true feelings about any humiliating treatment they received from social superiors. In a fascinating study of ancient suicides, it was found that 'losing face in general is a major motive in recorded suicide in the ancient world'.[48] Although this work mainly covers the elite, the shame of public humiliation was clearly deeply felt. The orator Quintilian describes a fictional case of a freeborn boy who is sexually assaulted by another man and then hangs himself. The legal question for Quintilian is whether the assailant caused his death.[49] From our point of view, it is noteworthy that suicide was considered a plausible response. As with women who had been raped, the victim bore the shame of the violation.[50] Incest may have been common with so many families crammed into small living spaces, which brought with it a terrible psychological trauma: 'A woman dreamt that stalks of wheat sprouted from her breast and that they bent back and went down into her vagina. Through some mishap, she unwittingly had sexual relations with her own child. Afterwards she committed suicide and died a wretched death.'[51] There was no sympathy even for a 'tender young girl' who died after having an abortion: as she was carried to the funeral pyre, 'everyone who sees her shouts, "She deserved it!"'[52] The Romans were 'acutely sensitive to shame in life', which acted as a very powerful social sanction and enforced conformity in a society where official justice was largely unavailable.[53] In a society where social status was so highly valued, public humiliation probably significantly undermined an individual's mental health.

Infant mortality stood at something like 300 per 1,000 live births in the first year. This compares with below 10 in the West today. One of the consequences of this high death rate was that it placed enormous societal pressure on women to have children. Statistically, each woman would need to produce five or six live births if the population as a whole was to remain stable. The risks associated with birth in an age of very limited medical help probably reduced female life expectancy considerably below that of men. Apart from the physical stress that frequent pregnancy and birth produced, women also faced the emotional pain of losing half their children in the first few years of their lives. Husbands deciding to expose infants cannot have been a psychological benefit, even if it was not necessarily as stressful as we might at first imagine. The need to get girls reproducing quickly meant that the average age of marriage was low, probably mid-teens, often to a significantly older man.[54] Then there was the pressure of being a young wife in an alien household. One bride was devoured by the watchdog as she fled the house on her wedding night 'dreading the first coupling of love' – a terror 'common to all maidens'. Another was abruptly deflowered by her hot young husband, earning from his wife 'the timorous hate that follows unnatural complusion'.[55] Pressure was in fact high on both sexes to marry. Marriage was nearly universal and seen as necessary to becoming a full member of society. As we saw in the Oracles of Astrampsychus, though, marriage could be anything but a bed of roses. Artemidorus interprets a bachelor's dream that he is being crucified as indicating marriage since 'it is a bond but not an easy one'.[56] Nor were Roman wives in an enviable position: status was low, the work was dull, control was exercised by the male partner and it was often lonely. Widowhood was even worse as it destroyed sources of both income and social status. One male poet empathizes with the fate of girls: 'we are not even allowed to see the daylight, but are kept hidden in our rooms, the prey of sombre thoughts'.[57] The wife was subject to her husband's whim. Domestic violence was probably common in that environment. Augustine describes how 'Many women bore the scars of beatings on their disfigured faces', which they had received from their husbands. When they complained to Augustine's mother, she said they should think of their marriage tablets 'as the instruments by which they had been turned into slaves . . . and they should not be insolent towards their masters'.[58] It was natural to associate an act of adultery on the wife's part with a violent reaction by the husband: hence to dream of beating one's wife was inauspicious, for 'it means she is committing adultery'.[59] Most women were sufficiently cowed that they suffered in silence; like the wife who will be 'subject to all kinds of injuries from her husband', but will be 'of such a temperate character that she patiently bears these injuries to the last day of her life'.[60]

Wives were pressed to be chaste and obedient: 'If a man dreams that he has sexual intercourse with his wife and that she yields willingly, submissively, and without reluctance to the union, it is good for all alike.'[61] Wives were expected to suppress their true feelings: 'A wife should have no emotion of her own, but should share in the seriousness and playfulness and melancholy and laughter of her husband.'[62] Likewise, Augustine recounts how his mother 'served her husband as if he were her master . . . She even endured his sexual infidelities so patiently that she never had even a quarrel with him on this account.'[63] This reflected the weight of emotional work that

Roman society placed on its women, as a seemingly natural extension of the traditional division of labour.[64] Women were expected to manage their feelings to produce an appropriate public display. At times this required deference, at others vigorous outbursts of emotion. Bishop Synesius recounts how when they saw the enemy attacking, women reacted by shrieking, beating their breasts and tearing their hair.[65] Grief, in particular, was seen as a womanly task. Bereavement customs assigned women the role of extended, ritualized periods of mourning, lasting well after the funeral had taken place. This burden of grief work helped drive some to suicide by means of starvation.[66] Emotional work of this kind put the woman's mind and body to work for the body politic, producing feelings that were useful for maintaining the status quo. Women's feelings themselves, though, were dismissed as irrational and unimportant. As we shall see with slaves, the lower the status group in Roman society, the more their feelings were discredited. None of this can be expected to have been beneficial for the individual's mental well-being.

Children were also subject to physical abuse. Beatings were frequent. We might be tempted to think that they were to some extent inured to violence, but Lucian's 'The Dream' suggests otherwise. When first sent, aged about thirteen, to his uncle to learn how to be a sculptor, he was beaten for breaking a table: 'I ran away and went home, sobbing continuously and my eyes full of tears. I told them about the stick and showed them my bruises and I accused my uncle of great brutality ... That night I fell asleep still crying and thinking of that stick.' But such brutality could be a laughing matter. The Philogelos contains the following joke: 'A bungling apprentice began to cry when ordered by his master to manicure a gentleman's nails. When the latter asked him why, he replied, "I'm crying because I'm frightened. I know I shall hurt you, I know you will hurt me, and I know my master will beat me into the bargain."'[67] The most extreme example of child abuse is Seneca's description of men who make a living raising exposed infants and mutilating them to send them out to beg.[68] Roman methods of child socialization can be expected to have created substantial self-esteem problems. But Roman society was by no means unique in the pre-industrial world for that.

High female mortality rates, especially of young wives from complications in pregnancy or labour, meant that stepmothers were commonplace. They became infamous for the harsh treatment they meted out to the children they took on from a previous wife. A stepmother 'would never love her stepchild by inclination or by choice'.[69] Stepmothers were assumed to dole out food within the family in a way that favoured their own offspring: like a stepmother 'she lavishes affection on the rearing of the children she has borne, but out of jealousy she hates the ones produced by someone else's birth pangs. Moreover, she shortens the rations for the latter and gives them to her own children.'[70] When the gardener in the Aesop fable, out watering his plants, asks why the weeds grow strong but his own crops are weak, he is told by way of explanation: 'The earth is mother to the one but a stepmother to the other.'[71]

At the very bottom of the Roman social pile stood the slaves. Roman society had substantial numbers of slaves, with perhaps a quarter of the Italian population being of servile status.[72] Bradley has noted that the life of a slave was not very different from that of an ass: a life consisting of beatings, hard work and little food, as well as being the object of sexual abuse, with scarcely any rights or status.[73] If slaves came before a court, even as witnesses, they were tortured to ensure that the evidence they gave was truthful. The slave was brutalized and suffered total psychological humiliation. They were no more than 'articulate tools'.[74] Even though slaves were meant to be naturally submissive, masters still felt the need to give them frequent and forceful reminders of it. Their treatment could be astonishingly brutal. Diodorus Siculus describes slaves in the mines who are 'physically destroyed . . . and are forced by the whiplashes of their overseers to endure the most dreadful hardships'; often, they 'pray for death because of the magnitude of their suffering'.[75] Violence became routine: an inscription from Puteoli lists the standard terms for floggings as four sesterces (about the price of 10 kg of wheat), which included a gibbet for binding the slave.[76] It was bad for a slave to dream of beef, 'as both straps and whips are made of oxhide'.[77] 'Why', asks the philosopher Seneca, when criticizing norms of behaviour towards slaves, 'do I have to punish my slave with a whipping or imprisonment if he gives me a cheeky answer or disrespectful look?'; 'Why are we so anxious to have them flogged immediately, or to have their legs broken on the spot?'[78]

Physical abuse could be almost comically callous – the emperor Hadrian once poked a slave's eye out with his pen. Galen claims that, 'Never did I lay hand upon a servant – a discipline practised by my father too, who frequently berated friends who had bruised their hands in the act of hitting servants in the teeth.' As Galen says, if only they had waited for their anger to subside they could then have 'applied the number of blows they wished, carrying out the task in accordance with their judgement. Some have even been known to use not only their fists but even their feet on their servants, or to stab them with a pencil which they happened to be holding.' A friend of Galen's, a 'worthy man', had such a temper 'he would regularly use his hands on his servants, and sometimes his legs too; more frequently, though, he would attack them with a leather strap, or with any wooden object that came to hand'.[79] The fact that some 'wear out their own slaves by famine, torture, disease, or constant toil',[80] did not for most Romans mean that they were having any impact on the slaves' inner self: 'slaves are ruined by their own evil natures, not by a master's cruelty'.[81] Masters easily overcame any pangs of conscience they might feel: 'If one is sorry for a blow, whether inflicted by hand or missile, and at once spit into the palm of the hand that gave the wound, the resentment of the victim is immediately softened.'[82] There was absolutely no need to apologize.

Sexual abuse was rife. Indeed, dreaming of having sex with your slave was auspicious because it shows the dreamer will 'derive pleasure from his possessions'.[83] Unwanted slave pregnancies were sufficiently common to joke about: 'When an egghead had a child by a slave girl, his father advised him to kill it. But he replied, "First, you kill your own children, then you can talk about me killing mine."' It was something that slaves dreamt about: 'I know of a slave who dreamt that his penis was stroked and aroused by his master's hand', although in this case it signified that he would be bound to a pillar and 'receive many strokes'. There is a hint of the resentment this kind of abuse could cause in the *Satyricon*, when a freedman notes that, 'I bought freedom for the slave woman who had shared my bed, so that no one could get his filthy hands on her.'[84] Many slave boys and girls were used for sex by their masters. The ex-slave Trimalchio says that when he was 'no taller than a candlestick ... I became my master's favourite', but defends it saying, 'I mean, what's wrong with doing what your master wants?'[85] That is probably how most masters justified their acts, or at least they would have if they had felt that any justification was required. As they saw it, their slaves were their possessions to be used as they saw fit.

Other problems the slave could face ranged from the absurd boredom that could result from being one of the slaves the rich used to do ostentatiously pointless tasks – such as announce the hours, a life literally spent clock-watching[86] – to coping with owners with mental problems, such as the proprietor of a woolshop in Rome who threw his slave out of the window to amuse the people passing the street in front of his house.[87] The dominance of the figure of the master in the average slave's life meant that an imminent or suspected change could cause great concern. An Abderite (people from Abdera were ridiculed for their stupidity) was trying to sell a pot without a handle or spout; 'Why did you cut off its appendages?' asked someone. 'So that it wouldn't hear that it was going to be sold, and so run away.'[88] Running away carried grave risks for a slave: regular runaways were branded or tattooed on the forehead so they would be easily spotted,[89] or collars were fitted on them embossed with the initials TMQF (*tene me quia fugio* – hold me because I'm a runaway). The astrologer Dorotheus included a section on runaways, and their fates make for grim reading: the runaway will 'hang himself', 'kill himself', be sent back to his master where 'misery and chains will reach him in this running away of his'; he will suffer 'beating and imprisonment' and 'fear of death will be immoderate in him'. Justifiably so since he will suffer an 'unpleasant death' and 'his hands and feet will be cut off' or he will be strangled, crucified or burned alive.[90]

A hierarchy existed even within the slave world. By no means all slaves were of equal status: there were field slaves, house slaves, the home born, barbarian imports, those who had received some education and those who had personal contact with the master or were entrusted with positions of authority. Slaves were sometimes no more tender than their master towards other slaves: Salvian describes how some slaves are 'terrified of their fellow slaves'.[91] Indeed the caricature of an ex-slave is one who is particularly brutal towards his own slaves, as with Trimalchio in the *Satyricon* who calls for beheadings and floggings as a means to overcompensate for his own former servile status.

Even in this environment, many slaves managed to have a family life, although their partner would mostly have been assigned to them by their master. Having children was not without its rewards: Columella gave a slave woman who had three sons 'exemption from work' and 'a woman who has more, freedom'.[92] They then lived in constant fear of having members of their family removed by means of sale. The moral of the fable of the dove and crow states: 'the most pitiful slaves are those who beget children in servitude'.[93] Conversely, their children might see their old or sick parents sold off: 'sell off old slaves, sick slaves and whatever else is superfluous', advises Cato.[94] Cato was a hard old bastard, but the practice was sufficiently common that the emperor Claudius had to act to try and stop people in general dumping their sick and worn-out slaves on the Tiber island in Rome.[95]

The dreadful treatment and routine humiliations that slaves underwent will have had a significant psychological impact. Seneca thought that home-bred slaves were best because they knew no other life. By contrast, a newly captured barbarian would need to be broken. He feels that such a slave should be pitied, when 'he holds on to some remnants of his former free status and fails to hurry to perform sordid and difficult services'.[96] But Seneca writes as a philosopher trying to persuade an audience of his case. There can be little doubt that most Roman masters would have shown anything but pity. The effect on most slaves of constant intimidation and brutalization was to leave them demoralized, deferential and unassertive. In dream interpretation, a mouse signifies a household slave as it lives in the house and is 'timid'.[97] It was not until Hadrian's slave had his eye poked out that he 'grew bold' and refused the offer of a gift in compensation: 'for what gift can compensate for the loss of an eye?' Varro also advises masters not to buy too many slaves of the same nationality, 'for this is very often accustomed to cause domestic quarrels'.[98] Many foreign slaves therefore found themselves in situations of isolation and loneliness, lacking any support networks to help them cope with their dire situation. One of the bugbears of slave-owners was that they had to rely on people who were always breaking down in tears and cursing.[99] Suicide attempts were sufficiently common to merit legal opinion, which stated that sellers were obliged to reveal to prospective buyers if the slave had tried to kill him- or herself.[100] In the comedies, slaves in tough situations almost routinely think of suicide. Some captured runaways would prefer to 'thrust iron through the bowels' than be brought back alive or 'return to his master submissively'.[101] Suicide and attempted suicide are not in themselves a sign of mental illness. Many of the suicides of the elite were carefully staged political acts. But killing oneself does point to tensions and stresses within an individual's life, and in the world of the Roman slave these could easily become overpowering.

Could it be argued that most Roman slaves had no real sense of self, and so will have been affected far less by the kind of treatment we have seen? If they had no sense of self-worth to begin with, then the psychological impact of maltreatment might have been lessened. Only someone with a sense of their own value can be humiliated and degraded. The evidence suggests that many slaves had strong views about justice and their own worth. Androcles, of lion fame, says that he had been forced to flee from his master because of the unjustified beatings he received every day. So he fled into the desert to look for food or, if all else failed, to kill himself.[102] The pain of these assaults was more than physical. Similarly, there were many slaves who 'long for freedom' and made great sacrifices to acquire it.[103] Seneca talks of 'The money which slaves have saved up by robbing their stomachs, they hand over as the price of freedom.'[104] Some household slaves were paid a small wage and many chose to save hard to achieve their long-term goal of liberty, even if it meant going short of food. The Delphic manumission inscriptions show that many slaves paid large sums to secure their freedom, often at an uncertain future date, typically on their master's death.[105] Some of these contracts also stipulate that slaves will have to hand over one of their children as a replacement, but they wanted it badly enough to agree. If they did reach their goal, the paranoid ex-slave was a sufficiently recognizable character-type to be caricatured as one who shudders at the thought of shackles and prays reverence to a mill-house as if it were a holy shrine, in reference to slaves being punished by having to turn the millstones instead of animals.[106] Freedmen also tried hard to conceal the physical marks of their servitude: some doctors specialized in concealing the 'tax-paid' signs tattooed on the foreheads of exported slaves by digging them out and burning the flesh so it would scar over.[107]

The evidence from Rome is that the non-elite faced powerful social stressors. Moreover, the lower down the social hierarchy individuals sat, the more intense these stressors became. Modern mental health research, and perhaps even common sense, tells us that we should expect such conditions to have had a detrimental impact on their psychological well-being, resulting in a generally poor level of mental health. It also tells us to expect a high incidence of mental disorder for the lowest-status groups, especially slaves. What it cannot do is tell us the forms that such mental disorders would have taken. Mental illness is sufficiently affected by societal influences that it will be expressed very differently from culture to culture. Each particular context will produce a certain style of psychiatric expression. Nor can it tell us how this unique form of expression will have helped Romans to understand and shape their world.

Mental discourse in Roman society

Roman medical writers have numerous accounts of patients suffering from various kinds of delusional disorders. Galen describes a patient who thought he was a pot and was scared he would break. Another believed he was a chicken, while some identified themselves with Atlas, bearing the burden of the world on their shoulders.[108] Alexander of Tralles mentions a patient who bound up her little finger because she was worried that the world would collapse if she bent it.[109] Caelius Aurelianus writes about a wealthy man who lived in constant fear that he would lose his wealth and status. The doctor arranged for pretend legacies to be announced to him from time to time as a way of relieving his anxiety.[110] Horace also mentions a delusional man of 'some rank' at Argos who 'used to fancy that he was listening to wonderful tragic actors, while he sat happy and applauded in the empty theatre'. When he was cured he actually complained that he had been deprived of his dearest illusion and pleasure.[111] A case of happy-clappy if ever there was one.

Quoting these examples is of course following in the footsteps of those who went to Bedlam to laugh at the lunatics, now just safely removed by time and text. Mental health problems for most Romans, though, did not involve costly treatment by such medical doctors. The severely affected were left to wander, abandoned by their families. Like the Gerasene demoniac, who went out into the desert after he had broken the bonds that had been used to fetter him: there he lived among the tombs, naked, crying and bruising himself with stones.[112] For a poor man to dream of singing songs in the street or marketplace was a sign of future madness, because this was how madmen acted when they wandered about.[113] Aretaeus describes 'those whose madness is associated with joy, laughter and play, who dance night and day, and sometimes go to the market-place wearing a crown, as if they had won some contest'. He says that most people found this behaviour 'inoffensive'.[114] The mentally ill would, however, probably have been spat at. It was customary to spit on the mad, as spitting was believed to repel any mental contagion.[115] Some people put spit behind their ears to 'calm mental anxiety'.[116] Another common means of avoiding contact with the mentally ill was to throw stones at them.[117] Children teased them and chased them. Artemidorus explains that dreaming of being insane is auspicious for those that want to teach 'since children also follow the insane'.[118] Sometimes they fired back: Libanius complains that, 'One of the artisans began to go mad and he would annoy people from a distance or would even man-handle them,' and whenever he saw Libanius the artisan would throw stones at him.[119] Severe mental disorder like this was associated with random violence and people generally kept clear; 'Being insane is auspicious for those who are undertaking a business venture, for madmen are not hindered in anything that they set their hearts on.'[120] Similarly, Matthew refers to a pair of madmen too fierce to go near.[121] Others would suffer by being 'over-anxious in mind and body and will be attacked by constant tremors. They are afflicted with slight tics and shake with terror at trivial messages.'[122] The physical burden of life was so great that the mental disorders more generally associated with old age were not widespread, if only because few people lived that long. Short life spans meant that, on comparative data, only about 7 per cent of Romans lived to be over sixty, 2 per cent over seventy and just 0.25 per cent over eighty.[123]

A whole hotchpotch of opinions and beliefs built up about what caused mental disorders. There were no Roman specialists in madness and, as Chadwick says, 'The ancients were not students of neuroscience and did not comprehend the extremely intricate workings of the brain.'[124] Explanations included both natural and supernatural causes. The action of the stars and planets could work to make those born under a particular sky insane: if the Sun is in opposition to Mars in the fourth house, evils will be greater and more frequent, and those born then 'will be madmen'.[125] Likewise, 'if the hour in which birth is completed has either an earthquake or a thunder storm', then the natures of those born at that time,

> will always be unstable with trembling bodies and shaking steps; through all minutes of the day they will fear the fall of threatening ruin. Their eyes will flash, they will shrink from everything; they will not be able to keep a definite order of words but the sound of their voice will be impeded, and they will hiss a tremulous murmur; or between clenched jaws their words will die on utterance. They will always think it is going to thunder or that the earth is about to move and that everything is falling. By these fears the correct order of their speech is disturbed.[126]

Health was a major source of concern in the ancient world, which is reflected in the size of the corpus of medical literature. Medical writers such as Galen, Aretaeus, Caelius Aurelianus (who produced a Latin version of the Greek work of Soranus), Celsus, Alexander of Tralles and Paul of Aegina all include references to mental symptoms and their treatment. Medical theory looked for physical causes of mental illness, primarily in an imbalance of the humours. The types of illness a patient suffered reflected the different levels of heat and moistures within the body: mania was characterized by heat, dryness and an excess of yellow bile; melancholia by coldness, with the black bile in the ascendancy. Phrenologists studied the shape and features of the head to reveal its inner heat: too much heat and moisture in the brain would lead to madness and would be reflected in 'thick, strong, black hair'. Bald people, by contrast, have cool, dry brains which makes the hair wither, but they are kept sane as a result.[127] Caelius Aurelianus argued that the causes of mental illness were not always observable but could be hidden: the origins of disorder could lie in exposure to intense heat or cold, indigestion, frequent and uncontrolled drunkenness, sleeplessness, excess of love, anger, grief, anxiety, superstitious fear, shock or blow, intense straining in study, business or other ambitious pursuits, love potions, the removal of long-standing haemorrhoids, or the suppression of menses in women.[128]

There were as many treatments suggested as there were causes. A whole supermarket in medical services sprang up. Treatments included diet, drink, drugs, incubus, chains, floggings, bloodletting and purges. White hellebore was popular as a vomitive, black as a powerful laxative. Caelius Aurelianus attacks other medical sects for treating epilepsy by binding limbs, or making the patient eat weasel, smoked camel's brain or the testes of a beaver, or placing a flame close to the patient's eye and tickling him.[129] Humoral techniques often sought to counteract the inner coolness or heat of the patient. Hence for phrenitis, a hot and dry complaint, Galen preferred to drain blood from the middle vein of the forehead. The heat of mania was best treated by applying cooling remedies directly to the head. Galen also looked for hidden causes. Once a woman 'lay awake at night, constantly tossing and turning' to the exasperation of other doctors. Galen noticed that her pulse quickened whenever he mentioned the name of the heartthrob actor Pylades, and so was able to diagnose love-sickness.[130]

Some treatments could be severe. Celsus advises that the insane are 'best treated by certain tortures. When he says or does anything wrong, he is to be coerced by starvation, fetters and flogging.' He further claims that, 'to be terrified suddenly and to be thoroughly frightened is beneficial in this illness'.[131] By contrast, the treatments of Caelius Aurelianus appear almost modern in their sympathetic approach. Patients should be massaged and kept free from stress. Attempts were made to alleviate the anxiety which the patient was feeling. One woman believed she had swallowed a snake that caused her great pain if she did not eat large amounts of food. The doctor gave her a vomitive but slipped a snake into her sick-bowl when she was not looking and so cured her (although other versions of this story say that she later came back saying that unfortunately the snake had laid eggs). Those who were depressed should see a comedy, or a tragedy for those whose madness involved playful childishness. Practical measures should also be taken: keep phrenitis sufferers in a place where the windows are high, 'for it often happens that unguarded patients in their madness jump out'.[132]

Caelius alone among the medical writers treats homosexuality as a mental illness, as DSM I-II did.[133] 'People find it hard to believe that effeminate men really exist ... This condition is an affliction of a diseased mind.' Similarly, *Tribades* are what he terms women who 'are more eager to lie with women than men and in fact pursue women with almost masculine jealousy ... they rejoice in the abuse of their sexual powers' and are also victims of an affliction of the mind. Not even Caelius can help: 'There exists no bodily treatment which can be applied to overcome the disease; it is rather the mind that is affected in these disgraceful vices, and it is consequently the mind that must be controlled.' This was difficult because he believed homosexuality gets stronger with age and causes 'a hideous and ever increasing lust'.

Another, non-medical, approach to mild mental problems was the folk psychiatry offered by the cult of Asclepius. In the second century, Aelius Aristides had a lifelong devotion to this practice, which involved sleepovers in the temple of Asclepius, so that the god could make known his thoughts via dreams, dream interpretation, rituals and group activities, all carried out within the institutional framework of the Asclepeion. Aristides kept a detailed journal of his treatments. It is a relentless account of exhaustive, some say neurotic, attention to every physical detail of his life: 'On the following day I bathed again. I dreamt my food had not digested properly . . . I consulted the priest and I vomited in the evening'; 'The god ordered us to do many strange things . . . when the harbour waves were swollen by the South wind and ships were in distress, I had to sail across to the opposite side, while eating honey and acorns, and then vomit.'[134]

The treatments we have seen so far reflect a strongly somatic culture. All illness and anxiety was given a physical form. A strong sympathy existed between body and mind. Such a holistic conception meant that any influence – moral, physical or mental – could individually or in combination cause illness anywhere in either body or mind. Hence physical remedies seemed a perfectly natural solution to mental problems; all sought to restore the natural balance that had been disrupted. The placebo effect of receiving detailed attention within the healing context was itself doubtless sufficient to cause an improvement in many cases.

But medical theories of what caused mental illness and how it should be treated were largely reserved for the wealthy in Roman society. Doctors were expensive and treatment at home even more so. We should therefore be careful not to attribute these beliefs to all the non-elite. There is some evidence that wealthier members of the non-elite did seek treatment: Galen refers to one joiner who was a skilful artisan and 'while on the spot where the work was performed' was completely sane but went mad if he left and went out of sight of the workplace. Caelius also recommends that if patients are unacquainted with literature, the doctor should give them problems appropriate to their particular craft, such as agricultural problems for a farmer or let him play *ludus calculorum* (a Roman game similar to backgammon). But it suggests that being unacquainted with literature was not the norm. Most patients came from the top section of society. The popular culture mocked some of these theories: a patient said to a doctor, 'I'm passing blood in my stools, something must be wrong with my humours'; the doctor replied, 'Oh, go ahead and shit your guts out, you won't spoil my good humour.'[135] The non-elite could not afford the genteel treatments of a Caelius, nor the brutal ones of Celsus for that matter, but they may have helped out the mentally ill where they could: one astrological forecast is that the retarded in mind, speech-impaired or deaf will be 'wretched paupers, wanderers, or travellers, who never have a settled home', but later 'they acquire some protection in life from various occupations'.[136] Similarly, if a poor man dreams that he is mad it signifies he will become richer, 'For a madman receives something from everyone.'[137]

The medical profession served to differentiate the elite from the people. It flattered the wealthy by pandering to their needs. But, more importantly, it established a different body of illnesses for those who could afford them. The non-elite were left to have their own traditional illnesses.

Popular notions of mental illness were dominated by possession.[138] Mental disorder was believed to be caused by demons, creatures halfway between heaven and earth, who could be found anywhere. The mentally ill were, in this way, literally demonized. That is not to say that demons were only used as ways of discussing mental disorders. Demons were capable of bearing the brunt of people's understanding concerning a whole range of issues. They were a powerful catch-all to help explain the inexplicable, and in a world where the human and divine were inextricably linked, it was natural to understand mental phenomena in a religious context. Even multiple deaths resulting from food poisoning could be attributed to 'a troop of demons passing through the pot cooking a slaughtered ox and killing all who had eaten it'.[139] No one was quite sure what a demon was: an unclean spirit of the underworld, or the souls of those who had met a violent, untimely death were two common explanations. *The Life of Theodore of Sykeon* describes them as unclean spirits coming out of the ground, like a primal force of nature.[140] The high level of mental disorder that we would expect to find in the non-elite world required a causal agent that was easy to catch. How else would it be useful as an explanation? It was all too easy to be possessed by a demon. In Xenophon's *Ephesian Tale*, Anthea feigns the 'sacred disease', epilepsy, to avoid being used as a prostitute and describes how she succumbed to it:

> When I was still a child ... I came upon the grave of a man who had recently died. There it seemed to me that someone leapt out of the grave and tried to lay hold of me. I shrieked and tried to flee. The man was frightful to look upon, and his voice was more horrible still. Finally, when day broke, he let me go, but he struck me on the chest and said that he had cast this disease into me.[141]

Or another man was simply standing outside his inn, 'when a black dog came up and stood in front of me and yawned, which made me yawn too, quite against my will, and immediately the dog disappeared from sight and I was seized with fever and my face was turned round backwards'.[142] Beliefs such as this, incidentally, may be the origin of people putting their hand in front of their mouth when they yawn.

Demons were objectivized so as to make them more readily understandable. In the same way, bugs in dreams were taken as symbols of

6. Bronze tintinnabulum in the form of a gladiator or animal-hunter fighting his own phallus. Phallic wind-chimes like this were often hung in doorways to protect against evil spirits

cares and anxieties for they 'keep people awake at night'.[143] So when Theodore drove out a host of unclean spirits that had descended on a village, people could actually see them, 'and to some who saw them they looked like flying blue-bottles and dormice'. They took on the shape of the pests that troubled people in their daily lives. Others saw them as hares, presumably because that was the fastest creature they encountered regularly and so provided the best way to portray their demonic speed. Elsewhere, a sea captain is afflicted by a demon under his skin in the shape of a mouse. Demons are described as being like beasts and, in the *Life of Anthony*, reptiles breaking through walls, and even the devil himself is 'bound by the Lord as a sparrow for our amusement'.[144] This was how people used everyday things to think with: a process of 'thingking'.

The chaos that demons could create was considerable. Their attack was 'full of confusion, accompanied by crashing, roaring, and shouting: it could well be the tumult produced by rude boys or robbers'. The psychological impact of such an assault on St Anthony was profound, as it caused 'terror in the soul, disturbance and confusion of thoughts, dejection, hatred of ascetics, indifference, sadness, remembrance of kinsfolk, and fear of death'.[145] The popular understanding of mental disorder was not as a purely personal affliction of the mind and self. It reflected a disruption of the proper ordering between the individual and the divine. Mental disturbance happened when a tear had formed in the fabric of the universe, allowing chaotic, demonic powers to break free from their correct place and pour into the human sphere. In an environment where it was natural to see mental illness as inextricably linked with the divine, so it was natural to turn to the divine for its treatment.

The popular view linked mental disorders to the effects of an invasion of evil spirits into the body. It was only logical, therefore, for treatment to consist of trying to lure or force the demons back out again. Some approaches relied on strong-arm physical tactics, including beatings, trepanations (drilling holes in the head) and venesections (bloodletting). Fortunately, the demonic world could also be influenced by magic, such as incantations, spells and exorcisms. Magical healers were easy to come by and were cheap enough to be used by all but the destitute. One such spell, a self-styled 'Excellent rite for driving out demons'[146] calls on the evil spirit to leave: 'I conjure you, demon, whoever you are, by this god, SABARBAR-BATHIOTH SABARBARBATHIOUTH SABARBARBATHIO-NETH SABARBARBAPHAI. Come out, demon, whoever you are, and stay away from him.' The magic words, like abracadabra, were meant to speak directly to the demonic powers in their own language; a kind of 'demonese'. The words became progressively more complicated as time went on, presumably as familiarity meant that users needed more 'gimmicks' to keep them awe-struck.

Protection was seen as better than cure. Amulets worn on the body were believed to keep the demons from entering in the first place. One from near Beirut, from the fifth century, reads, 'Protect Alexandra from demons, spells, dizziness, and from all suffering and from insanity.' Or another from the Negev desert: 'Save Esther from evil tormentors, the evil eye, spirits, demons and night ghosts'.[147] But the fact that demons could be influenced meant they could also be used for aggressive purposes. A spell to 'make mad any man or any woman', says to 'take the hair of the man whom you wish together with the hair of a dead man ... tie them to the body of a hawk and release it alive'.[148] In one spell, the motivation for the attack is revenge: 'vengeance be exacted on the man who caused me to be expelled from the household of Demetrios, due to my headaches and other pains'.[149] The general belief that magic worked meant that magic spells can be expected to have had some effect, either as placebo or by causing anxiety. Amulets provided a means of reassurance and self-confidence. Aggressive magic functioned as a mental health strategy, which allowed the user to offload his or her feelings of anger and frustration. As Gager says, this was a litigious society that provoked strong emotions of fear, shame, guilt and panic in its members, and magic allowed them to personify their unacceptable feelings by ascribing them to demons.[150]

Most people believed in demons and magic because it explained how their universe worked in a way that made sense to them. It was natural to see mental disorders as demonic or divine punishments: one inscription tells how a girl had been called by the god to do a service but did not carry it out swiftly and 'for that reason the god punished her and made her insane'.[151] When divine power was felt to be everywhere and no obvious earthly cause could be found, no other explanation was needed. Treatments could evolve from these beliefs, making use of any influences that human agents had on supernatural forces.

7. A folded lead curse tablet that has had a nail driven through it to ram the point home

It is important to emphasize that many, probably most, of the elite also shared these views. They had access to most of the popular culture and had no intention of cutting themselves off from a powerful healthcare resource when the world they inhabited was so full of dangers. They saw no contradiction in using multiple sources of help when required, in addition to medical resources. That did not stop some of the elite from mocking what they saw as a general belief in false prophets and charlatans. The eponymous False Prophet in Lucian's tale feigns fits of madness, with foaming at the mouth caused by chewing the root of the soapwort plant. The sight of the foam 'filled the people with superstitious awe'. But we have already seen that the non-elite as a whole were too sceptical to fall for every charlatan who came along.

If demons provided an explanation for mental disorder, it was disorder itself that defined what most people understood as madness. It was 'monstrous attacks of madness' that made the individual turn away from the 'right path of life'.[152] All societies designate certain forms of behaviour or belief as insanity. The symptoms of insanity are culturally constructed, and mental disorders violate the social norms of a society. Nakedness was a common sign of madness in Rome, not in any absolute sense – it was fine to be naked in the public baths – but when clothes were lacking in the wrong context, such as the street, accusations of madness would surely follow. Sanity also established norms of space. Those madmen who we encountered earlier singing in the forum were humoured because they posed no real threat. But once they had left the settled, urban spaces to live in the tombs, such as the madmen in Matthew, the signs were mounting that their mental imbalance was of a worryingly profound nature. Random violence was a sure indication that a severe state of madness had been reached. Caelius describes the phrenitis sufferer as one who hates everyone, 'shouts, beats himself or tears his own clothing and that of his neighbours'.[153]

Ideas about insanity in the Roman world were shaped by the high value Romans placed on status. The mad had no interest in their status and to disregard or even voluntarily destroy social position in a society where most fought tooth and nail to improve their standing was a terrifyingly incomprehensible act. By shredding their clothing the mad literally ripped up their claim to recognition. In the same way, but taken to the other extreme, Caelius is incredulous that effeminate men 'even adopt the dress, walk and other characteristics of women'.[154] The mad gave themselves over to uncontrolled passions and were violent to no purpose. We have seen how violent the Romans could be when it suited them, but to resist authority with pointless fury was to be no different from a wild beast. Political change had similar connotations of mental instability: dreaming of being insane was 'especially propitious for potential demagogues, for those that wish to rule the masses, and for those who ingratiate themselves with the crowd'.[155]

Ideas about insanity were also shaped by the high value placed on traditional religious beliefs. Behaviour that wantonly insulted the gods posed an irrational threat to the peace of the gods, the *pax deorum*. Christians displayed most of the tell-tale signs of motive-less status-destruction that marked them out as insane. In Lucian's *Peregrinus*, he is imprisoned for being a Christian and brought before the governor, who is 'aware of Peregrinus's lunacy'. When he openly attacks the emperor, he is generally admired by 'the uneducated ... for his madness'.[156] From a Roman perspective, Jesus himself gave many indications that he was mentally deranged.[157] The founder of the Manichees, Mani, exacerbated the image of insanity he projected to the Romans by having a name that closely resembled the Greek word for madman (as in *mania, manic*). This led to his being the target of endless weak puns by opponents. Accusations of madness also became a way for the Christians to stigmatize heretics and astrologers once Christianity had itself become the official religion. They latched on to scapegoats to emphasize their own normality and create a psychological unity within the group, in the same way that Romans had done with them in the early empire.

Emperors themselves became a focus for discussions about ideas of madness. The uncontrolled insanity of emperors like Commodus, as in the film *Gladiator*, has become one of the stock images of Rome, and the works of Suetonius and the *Scriptores Historiae Augustae* are replete with tales of imperial breaches of the proper social order. Such transgressions are characterized by individuals having too much: they have too many luxuries, too many passions and, crucially, too much power. Rome in the late republic and early empire was a society that had undergone a revolution in the way its politics were ordered. Society too had been transformed by the benefits that accrued from empire, particularly in the capital city. These were major issues for a traditional, ordered society to deal with and the disrupting activities of emperors became a way for concerns to be personified into readily comprehensible, concrete situations. It may be that certain emperors were sent mad by the pressure of governing so large an empire, knowing they could be assassinated at any time; but it is more profitable to see the general level of accusations of imperial insanity as an index of strain within the social order. Madness was linked to the rejection of the proper social order, so Nero's decision to act on stage, when this traditionally carried legal loss of status (*infamia*), offered a simple way of discussing the social changes that had made this possible. It provided a ready-made opportunity to discuss the proper limits and exercise of imperial power and the relationship a ruler should have with his people.

Rome was a highly regimented society where alternative ideas about social ordering could be most safely expressed though expressions of mental disorder. This excused them from the full force of official repression by the state. Psychiatric expression, therefore, became a vehicle for communicating all manner of social differences and tensions. Madness had never been seen as purely a negative phenomenon. Plato talks of its four blessings: that which is associated with poetic inspiration, divine prophecy, love, and religious rituals such as the frenzy of the Dionysian rites.[158] As the medical writer Aretaeus describes, 'some cut their limbs in a holy fantasy, as if propitiating strange gods', but 'in other respects they are sane. They are roused by the flute, and mirth, or by drinking, or by the admonition of those around them.'[159] In this way, the mentally disordered could still function in Roman society, by making use of the symptom pool that was available within the Roman cultural context. Religion gave a clear, socially acceptable route for the expression of mental differences, without having to incur stigma.

The basic element of the popular view of mental abnormality was the belief that it resulted from the action of a supernatural power which had either entered the body or produced its effects by action from outside. When madness was linked to demonic possession in this way it is not surprising to find that the mentally disturbed could be treated with some awe. But contact with the supernatural could be double-edged, for with awe came fear. Stoning the mad was a way of keeping an anomalous power safely at bay. The fact that Romans could feel the world throbbing with the demonic and the supernatural made it seem quite natural for delusions to occur. Delirium gave people a means of communicating their distress, and relieving the tensions it caused, by talking nonsense. Often these feelings were personified into the forms of demons and unclean spirits. Such speech could also be used to express socially unacceptable ideas. But in and of themselves these expressions carried no weight. They were the mystic ramblings of marginal figures that lacked any sense of authority.

Hysteria was thought to be an affliction of women caused by the womb's propensity to wander in the body. Found mainly in virgins and widows, the symptoms included shortness of breath, chest pain, pain in the legs or groin, and seizure. Its treatment consisted of the application of strong smells to try and either lure the uterus back down or drive it up again into its proper place. Magic could also be tried: 'I conjure you, O womb ... do not gnaw into the heart like a dog, but remain in your own intended and proper place.'[160] It is hard not to see the womb as a metaphor for women in Roman society. Women faced irresistible pressure to reproduce and rear children. The physical and emotional stress this generated will have overwhelmed many. Hysteria served as a permissible way for women to manifest their tensions and distress. The method was allowed because it worked on men's own notions of how a woman was thought likely to behave: inconsistently, unpredictably, emotionally. Male writers medicalized these expressions of disorder according to their own preconceptions of the proper behaviour for a woman. Hysteria was seen as being caused by miscarriage, premature birth, long widowhood, retentions of menses and the end of ordinary childbearing. Hence the only real cure was childrearing, being a wife and having sex.[161] Likewise, Galen thought much male hysteria was due to the retention of sperm and lack of intercourse.[162] The male medic's view of female mental health was that it depended on reproductive activity and women fulfilling their proper social role. For the woman, hysteria represented a rejection of these very same values. It provided her with an acceptable way to express frustration and dissent, and acted as a somatic representation of inner conflict.

For some, mental disorder could act as a survival strategy. Life for those at the bottom of the social pile took place against the backdrop of a hostile environment, and aggressive, antisocial behaviour could help in creating a protective barrier. Defence mechanisms that others saw as indications of mental aberration, such as violence, swearing and aggressive humour, could all serve the individual as ways of coping. Such styles of behaviour could also be used to work on people's sense of pity and eke out a meagre living. John Chrysostom describes how:

> There are other poor men, empty-headed and of unsteady mind, who do not know how to endure hunger, but will do everything rather than undergo this. Frequently they accost us with pitiful appearances and words, and when they achieve nothing, they dispense with these appeals and in the end surpass our magicians, some chewing the leather of worn-out shoes, others driving sharp nails into their heads, others entering water frozen from cold up to their naked stomachs, and others undergoing things even more bizarre than this, in order to gather round them a wretched audience. But you, while this is going on, stand laughing and amazed, celebrating the miseries of others ... Then so he will do this more eagerly, you give him a generous amount of money.[163]

As Augustine bemoans, 'What things men do that they may live a few days.'[164] But for all the desperation of this approach, it worked in that people gave. Paul of Aegina, in his Appendix to Book Five, includes a section 'On Feigned Diseases and their Detection'. We have also seen how Anthea, in the *Ephesian Tale*, feigned epilepsy to avoid being used as a prostitute. The fact that this tactic may have been commonplace does not necessarily mean that the people in the audience were entirely taken in. That is why they were so demanding in the extremes to which they demanded the 'madman' went. Hammering nails into one's head can hardly be described as a free lunch.

Individuals were able to play on perceptions of mental disorder to find relief in aggression or even complete social withdrawal. Aretaeus describes how, 'some flee the haunts of men and going into the wilderness, live by themselves'.[165] Abandoning society in this way represented a disturbing rearrangement of accepted practices of habitation. People could not understand such a voluntary destruction of social status. Some of these individuals were happy to remain, if not outside, on the margins of society for good. Bringing them back into the community posed a difficulty for which there was no accepted mainstream practice. Exorcism provided such a route back into the ordered, settled world of society. By ritually driving out the demons that had caused the aberrant behaviour, the mad individual was able to be reintegrated into normal life. The act of exorcism re-established the social order by ridding the sufferer of the infernal powers that had caused the disorder to begin with. Exorcism therefore offered a means for the individual to change his or her selection from the symptom pool, whether consciously or unconsciously, away from those which signalled mental illness to those which indicated a recovering victim. For marginals, such as prostitutes and cave-dwellers, it was a way to express regret and wipe the slate clean. The demon became a face-saving device, whereby the former wrongdoer could pin the blame for their poor behaviour on an external malevolent force.

The later Roman Empire saw an explosion of psychiatric expression. Mental phenomena, in the form of possession by demonic power and its exorcism, came to play a central role in how society discussed sensitive issues. What caused this? Was it a direct result of an increase in both the number and the degree of social stressors? It is certainly not difficult to draw up a list of factors that may have intensified stress in the later empire: the inflation and chaos of the barbarian invasions of the third-century crisis; the impact of a tougher, more centralized government and bureaucracy that was designed to extract a bigger surplus from an already oppressed peasantry; the widening gap between society's powerful and the mass of the people; a decline in the legal status and privileges of the citizenry; an economic decline which may have set in in the West; a population decline which may have set in more generally. The impact and indeed the existence of many of these factors is hotly disputed. Brown suggests that life in the later empire may have done no more than turn 'a slightly deeper shade of the ever expected grey'.[166] But in a world where even small differences in income could have a major impact on the quality of life, that in itself could have brought a considerable change in overall levels of mental health. Small, subtle changes from our viewpoint might well have been seen as monumental and cataclysmic events from a position at the bottom of society. If the social and economic changes of the later empire did have an impact on mental health levels, the effect, as Brown also says, will not be seen in pervasive empire-wide moods of anxiety, but in the details of small-scale events and traumas. It will have been the thousands tipped over the edge who were at the front line of any society-wide assault on sanity.

The move to centre-stage of mental phenomena did much more than reflect any possible increase in mental health problems resulting from a rise in macro-social stressors. It reflected a disruption of the entire social order. In a society undergoing rapid change, people turned to tried-and-tested methods to try and pinpoint exactly what was going on, isolate it and deal with it. The huge increase in possession and exorcism in the later sources cannot simply be seen as a result of an exponential growth in mental illness. Accusations of mental disorder and its treatment via demonic expulsion served as a scale of tensions within a society that was shuddering under seismic shifts in its structure. They clustered around the areas where the stresses created by society's re-ordering were most keenly felt. People needed to be able to gain access to those who could influence the demonic world, which seemed to have grabbed hold of the human realm. But they also needed access to be able to relaunch their own lives, refashioned into a style that would be better adapted to the new environment. Simply being a good citizen, or even a citizen, was no longer sufficient. People had to find new ways to express their place in society that forged a definite link between them and a higher power.

Mental phenomena had a major impact on popular perceptions of their world. It was for this reason that people turned to traditional means of dealing with mental disorder when their social order seemed to be behaving so strangely. They had a pressing need to understand and, if not control, at least influence what was happening. Exorcism had always offered a more powerful cure than other approaches to dealing with mental illness, in that it relied on access to an overwhelming divine power to evict the demons from their human home. In a society focused on supernatural explanations, a cure that not only brought the divine into human form but allowed its power to be directed for human benefits had always been genuinely awe-inspiring. And in a society where social change meant that people needed influence to try and establish their place in the new order, exorcism became a critical means of accessing power.

The later Roman Empire saw power and wealth drift steadily upwards into the hands of a smaller elite. This special group of privileged individuals became the norm for what people expected those with power, any power, to be like. So it was inevitable that when the search began for ways of accessing the holy, they would look to an extraordinary group of religious men to provide it. The people needed leaders, champions and heroes because it was only through elites of this kind that they would have any hope of influencing events. Only truly powerful individuals had any chance of getting things done, and it was only by attaching themselves to these top people that the non-elite could have some influence too. Holy men, therefore, came to act as the necessary mediators between the people and a God more distant than the old deities. Unlike the traditional, open-access treatments for mental disorders, which relied on dream interpretation, incantations and magical rites, it became necessary to enter into a relationship of dependence with these holy men, those who had been 'driven into the desert by a crisis in human relations'.[167] It was through them that demons could be driven out, through them that order be re-established.

The power to exorcise also became critical to establishing the credentials of the holy elite. Such an overwhelming force did not come easily. Holy men had to undergo exceptional hardships to establish a special relationship with God, from whom flowed the divine energy to deal with demons. Brown has shown how Christians believed that the body could be changed and with it the society it represented.[168] But the early monks also sought to show that the psychological self could be refashioned into an independent entity, untroubled by the mundane. They made use of the symptom pool of mental illness to reject traditional society, and they battled against the psychological stresses that life in the status-riven society had routinely created. This is not to say that the early monks were schizophrenic, though some probably were, but that modes of behaviour and expression which the Romans recognized as signs of mental deviancy acquired a new meaning that was appropriate for a changed world. As Brown says, living in 'states of prolonged depression and anxious self-searching', Anthony grappled with his personality 'in a situation of self-imposed sensory deprivation, where one may suspect that hallucination and extreme emotional states were deliberately courted so as to be overcome'.[169] In effect, these monks underwent a voluntary mental illness to show that they had mastered the stresses of normal life. They had recast their minds into a tool as hard as granite.

The anxieties that holy men struggled against came in the form of demons that exaggerated the daily concerns of the people into a highly intensified, dramatic form. The holy man delivered almost mundane miracles: saving people from fires, droughts and famine, and healing their ailments. He helped out when they faced monumentally laborious tasks. He stood up to injustice and bad government. A kind of moral magician, he became the hero of the popular culture: competitive, tough, resilient, resistant to authority, he was the concrete expression both of the values that ordinary people needed to show to survive and their ideals too. By overcoming the kinds of threats and anxieties that plagued the people in their daily lives, the holy man established his right to mediate between them and the divine. He became the true patron of the people.

The result of their great labours was also to give them the power to adopt Jesus's role as an exorciser of demons. Some tried to fake this power, as when some itinerant Jewish exorcists tried to invoke Jesus's name to drive out some demons from the afflicted. The evil spirit simply refused to recognize their authority: 'Jesus I recognize, Paul I know, but who are you?' The demon then made the possessed person attack them so ferociously that they had to flee naked.[170] But such humiliating failure did not affect the true holy man, who had established his authority through the rigorous subduing of his body and mind. His visions and actions provided a way for society to be reintegrated. As such, it was a kind of creative madness that relieved social tensions by re-establishing order. The possessed themselves played more than a walk-on part on this drama. To be sure, they acted as literary foils to show the power of holy men at its best; but they also provided a mechanism for the expression of controversial opinions and public sentiment as they had always done. They often appeared at times of intensified social tension when people needed leaders,[171] and possessions increased in the run up to religious festivals, since they gave an opportunity for plain speaking.[172]

Mental disorder had always acted in some guises as a positive social force. Possession and exorcism acquired the power to change the individual and then reintegrate him or her into society in a new form of dependency with certain divinely blessed healers. The Church was keen to control such an awesome power, particularly because it showed that physical and spiritual healing had to go through a religious intermediary. Individual holy men were not always keen to have their power so controlled. Between them, the church and the holy man profited the non-elite because they reduced anxieties, gave vent to their concerns, promoted social cohesion and helped establish new social identities, all of which were keenly desired in a society where the distribution of power had shifted. That is not to say that this new mode of social relations did not itself create new concerns – such as heresy, guilt and the problematization of sexuality – but it established a more stable social base on which people could carry on their lives.

The aim of this chapter has been to explain some of the factors that lay behind the peculiarly Roman style of expression regarding mental phenomena. Modern research into the social causes of mental illness strongly suggests that the general population would have had a poor level of overall mental health. But the difficulties involved in applying such a concept to the ancient world mean we cannot use modern evidence to predict the degree or the forms that such ill-health would have taken. Theirs was a context in which the psychiatric had always been able to provide certain socially acceptable benefits. It had provided a means of expressing difference and tensions, of raising new ideas and discussing contentious issues, and of ritually resolving difficult social problems. The mind lay on the borders of the human and the holy and, as such, was the site for constant skirmishing between the demonic and the mundane. Roman society was a strongly somatic culture at the dominant level, whereas the popular placed more emphasis on the demonic as an explanatory agent. We cannot, though, draw a simple equivalence between demonic possession and mental illness. Demons provided an explanation for all manner of socially unacceptable behaviour and feelings. And when, in the later Roman Empire, the notion of humanity and its relationship with the divine was itself being re-evaluated, psychiatric phenomena were crucial to that debate.

3

The World Turned Bottom Up

So far belonging to the non-elite has been a serious business: battling to survive and coping with the stresses generated by living in an often brutal society. This chapter is about how the people had their own way of enjoying themselves. It was the spirit of the Saturnalia that epitomized how the people had fun, a festival where 'the serious is banned, no business is allowed', and the fun centred on 'drinking, noise and games and dice, electing kings and feasting slaves, singing naked, and clapping frenzied hands'.[1] It was a time when 'the whole mob let itself go in pleasures' and celebrated the unofficial culture.[2] This was a festival driven by what Bakhtin called the spirit of carnival: it delighted in pulling the high-and-mighty down from their pedestal and putting whoever and whatever was at the bottom of the social and cultural hierarchy at the top;[3] it revelled in the functions of the body to emphasize that everyone was fundamentally the same; and it delighted in mocking, ridiculing and generally laughing at everything serious. Stylistically, this was a very different way of enjoying the world from the elite fashion. In fact, the popular style reversed the elite mode almost exactly: coarse and rough instead of refined, overblown and showy instead of subtle and sublime, driven by acts and events not ideas, strongly and openly emotional instead of disciplined and controlled. Firmly rooted in the here-and-now and boisterously cheerful, this was how most people liked to take their pleasures. Again, it should be emphasized that this does not mean the elite never participated in certain non-elite activities or even on occasion adopted the same approach. But, for the most part, what characterized the great tradition was at odds with what characterized the little tradition.

The Saturnalia, starting on 17 December and lasting for several days, was a time of great excitement: 'all Rome is at fever-pitch'.[4] A public feast was held at the temple of Saturn and shouts of 'Io Saturnalia' filled the air. It is easy for us in the Western world to underestimate the vitality with which festivals of this kind were celebrated. Augustine describes the revellers at the New Year fun: 'Carried away by worldly and carnal excitement, they celebrate to the sound of frivolous and obscene songs and by dissolute feasting and licentious dancing.'[5] The killjoy Pliny was forced to take himself off to a quiet room to escape the noise emanating from the household party.[6] The Saturnalia were more than a mere holiday; they were an alternative world sanctioned by the authorities. Everything that was culturally dominant was overturned, meaning that people's behaviour became blasphemous, coarse, dirty and drunken. A new world order was established in direct opposition to the serious high culture. Three methods were used to express this transformation: first, the spectacles, pageants and comic shows of the marketplace, then parodies and jokes that debunked the official culture and, finally, swearing. All three forms were based on the principle of laughter.

The Saturnalia incorporated a number of interrelated themes. The first was equality. The Saturnalia represented a return of Saturn's golden age, which had existed before rank and order had entered society. There was neither slavery nor private property and all men had everything in common. People wore the brightly coloured synthesis rather than the toga, and they donned the *pileus*, the felt cap of the freedman, to symbolize the licence of the occasion and the abolition of hierarchy. Slaves could not be punished. Gambling was permitted. It was the time of the year 'when the equestrians and senators show off their party clothes and even the emperor wears a freedman's cap, and the home-bred slave is not afraid to look straight at the Aedile and shake the dice-box'.[7] Presents were exchanged as was done between equals. People sang in the marketplace or street, a practice that would usually signal 'disgrace and ridicule for a rich man and insanity for a poor man'.[8] A whole range of itinerant entertainers, jugglers and snake-charmers filled the forum. The feast reflected the fact that this was a time of plenty for all, not just the elite whose 'jaws are always at Saturnalia'.[9]

Inversion also ran as a strong current through the proceedings. If proverbs expressed a fatalistic resignation to the world as it was, at carnival the world was turned bottom up. A mock king was elected by lot, that in itself underlining the egalitarian spirit, then was killed in a mock ritual at the end of the festival. Slaves could sound off at their masters, who served them at table, while the king issued stupid commands telling people to drink, sing, dance, ridicule themselves or give a flute-girl a piggyback round the house.[10] Men cross-dressed as women. On 7 July, the day Romulus had died, female slaves could take liberties in the *Nonae Caprotinae*. Dressing as free women, they went out of the city scoffing and jeering at all the men they met, and fought among themselves with blows and stones before feasting under a wild fig tree.[11] At the festival of Anna Perenna girls chanted obscenities.[12] On 13 June, the guild of musicians travelled though Rome wearing masks and female dress, drunkenly singing parodies of ancient tunes. This was institutionalized madness, which ruptured the norms of everyday life. But it was also a populist utopian vision that critiqued normal life by inverting it. Power relations were symbolically overturned so that the cornerstones of the social structure – male/female, animal/human, master/slave, wise/fool – were pulled away.

The pure lines and beauty of the classical form were replaced by a delight in grotesque realism. The physical was used to bring every-one down to the same level by emphasizing bodily orifices, touch and everything associated with what Bakhtin delicately called 'the lower stratum'. To put it crudely, the arse ruled the head. Everything was degraded by lowering all that was high to a base, material level. The physical was exaggerated into a grotesque parody of normality. By focusing on bodily functions, the carnival culture also celebrated the changes in human life in contrast to the stasis of normality. Such physicality was also reflected in the use of violence. The 'other' – be they women, animals or social outsiders – were violently abused. People violated the language by swearing, showing no deference and making rude gestures. They threw things at each other and they tor-tured animals, which usefully served to define the human at a time when all were equal and the normal status hierarchy had disappeared. The domestic and local were juxtaposed with the bizarre and exotic to help in specifying what the new normality had become.

Lewdness abounded. Sex worked thematically to symbolize fertil-ity, abundance and growth. Everything was done to excess – food, drink, gambling, song and dance – all to invert the lack associated with ordinary life. John Chrysostom warns his flock about the festival demons in the marketplace and urges them to stay at home away from 'tumults, disorders, diabolical processions, and the marketplace filled with evil licentious men'.[13] People mocked everything. Any-thing serious was laughed at, even the gods. The pagan emperor Julian was ridiculed at the Saturnalia and New Year celebrations in largely Christian Antioch for his beard, his ascetic lifestyle, his dislike of the theatre and horse-racing, and for the fact that he slaughtered so many animals at his sacrifices. Libanius describes the New Year's Eve fun:

Night falls, but no one sleeps. The common people engage in songs, wild dancing, and mocking jests. They do this even in the commercial district, barging in, pounding on doors, shouting and mocking. They make it impossible to sleep. And some people are angry with what they hear but others consider it an occasion for laughter, and no one present is so austere that he censures these goings-on: even he who is too self-controlled to laugh breaks out laughing.[14]

Farces overturned the usual rules of polite behaviour, jokes ridiculed those in authority and even puns transgressed the grammatical order. The fool summed up this spirit of mockery, being free to make public what was normally private, and to tease the powerful about their weaknesses and indiscretions. He was frank, unofficial and rude.

The crowd did not simply stand there watching. They joined in with gusto, revelling in the transgression. The division between the performer and spectator was largely knocked down, suspending the social distance that normally existed between people. Every good festival had a procession, which anyone could join, a sacrifice and a set of games. At the *pompa circensis*, the New Year procession before the day's games, the people dressed up as various gods or, in Rome, as satyrs and sileni and 'ridiculed and mimicked the serious movements of the others, turning them into something ridiculous'.[15] The carnival of Saturnalia was not in that way a festival given for the people but one they gave themselves. It was a product of the vast difference between the lives of the people and the elite. Peter Chrysologus describes the pompa at Ravenna in about 480 CE, which reflects all the essential elements of the carnival spirit. The people impersonated gods and monsters, men dressed in animal skins or as women, and unnatural deformities were put on show: 'They ridicule decency, they violate judicial authority, they laugh at public opinion, they make sport with the whole world watching, and they say that in so doing they jest.'[16] Other public rituals – executions, imperial birthdays, triumphs – all gave similar opportunities for carnival excess, where an alternative set of passions and interests were celebrated. With its own internal logic of reversal, which put the bottom of society at the top, carnival provided a blueprint for a more equal society.

Or did it? What exactly did such festivals mean within Roman society? Were they simply holidays? It is possible to see carnivals as mere safety-valves that allowed the people to let off a bit of steam without harbouring any pretence of bringing real change. Inversion without subversion. To the extent that they provided temporary outlets for conflicts about authority, it can also be argued that carnivals actually reinforced hierarchy because they underlined the norms of order that were expected for the rest of the year. In other words, they did not generate any real change in behaviour. Libanius describes how the Saturnalia 'reconciles citizen with citizen' and 'settles family feuds'. By allowing a space for the safe expression of tensions that threatened normal life, carnival helped society function better. It created community by destroying it and defined norms by challenging them. Moreover, carnival sometimes exaggerated existing hierarchical relationships, as with men's treatment of women. Carnival was mainly for men's pleasure, and the abuse of women, which was commonplace in normal life, was if anything increased though mockery. Men might have dressed as women to signal the disorderliness of the carnival atmosphere but there was little by way of liberation for the women.

It is probably wrong, though, to see any one, single meaning in carnival. Inversion provided an ambivalent image. From the elite's point of view, it showed the stupidity of changing the existing order because the result was just a chaotic and foolish mess. But it also gave the dissatisfied an image of the official culture being ridiculed. It showed that things were not set in stone and could be changed. It gave hope of revenge and of future justice. This universal appeal was part of the reason for its success. Nor were the meanings of carnival fixed: mostly it provided a stable way of having fun, at other times it became a focus for expressing discontent. So it is not correct simply to see carnival as reinforcing normality by allowing hostilities to be resolved and showing that change was futile, if fun. To be sure, nothing was really forgotten but it did create a symbolic space of equality and freedom, which was threatening in a society where respect for hierarchy was the norm. People expressed this sense of freedom in their disorderly behaviour and, no matter how ritualized and routinized such excess became, it asserted that social difference was a part of the ritual order. Carnival did also spill over into the real world. When tensions were being brought out into the open, it was inevitable that these would sometimes get out of hand. The riots in Antioch that accompanied the emperor Julian's visit over the festive period attest to that. But people did not always grab at the opportunity to complain. At one festival, a madman seized Caesar's crown and put it on. He caused such outrage that he was lynched.[17]

The Saturnalia were the extreme expression of the principles of non-elite fun. They emphasized laughter, the physical, the profane and the unofficial, all of which stood in direct contrast to the dogmatic immutability of the official culture. But these principles were not simply confined to a few festivals, even if these allowed their fullest expression: they informed the way the non-elite took their pleasures throughout the year.

Laughter was perhaps the defining characteristic of the spirit of non-elite entertainment. It mocked the pretensions of the official culture. Election graffiti in Pompeii announce that 'The petty thieves urge you to elect Vatia as aedile', a candidate who also got support from 'the late sleepers'.[18] In another, Late Drinkers United (*seribibi universi*) announced their favoured candidate.[19] It is impossible to be sure whether this last scrawl represented an attack on a rival candidate, a funny name for a club or pure mockery of the whole election process. Whichever is true, it is the kind of irreverence that epitomizes popular humour. A fine example of this is found in the Tavern of the Seven Sages where, painted above pictures of twenty or so ordinary men sitting on latrines, the wise sayings of the philosophers were reinvented in popular terms: 'Thales advises those who shit hard to push hard'; 'Cunning Chilon taught how to fart silently'.[20]

It was usually a case of laughing *at* rather than laughing *with*. Plutarch recommends loud speaking as a means to maintaining good health but says that if you carry on speaking loudly in an inn you will have to ignore the jeers of sailors, mule drivers and barmen.[21] Likewise, one high-living aristocrat 'had so dreadful a reputation for licentiousness, that his behaviour had been the subject of rude street corner songs'.[22] A fable describes how 'A fox, seeing a caged lion, stood close by and offered him frightful insults', which shows, as the moral explains, that 'many persons of distinction, when they fall victims to misfortune, are treated with contempt by men of no account'.[23] Nor was humour only aimed up the social ladder. Numerous jokes mock the misfortunes of others, such as hunchbacks.[24] Then there was the man who saw a Spartan beating his slave and shouted, 'stop treating him as your social equal', in reference to the Spartans' harsh upbringing.[25] In a culture where shame acted as a powerful social force, humour could help to reinforce norms of behaviour. In the fable of the ass in the lion's skin, an ass pretends to be a lion but is discovered and beaten: as the moral states, 'a poor common man should not imitate the wealthy for fear of being laughed at and getting into trouble'.[26]

Humour also provided a way for people to enhance their status, especially as wit was highly prized. People went so far as to use magic against people who were mocking their misfortunes and so undermining their standing in the community.[27] Laughing in the face of overwhelming power was a way of saving some face from the situation. In one fable, an old man struggling under a burden of wood asks for death to come to relieve him. When death duly appears, the old man asks him to relieve him by carrying his load of wood.[28] The fact that 'Lucky' was a popular name for slaves reminds us that masters were also able to use humour as a means of enhancing their own status at the expense of another. Nicknaming was another popular tactic to reduce an individual's character to caricature by focusing

on any distinguishing trait and mocking it. The nickname was a kind
of carnival mask that overturned the normal personality of the individual in favour of a ridiculous and reductive travesty. The people
christened one rapacious tax-collector in Lydia 'Leaden Chops'
because of the excess flesh on his face which 'hung down in folds like
a cloak'.[29] The late fourth-century bishop, Synesius of Cyrene,
describes how the crew of a boat, comprised of Jews and a collection
of peasants, spent their time 'jesting with one another, accosting their
comrades not by their real names, but by the distinguishing marks
of their misfortunes': 'Lame', 'Ruptured', and 'Goggle-eyed'.[30] The
popular culture mocked everything including itself, but in this situation nicknaming also helped to create a small well-knit group. In
other situations it provided an effective means of enforcing norms of
personal appearance and personality. The public teased the elite
Quintus Hortensius Hortatus by calling him 'Dionysia', because his
effeminate voice was thought to resemble this famous actress.[31]
Nicknaming could also mark out certain individuals as contemptible
non-people. The description of the native Britons as 'Brittunculi',
nasty little Brits, in the Vindolanda tablets is an example of this. Many
jokes feature the inhabitants of Kyme and Abdera as being naturally
stupid, making them the Roman equivalent of the Irish or Polish
minority mocked to produce a stronger sense of central identity. One
Abderite, so the joke goes, saw a eunuch chatting with a woman and
asked him if she was his wife. The eunuch replied that people like
him couldn't have wives. 'Ah', said the Abderite, 'then she must be
your daughter.'[32]

Travesty and parody were essential elements of popular humour.
Big issues were trivialized into irrelevance, as with the sayings of the
Seven Sages. The anonymous 'Cyprian's Supper', from the fifth or
sixth century, even parodied biblical characters, such as Adam and
St Peter, caricaturing and ridiculing them at a great banquet. Pigs
seem to have featured highly in popular wit, perhaps because in the
country they often lived side by side with humans, almost in the house
itself. Pork was the popular food of choice and for this reason was
given out free in Rome in the later empire.[33] Each citizen received
5 lbs per month for five months of the year. This might not seem much
– as one of the laws states, the pork-dole was a 'titbit' by which 'the
populace can be cheered rather than nourished'[34] – but even this
small addition to their diets was, in the context of struggling to maintain subsistence levels of food, a useful benefit that could have kept
thousands on the right side of the subsistence divide. One fool, noted
for his urbane wit, 'would suddenly put his head beneath his cloak,
and imitated a pig with his voice so well that the onlookers claimed
he had a real pig under it and demanded that he shake it out'.[35]

Porcus was also used as slang for the female genitalia. Pigs featured in a parody of a will known as the *Testamentum Porcelli*, 'The Piglet's Will', or, as it should perhaps be called, 'Pigswill'. This widely known text, 'unlearned and silly' according to Jerome but so popular with the 'simple multitude' that it left them 'shaking with laughter', is full of 'high spirits, low humour, and bad Latin'.[36] It features a pig called Corocotta, named after a famous first century BCE fighter who was so successful at resisting Rome that a one million sesterces bounty was put on his head.[37] A flavour of it is given below:

> Marcus Grunter Bin Lardon the piglet has made this will. As I cannot write myself, I have dictated it. 'To my father Lardy Pig, I bequeath 30 pecks of acorns, and to my mother, the Old Sow, I leave 40 pecks of wheat, and to my sister Gruntress, whose wedding I shall be unable to attend, I give 30 pecks of barley. And of my organs I leave my bristles to the cobblers, my thick skull to the fighters, my ears to the deaf, my tongue to the lawyers and gossipers, my innards to the sausage-makers, my thighs to the stuffing-makers, my loins to the women, my bladder to the boys, my tail to the girls, my muscles to the gays, my heels to the runners and hunters, my claws to the robbers ... And I want a monument inscribed with golden letters – M. Grunter Bin Lardon the piglet lived 999 ½ years; had he lived another half year, he would have made it to a thousand ... My very good friends, I ask you that you look after my body properly, season it well with good flavours of nut, pepper and honey, so that my name will be famous for all time. My masters and relations, who are present at the making of this will, sign it as witnesses.' Porkchopper signed. Oinky signed. Squealer signed. Sausage signed. Bacony signed. Porkscratching signed. Wedding-pig signed.[38]

Witty chitchat characterized the people's public life. Dio Chrysostom describes how fake Cynic philosophers would work a crowd: 'They pass round the hat and play upon the credulity of lads, sailors and crowds of that sort, stringing together rough jokes and a lot of chatter and the low-level banter that smacks of the market-place.'[39] But the people were not that credulous and Dio tells how they mocked them back, ridiculing their claims. This kind of two-way commentary was an integral part of life in the forum and it could be anything but deferential. John Chrysostom complains that, 'Baths made the peasants more effeminate and inns give them a taste for luxury ... Markets and festivals make them insolent.'[40] The use of humour to undermine supposed authorities can be seen in anti-doctor jokes in the *Philogelos*. One runs: 'Then there was the doctor from Kyme who switched to a blunt scalpel because the patient on whom he was operating was screaming so much from the pain.'[41]

Humour provided a socially acceptable and reasonably safe means of speaking truth to power. Wit provided protection even when joking about emperors. Suetonius describes how Vespasian was well-built, with strong, sturdy limbs, but had the expression of one who was straining on a toilet. So when the emperor asked a well-known wit to make a joke about him, he replied: 'I will, when you have finished relieving yourself.' Why did he put up with this? It was because of the role of humour in festivals as a mediator between ruler and ruled. Even emperors were mocked in the carnival atmosphere of the army's Saturnalia: 'they mock and ridicule the emperor, using a wagon as a stage, and elect him a bogus bodyguard', which consisted of soldiers dressed as women.[42] One holiday crowd in fourth-century Edessa resented some treatment they had received, so overturned a statue of Constantius and thrashed its bronze backside.[43] The emperor ignored this because it had occurred at a period of carnival licence. Similarly, Constantius showed his *civilitas*, his common touch, in the circus at Rome by enjoying popular jokes at his expense.[44] It is hard to reconcile this image of the jovial emperor with the hard-faced ruler whose arrival at Rome expressed a ferocious dominance: 'For although he was very short, he bowed down when passing through high gates, and he looked straight before him, as though he had his neck in a vice, and he turned his eyes neither to the right nor to the left, as if he had been a statue.' But reconciliation is possible because carnival gave people the ability to mock in limited circumstances. It was the fool's privilege.

In the post-republican empire, the people took full advantage of this privilege. The power of the emperors forced politics into new areas such as humour, and it was during the carnival atmosphere of the games that such views could be most safely expressed. Wit effectively became an alternative political forum. So when a line was delivered in the theatre that said, 'The old goat was licking the does', and frantic applause and laughter broke out, we can only understand what was happening when we realize that the crowd were actively interpreting the line to refer to the emperor Tiberius's reputation for his sexual exploits and so provided a negative commentary on them.[45] Likewise, when a well-known theatre song with the line 'Here comes Bumpkinus down from the farm' was sung at the time when the provincial, unsophisticated Galba had taken the throne, the whole crowd took up the chorus.[46] After it was learnt that the emperor Maximinus knew no Greek, the theatre crowd insulted him in it.[47] The emperor Julian's *Against the Beard Haters* was a reply to scurrilous verses that had been put about during the festive season.[48] Although Suetonius ascribes it either to his lack of shame or to his fear he would encourage even worse gossip, Nero was sufficiently in tune with the people's sense of humour that, 'he bore nothing more patiently than the scurrilous language and railing abuse which was in every one's mouth, treating no class of persons with more gentleness than those who assailed him with invective and lampoons'. He only exiled a comic actor, called Datus, who while saying the lines 'Farewell, father! Farewell, mother!' had pretended to be drinking and swimming, alluding to the death of Claudius, allegedly by poisoning, and Agrippina's near-death-experience by drowning in a collapsible boat that Nero had had built for her.[49] It was the sign of a 'bad' emperor that he did not grant the fool's privilege. Hence, Domitian had a spectator, who said that a Thracian gladiator was a match for a myrmillo but not for the arbitrary giver of the spectacles, hauled out and thrown to the dogs with a label round his neck saying 'a fan of the Thracians who has spoken impiously'.[50] In the same vein, Caligula had an Atellan farce writer burnt alive for one ambiguous line.[51] Taking jokes well was part of what made a good emperor, and by displaying such inappropriate behaviour in the context of the games, Caligula and Domitian merely underlined their lack of necessary qualities for the job.

The people's humour was expressed in a coarse, rude manner. The popular culture was primarily an oral culture and as such stood in opposition to elite textuality. Poor spelling was part of the orality of graffiti texts. There was no need to spell or be grammatically correct so long as meaning was imparted: if it wurkt it woz gud inuff. The orality of the culture was also reflected in their love of song and verse. Sometimes these were lampoons with political content,[52] while at others they were simply the dirty songs sung by workmen as they dug.[53] Popular speech was full of slang, which reflected the niche roles many had, and served to exclude outsiders. It was also full of swearing. Swearing acted as a linguistic inversion in that it overturned the normal rules of polite expression. It reduced everyone to the same physical level, both in the acts it denoted and also in the way it exaggerated mockery. One graffiti claims, 'I butt-fucked Nisus ten times.'[54] Some lead sling bullets survive from the siege of Perugia by Octavian's troops in the winter of 41/40 BCE, which the defenders fired at their attackers: 'I'm heading for Octavian's arsehole', is scratched on one; and on another, 'Hi, Octavian: you suck dick'.[55]

These grotesque insults, concerned with bodily exits and entrances, reflected the popular focus on the physical. The body was common to all, which in elite eyes was what made it inherently vulgar. But for the people, physicality was a practical reality – most had to work hard manually to make a living. It was natural, then, that they would delight in excessive, physical and materialistic pleasures. And the celebration of ugliness that the grotesque images of carnival presented can be seen as a defiant statement against the refinement and sensitivity of the elite. The popular grotesque was therefore implicitly political because it ridiculed the official aesthetic.

Comedy relied on the physical world of violence and bodily movements. In the *Golden Ass*, the hero would have been flogged to death, but all the blows to his stomach made him fire his faeces into the faces of his tormentors.[56] This was a culture which explained the concept of modesty to itself by means of the following fable: Zeus made man but forgot to include Modesty and as there was no room left he told her to go in though the arsehole. At first she refused and stood on her dignity but when he insisted, reluctantly she agreed on the condition that if anything came in after her she would leave immediately. Hence all perverts, it was stated, lack modesty.[57] The popular culture also had a fascination with variety, with a strong focus on the fabulous and fantastic as opposed to the routine and mundane. Augustus, 'if anything rare and worth seeing was ever brought to the city, used to make a special exhibition of it in any convenient place'; hence a rhinocerous was displayed in the Saepta, a tiger on the stage, and a 50-cubit snake in front of Comitium.[58] Earlier, Julius Caesar had been keen to ally himself with the special forces often attributed to the deformed by riding a horse with five part hooves, since the soothsayers had said that its master would rule the world.[59] Grotesque figures of all kinds were popular to counteract the effects of the evil eye – terracotta, bronze and ivory statuettes of pygmies, hunchbacks and dwarfs have all been found. The distorted body was a popular marker of the animal/human divide and represented a physical discussion of what it was to be human. It also had strong connotations of carnival fun, and for that reason some of the wealthy kept half-witted and deformed slaves for entertainment.[60] A market for them sprang up where it was possible to buy 'people who have no calves, or who are weasel-armed, or who have three eyes, or who are ostrich-headed'.[61] Their location on the borders of notions of humanity meant that the deformed also became associated with the privilege of the carnival fool. Tiberius was once asked aloud by a dwarf at a dinner why Paconius, who had been prosecuted for treason, was still alive. Tiberius reprimanded him for his insolence but then wrote to the senate telling them to punish Paconius without further delay.[62] The deformed fool, like carnival itself, turned the tables on the powerful, but did so in a way that left them outside the law, not against it.

Popular notions regarding sexuality revealed themselves partly in the often grossly enlarged phalluses that were used to ward off evil spirits. Here again we see a love for the grotesquely physical. It is tempting to think that the people's sexuality differed from that of the elite – that the non-elite acted in a more 'straight', heterosexual

8. Happiness lives here, not in a brothel, but a bakery

manner than the elite, whose adoption of Greek homosexual practices was itself an act designed to differentiate themselves from the
masses. But there does not appear to have been a distinct popular
attitude about what constituted the correct object of sexual desire.
The people seem to have shared the same active/passive divide that
characterized elite ideas about sexuality. What mattered most was
who was doing what to whom, with those being done bearing the
mark of shame. This was a far more status-oriented concept of sexuality.[63] In discussing the Tavern of Salvius in Pompeii, Clarke argues
that 'Non-elites, in particular slaves and former slaves, were the usual
passive partners of freeborn elite men.' Therefore, he concludes, a
large percentage of the males in the tavern – slaves, former slaves

and foreigners – 'had experienced being penetrated anally and had also been penetrated orally; that is, they had fellated males'.[64] This might be an exaggeration, given that a majority of slaves are unlikely to have had much direct contact with their masters and that masters themselves appear to have preferred smooth, young, pre-pubescent boys to hard, rough-skinned slaves, often being willing to pay high sums for particularly attractive slave-boys. That, though, suggests that perhaps the real difference between elite and non-elite sexuality lay in the manner of its expression. It was a matter of style. The elite male tried to emphasize his taste by enjoying partners of either sex who were characterized by beauty. In this way a physical act was raised to a higher plane of artistic appreciation. The elite were also able to take their pleasures in private rooms within their household. The non-elite, by contrast, were compelled by force of circumstance to enjoy their sexual relations in a far more crowded environment. Cramped living conditions meant that sleeping together often took place in close proximity to the family group. The non-elite's large cohort of young, unmarried labourers relied on prostitutes. The prostitutes' work was carried out in a semi-public environment, often closely associated with taverns and inns, which meant that such sex acts were easily overheard. The elite found this behaviour revolting. Dio Chrysostom censured the people of Tarsus for their habit of snorting because it was reminiscent of the bestial, immoral noises that were associated with brothels.[65]

In many ways, the character of Aesop in the *Aesop Romance* epitomized the popular principles of carnival. Potbellied, misshapen of head, snubnosed, dwarfish and bandy-legged, he was a monstrosity who his fellow slaves assumed was being used 'as a horror to protect the market from the evil eye'.[66] He physically embodied the confrontation between the high and low cultures and expressed the tensions between master and slave, philosophy and natural wit, vulgarity and refinement. He is openly sexual and even his religion was the new, popular Isis worship, as opposed to the traditional, official Apollo cult. He breaks all the rules, which generates much of the humour. He is a trickster who wins small, temporary victories based on an intimate knowledge of how the powerful operate. He works constantly to invert the social order and even though he loses in the end it is only to overwhelming odds.[67] This was a character created over hundreds of years, representing an amalgam of all that the popular encapsulated. It is hard to say who read or listened to the story of Aesop's life, but that need not stop us from seeing it as a representation of popular culture in action.

Mimes also give a clear indication of the principles of popular entertainments. Although relatively little is known about them, the mimes were the most popular form of theatre in the empire. Only one, *The Oxyrhynchus Mime*, survives and it is clear from this that the text represents only the bare bones of a largely improvised performance, which included a variety show of acrobatics, song, dance, jokes and magic tricks.[68] These were short plays which ridiculed everything. They were full of violence and stupidity. As in carnival, everyday situations were inverted to generate comedy, which can be seen in the titles of various plays that do survive: *Wealthy Overnight* (the equivalent of today's *Lottery Winner*), *Millionaire Bankrupt*, *The Highwayman Crucified*.[69] One very popular mime, called *Beans*, told how the new god Romulus wanted to eat beans, not the traditional food of the gods, ambrosia.[70] Beans obviously held a high place in popular Roman gastronomy, particularly since four of the most famous Roman families were named after them: the Lentulus family (after lentils), the Fabius (after favas), the Cicero (after chickpeas) and the Piso (after peas). But in the context of a rude play, as any schoolboy knows, beanz meanz fartz. But perhaps the most popular subject was adultery. *The Locked-out Lover* had a simple plot: a married woman whose husband is away, lets in her lover, something of a smooth-operator, but then the husband unexpectedly returns so the wife hides the lover in a trunk, with his discovery providing the climax.[71] The show was full of ridicule for the stupid husband, who falls for the artful tricks of his clever wife. The denouement was usually simple: the lover ran away or the music just stopped.[72]

The plays were especially associated with the festival of Flora, where they were performed with female actors naked on stage.[73] The future wife of the emperor Justinian, Theodora, used to appear naked on stage before he 'discovered' her.[74] Not surprisingly, nudity led to sex acts both simulated and real.[75] The staging requirements were minimal: there was no scenery, which made it ideal for travelling groups of players to put on, and often the only prop seems to have been the trunk to hide the lover. No masks were worn, which gave free rein for grotesque facial expressions and contortions that were improvised on the spot. One comic actor, called Stratocles, who played nasty old men, clever slaves, parasites, pimps and all the ludicrous characters, had great agility, a booming laugh and an extraordinary ability to 'sink his neck into his shoulders'. 'It is', as one expert in elite public-speaking said, 'most unbecoming to distort the features or use uncouth gestures, which arouses such laughter in the farces.'[76] The character of the Fool, the *stupidus*, wore a multicoloured costume, had his head shaved, and was the target for general insults and slaps. Trained animals sometimes appeared, such as when in the theatre of Marcellus, in Rome, before the emperor Vespasian, a dog played the main part, took a drug, staggered and shivered and pretended to die, then at the correct prompt woke up to general astonishment.[77] Needless to say, the language was rough and the Latin vulgar in every sense. Obscenities were used, 'such as are spoken only by the dregs of the people'.[78] But witty and pithy aphorisms were also appreciated.[79] Indeed, the collection of sayings that survives of Publius Syrus derives from the mimes he wrote. But however it was said, everything was ridiculed.[80] Topical references and political comment were freely included.[81] Double-entendres and puns were also used in farces as a means of expressing political comment.[82] Double-talk of this kind subverted language's official meaning to reveal a truer popular meaning beneath. The crowd were therefore actively involved in interpreting what happened on stage.

The mimes aped and parodied normal everyday life, ridiculing family life like a bedroom farce. They mocked, as Shaw says, society's 'core institutions' – fathers, husbands and its sexual mores – in a physical and direct way, unmediated by any masks. Mime was 'a type of theatre that was anathema to public authorities'. Here were acts that emerged from below, from the popular culture that coalesced around the streets and marketplaces.[83] But, as Choricius, who wrote a defence of the mimes, claims, the mimes can be seen as morally harmless and perhaps even beneficial: 'when you watch adultery, then you also see the magistrate's court: the man who rashly committed adultery is tried with his lover, the judge threatens both with punishment'.[84] In other words, mimes served to reinforce normal morality not subvert it. The mimes provided 'simple pleasure, free of strife and disturbance', and were 'unlike horse racing and pantomime dancing in that they do not fill people with dissension'.[85] Cicero complained that the mimes were 'hackneyed', but the mimes reflected a culture where ritualized repetition helped fix what was known and understood.[86] By dealing with stock themes and simple polarities the mimes endorsed the normality of everyday life. But, as with carnival, alternative readings were possible. The mimes gave temporary freedom from normal life too, and showed that life could be different. This was not a textual tradition and improvization was given a higher priority than careful composition. This reflected the higher value the non-elite placed on instinctive thinking processes. Natural wit and the ability to think on your feet were much better survival tools than an educated brain. It also reflects a culture where community was seen as more important than individual creativity. The performer ranked higher than the author. Performers were not simple mouthpieces; they were free to improvise and it was in their performance that the creativity lay. Such repetitive performance of stock plays and themes can easily seem tedious to the modern ear, but the non-elite lived a repetitive life, where small breaks in the routine offered the greatest fun. They were far more attuned to the slightest variations in daily life because these could have a significant impact on their quality of life.

There is a risk that we see the non-elite as a wholly rough lot, who only enjoyed sex and farts. The Roman pantomime was utterly unlike the modern stage-show of that name and showed that many of the non-elite enjoyed a more sophisticated physical performance. These acts consisted of a graceful, ballet-type act, accompanied by music, and usually based on a well-known mythological scene. While not as widespread as the mimes, they reveal a far more discerning side to the popular. Apuleius describes one show, which dealt with the beauty contest between the gods that Paris adjudicated in and that led ultimately to the Trojan War:

> Then Venus appeared displaying to all her perfect beauty, naked except for a sheer silk scarf which covered, or rather shaded, her quite remarkable hips and which an inquisitive wind mischievously either blew aside or sometimes pressed clingingly against her ... Then two groups of attractive young maidens danced on to the stage, the Graces and the Seasons, who honoured the goddess by scattering flowers around her. They danced with great skill an intricate ballet movement. The flutes played sweet Lydian melodies, which soothed and delighted the spectators. But far more delightful was Venus, who began to move forward gracefully, rhythmically, slowly, swaying softly from side to side, gently inclining her head. As soon as she came face to face with Paris, the judge, she appeared by her gestures to promise him that if he chose her she would give him a bride who was the most beautiful of mortals and similar in appearance to Venus herself. And then the young Trojan prince gladly handed to Venus the golden apple and pronounced her the victor in the beauty contest.[87]

Any threat that popular theatre presented to the elite was contained by plays having to be staged, licensed and often paid for by a donor. Legal rights were denied to popular performers as a further way to contain, if only symbolically, their social status. It was when the people met off-stage in their own space that the elite became far more jumpy. A well-known correspondence between the emperor Trajan and the then governor of Bithynia-Pontus, Pliny the Younger, reflects these concerns. Trajan turned down Pliny's request that an association (*collegium*) be formed to fight fires at Nicomedia because 'We must remember that it is associations like these which have been responsible for the political disturbances in your province, particularly its towns. If people assemble for a common purpose, whatever name we give them and for whatever reason, they soon turn into a political club.'[88] In another exchange, the two agree to permit these groups so long as they are 'not used for riotous and unlawful assemblies'.[89] In reality, though, the elite did permit these clubs to exist and probably could have done little to enforce their disbandment. Most of their attempts at control seem to have been local responses to local problems, but these still reflect the underlying nervousness which the elite felt when they saw the non-elite gathering together unsupervised and on their own terms. These clubs actually seem have been no more threatening than a modern golf club. Many aped the elite, organizing themselves and their processions along elite lines and in order of rank. In Aphrodisias, they sat happily together in their allotted slots in the theatre.[90] One such statement of popular conformity can be seen in the rules concerning dinners and behaviour at a club in Lanuvium, near Rome: 'Chairmen for the dinners, four at a time, ought to provide one amphora each of good wine and bread worth two asses and four sardines and a room for the dinner and hot water and a waiter.' It was also stated that 'if any member moves about from one seat to another simply to cause a disturbance he shall be fined four sesterces. If any member speaks abusively to another or becomes obstreperous he shall be fined twelve sesterces. If any member is insolent to the club president he shall be fined twenty sesterces.'[91]

Collegia created a more private space for non-elite entertainment, and established an air of exclusivity by charging fees, granting membership and adopting ritual observances. Given that it cost 100 ses-

9. A shop sign in Pompeii showing the association of carpenters processing together

terces to join this particular club in Lanuvium, it may be that collegia were aimed mostly at the more well-to-do among the non-elite. Social life for most in the towns and cities took place in the less formal surroundings of taverns. They were the site for local leisure and, because most people did not have access to cooking facilities, for hot food. They were so popular that Pompeii, with about 20,000 inhabitants, had almost 140 inns and bars, or about one per 145 of the population. Their importance was such that the Romans had numerous names for these eating and drinking places: *taberna, popina, ganeum, caupona, hospitium, deversorium*. Often these places had other entertainments, such as music, gambling and prostitutes. Anyone could go to one: Synesius talks of a slave who 'wallowed in cock-fighting, in gambling, and in drinking in taverns'.[92]

Taverns acted as centres for boisterous popular entertainment. They were also centres for local gossip and rumour spreading.[93] Drink no doubt led to frequent addiction problems and destroyed many families. The *Philogelos* jokes about an alcoholic who was drinking in a bar when someone came up to him and said, 'Your wife is dead.' 'Bartender', he replied solemnly, 'some dark wine please.'[94] The other problem was that any popular gathering was viewed by the elite as politically suspect. The people standing round the bar came to represent, quite literally, a counter-culture. It was presupposed that the lower orders were given to disorder. Taverns, as centres for drink, dance, sex and bodily pleasures, centres that had been created by the people for their own enjoyment and sociability, were seen as a potent threat to the social order,[95] for even though the elite held political power they did not have social control. Popular leisure in the new urban environment of Rome seemed not simply to exceed, but to overwhelm the very limited forces of social control that the elite had at their disposal. There was little they could actually do to stop people using these dens of iniquity. The vocal and legal attacks of the elite on taverns and the foods they served, banning such things as cooked meats and the hot water used to dilute wine, acted as an index of social strain, reflecting the difficulties the elite had with the new forms of uncontrolled popular urban leisure that had sprung up.

Sumptuary laws, aimed at limiting what the elite saw as misplaced luxury, can in this way be seen as symbolic markers as much as genuine attempts to reform popular leisure. Their aim was to help protect the elite from popular influence and maintain a cultural apartheid. This was important in the late republic and early empire because urbanization had brought great change to popular entertainment. The city of Rome was far from being a folk society and it established a more varied culture for the non-elite. Many of the underlying differences that made the elite particularly nervous about tavern culture stemmed from profound differences between the elite and the popular cultures. Above all, lay the contrast between what the elite thought was acceptable behaviour in public. This difference was exaggerated by the practical realities of living in a city as crowded as Rome. Home comforts for most were minimal, while privacy was limited and may not have been desired. People had to go out for hot food and for sociability. It was a close, physical environment where the shame which the elite associated with many public acts was not a viable option. The chronic underemployment that was the norm for many urban manual labourers promoted an irregular, casual lifestyle spent lingering and loitering in the streets, meeting with friends and neighbours, waiting for the next bit of work to come along.

What was especially concerning for the elite about urban popular leisure was that the spirit of carnival seemed to be spilling on to the streets all year round. Drink was central to popular leisure, and also practical in that it was nutritional and warming, and dulled hunger, fatigue and pain. It acted as a social lubricant by creating a safe form of aberrant behaviour. Drunkenness created a clear public way to overturn normal codes of behaviour and bring social tensions out into the air. One of the problems for the elite was that this release of tensions inevitably sometimes spilled over into violence. Some of this fighting may simply have been for fun, but, where brawls were used to settle social differences, it shows that the people developed their own ways to settle disputes outside any elite framework. The fact that these methods were physical and violent should not surprise us. Being able to vigorously defend rights was a valuable skill to have in many non-elite situations. But the elite could not see past the fact that what was basically a safe form of social pathology had the effect of bringing violence into public spaces.

Drink and gambling were part and parcel of being a non-elite man in an urban environment. What they thought was worth fighting over can tell us something about what they really cared about. Gambling seems to have been a common source of arguments. As mentioned earlier, the laws concerning gambling are full of references to assault and the use of force. Various wall-paintings from taverns in Pompeii depict men fighting about the outcome of dice games. Gambling provided people with the necessary skills they needed in non-elite society: how to assess risk and solve problems under pressure. It involved cheating and arguing to protect one's interests. The frequent fights reflected the intense rivalry that social competition created between men of near-equal status as they struggled to assert their virility. Mockery was part and parcel of this process. Laughing at your opponent is captured in the gaming board that ridicules both competitors with its letters:

```
LEVATE    DALOCU
LUDERE    NESCIS
IDIOTA    RECEDE
```

'Get up from your seat; you don't know how to play; get lost you idiot.'

Even the counters used to play were abusive, with particular scores having names such as 'adulterer', 'fucker', 'tart', 'cunt-licker'.[96] Part of the fun of this came from subverting the phrases found on polite tables. But most of the enjoyment came from going head-to-head with a social rival in a heated contest, where status could be won. This was an unofficial status, unrecognized by any others than those in the gambling group, but its importance is reflected in the camaraderie that the historian Ammianus noted:

> It must be admitted that, even though all friendships at Rome are rather cool, only those which are forged by gambling are close and intimate, as if they had been formed during glorious struggles, and were firmly grounded in great affection; some of this group of gamblers live in such harmony together that you would think they were brothers. You some-times, therefore, see a low-born man, who knows all the secrets of the dice, put on a solemn and serious face because someone important has been preferred to him at a grand entertainment or assembly.[97]

By the late republic, the traditional Roman political system was breaking down in the face of its inability to cope with the influx of power, wealth and people into the city of Rome. Tensions between the people and the elite were exacerbated by the fact that the urban non-elite acquired new ways of enjoying themselves outside elite control, ways that brought the rough, boisterousness of carnival into everyday life on the streets. It was clear that new institutions and rituals were needed to reintegrate the people more fully into Roman society. Corbeill has suggested that populist aristocrats, the *populares*, adopted non-elite gestures to distance themselves from the more elitist *optimates* and align themselves politically with the urban plebs.[98] I want to suggest that the games developed as a way of incor-porating carnival into government. Bakhtin argued that carnival was incapable of full assimilation by the dominant culture because it was inherently opposed to anything official. The spirit of carnival would not be able to stop itself from mocking. But in Roman public enter-tainments, a cultural form was created that drew on many of the principles of popular entertainment to help lure the people into a new relationship with the official culture. As a result, the official culture itself was changed. This shows that the popular culture did have upward influence in Roman society, and was not just the benefi-ciary of cultural crumbs falling from the elite table.

That the games were successful in gaining the allegiance of the people seems clear: as Cameron says, 'The man in the Roman street positively lived for the thrill of circus and theatre.'[99] It is true that the disproportionate access to the Colosseum reflected society's power structure and made these contests an occasional treat for most, unlike the circus races which were easily available to nearly all. But the important point was that all were symbolically included, albeit in a way that also spelled out to them their social inferiority. It was one of the characteristics of the games as a whole that, like the festivals of which they were generally a part, they were aimed at everyone. The people responded by showing enthusiastic appreciation because that is what the sponsoring elite wanted. The people were in this way able to influence the direction of elite generosity by means of their

10. That most popular hero, the charioteer

vocal support for anything that met their standards. What met their standards were those entertainments which reflected the broad principles of popular entertainment we have been examining.

The spectacles had to have a wow factor. People wanted the same variety and novelty that they found in the carnival. Inversion of the human/animal divide was a common tactic. Trained monkeys wearing human clothing could act as human beings, riding chariots and balancing on the backs of dogs, or a goat might perform tricks.[100] In one show, tame lions caught hares but then, rather than eating them, brought them back to their handlers.[101] Or, in another, elephants walked a tightrope and one could even write Greek.[102] The crossing of the divide worked the other way too, with criminals being condemned to being ripped to pieces by wild beasts in the arena. The appearance of the grotesque also enhanced the carnivalesque atmosphere: dwarfs and pygmies fought as gladiators.[103] Or women fought, inverting the normal rules of combat.[104] In hostile Christian eyes, the inversion of normal rules of behaviour was one of the characteristics of the games:

> A man who will scarcely lift his tunic in public for the necessities of nature, will take it off in the circus in such a way as to make a full display of himself before all; a man who guards the ears of his maiden daughter from every smutty word, will himself take her to the theatre to hear words of that sort and to see gestures to match; the man who when he sees a quarrel on the streets coming to blows will try to calm things down, will in the stadium applaud far more dangerous fights; the man who shudders at the sight of of a body of someone who has died naturally, will in the amphitheatre gaze down calmly on the bodies of men mangled and torn to pieces.[105]

In the same way that gifts were exchanged at the Saturnalia, the givers of games often handed out presents. Tokens were hurled into the crowd and such *missilia* were extremely popular, if not with the super-rich Seneca who made a point of leaving before the 'trifles'.[106] That a *missilia* would be happening was a point worth advertising ahead of the games to increase their attractiveness.[107] Nero went further than most and gave out tickets for a wide range of items. The list shows general desires in approximately ascending order: birds, various foods, tokens for grain, clothing, gold, silver, jewels, pearls, paintings, slaves, beasts of burden, shops, apartment blocks, country estates.[108] Speculators would try and buy these gifts from spectators in advance in a kind of primitive futures market.[109] Most people would have been unable to cope with a gift such as an animal and so would happily have converted it into cash as soon as possible. Even items such as paintings and furniture may have been superfluous for those with little or no domestic space, and expensive goods such as jewellery would be difficult to keep secure. It was typical of the notorious emperor Heliogabalus that he subverted these expectations by giving out tokens for ten bears, ten dormice, ten lettuces and ten pounds of gold.[110] It is easy to imagine the violent scramble to get hold of these tokens when they were thrown into a tightly packed crowd. Herodian tells of the loss of life that could happen on such occasions.[111] The gifts were also spread evenly among the crowd, not according to the need of the recipients. The emperor Domitian had fifty tickets thrown to the senators and equestrians after most had gone to the crowd, although this may have been a calculated snub to an already wealthy elite.[112]

The Saturnalia harked back to a mythological Golden Age. In the games the emperors tried to manipulate this social memory. They reinvented mythology. On one occasion, Orpheus emerged from Hades, he enchanted nature with his playing so that animals crowded round him and even rocks and trees moved towards him; then, in a new twist to the tale, he was torn apart by a bear. The fun for the spectator lay in knowing the plot, knowing that it would be subverted but not how, and the thrill of irreverence when the twist finally came. Marcus Aurelius complained that the amphitheatre was boring because it always stayed the same, but the games showed the same popular method for innovation based around well-known themes.[113] They played with existing formats and plots to generate laughter and entertainment.

We have seen that violence was commonplace in the popular culture and provided a physical language the people could easily understand. Violence acted to express one's position in the social hierarchy. Treating slaves and criminals with great brutality was what those higher up the scale did; it made them feel important. Violence provided a physical indication of the gap between the spectator and the victim. The crowd had a high tolerance level for violence, and bloody punishment was seen as a good thing. The dramatic punishments of the games served to spectacularize the law. By scapegoating certain selected groups and individuals, the games created a world of excessive punishment that mocked the victims. When Nero executed the Christians, 'Their deaths were made farcical. Dressed in wild animals' skins, they were torn to pieces by dogs, or crucified, or made into torches to be ignited after dark as substitutes for daylight.'[114] The crowd delighted in the deaths of such criminals as a vindication of their own belief system. They ridiculed those who had dared to follow alternative rules.

The games provided entertainment in a medium that was carnivalesque in style, but their popularity also rested on the relevance of the messages they imparted to the non-elite. In the same way that a triumph expressed the idea of empire and conquest in concrete terms, with models representing particular towns that had been captured, so the games boiled things down to readily understood personal terms. It was easy to learn what mattered by looking at the dramatic and intense representations of the fights and chariot-races. They were in effect a Roman reality show. Charioteers and gladiators became the icons of popular culture, often accompanied by great crowds of followers.[115] These popular heroes postured, strutted and showed off like actors on a stage. They reflected the assertive masculinity that men needed to show to do well in competitive public life. It was a kind of somatization of belief. By taking carefully calculated physical risks, they won social status and wealth. In order to become an object of popular veneration, gladiators had to perform repetitious tasks with accuracy, skill and bravura. It was an approach that reflected the routines of non-elite life where the difference between life and death lay in paying attention to the smallest details of risk-taking. The division of gladiators into clear brands, based on their appearance and fighting technique, appealed to the many non-elite who relied on their own areas of niche expertise for a livelihood. Likewise, charioteers epitomized the attributes which people needed in their daily lives: technical expertise, resilience, strength, nous, the ability to jockey for position, to wait for the right time and to cheat. The games allowed the Romans to personify virtues in popular heroic terms. They were also full of specific situations where these heroes would have to show the right qualities to triumph. To be sure, it was formulaic. But the audience found satisfaction in the repetition of a familiar form, which allowed them to enjoy the details of the performance and increased their capacity for understanding. Originality was only welcomed to the degree that it intensified the experience they had expected to have in the first place.

Factionality was part of popular life. Local life produced local rivalries and the division of the races into factions reflected this. Those who followed the gladiators were also split into two groups, the *parmularii*, who backed the Thracians, and the *scutularii*, who supported the *myrmilliones*.[116] One of the benefits of factions and groupings was that it made head-to-head betting significantly easier. But in the eyes of the elite, hysterical and stupid fans provided an image of the social decline of Rome:

> I am astonished that so many thousands of grown men should have such a childish passion to watch horse-racing and men standing up in the chariots. If they were attracted by the speed of the horses or the skill of the men, one could understand their enthusiasm. But in fact it

is a bit of cloth they like, a bit of cloth that captivates them. And if the racers swapped colours during the race, the fans would change sides and immediately forget about the runners and riders they had been loudly cheering on by name just before.[117]

But such popular support reflected a subordinate system of cultural taste. The cultural criteria of the fans differed from the elite but that did not mean that it was necessarily stupid. In fact, knowledge was one of the distinguishing characteristics of the fan. Galen describes how the partisans of the Blues and Greens even smelled the dung of their racehorses to satisfy themselves that they were being fed good-quality fodder.[118] Such discriminating knowledge was a way of creating a hierarchy of status within the fans and also generated endless discussion points. Fierce competition between the factions would also mean that some would look to the supernatural for help, as one curse shows: 'Help me in the Circus on 8 November. Bind every limb, every sinew, the shoulders, the ankles and the elbows of Olympus, Olympianus, Scortius and Juvencus, the charioteers of the Red. Torment their minds, their intelligence and their senses so that they may not know what they are doing, and knock out their eyes so that they may not see where they are going – neither they nor the horses they are going to drive.'[119] Factionality reflected the reality of life for most of the non-elite: localism, expertise, intense rivalry within and between social groups, camaraderie too. Being a fan was a training for life. And supporting a colour was a way for an emperor to show that he was one of the people.[120]

The emperors were not simply reacting to pressure from below or trying to absorb the masses with watered-down elite culture. The development of the games articulated the change in leadership that had occurred within Roman society. The personal acts of gladiators were appropriated for society as a whole so that power could flow better to the emperor and down from him to those beneath. The popular performers were themselves changed by this rewiring, becoming the mediators between the ruler and the ruled. They became powerful in their own right, deriving their strength both from imperial patronage and also from their popularity with the non-elite. They became the intermediary between the humble and the divine. This special status gave them greater freedom, and they could even go around the city in masks, with raucous hilarity, playing practical jokes and stealing things.[121] The status of the charioteer as mediator between emperor and people invested their performances with far greater importance than mere horse races. The emperors liked to associate with the stars in public. Many of the elite wanted to appear in the games because that was where it was at. Almost everyone wanted to be a supporter of one of the colours in the races because that showed they were plugged into the social network.

The emperors used the games to try and inculcate habits of obedience and deference in the non-elite. The seating in the Colosseum was carefully arranged according to social rank. The equally ordered procession at the beginning of the entertainment acted as a ritualized affirmation of inequality. The spectators came to the games as would clients to their patron: demurely knowing their place, grateful for what they were about to receive. Such public performance of deference was so important to the imperial regime because this image of concord was how the emperors wanted their rule to be seen. It was not a lie, but what Scott calls a 'self-portrait', a very one-sided statement of power that sought above all to make it seem part of the natural order.[122] The games were also an attempt to create a new space which could be used for ritualized contact between the ruler and his subjects. By formalizing the relationship in this way, there was less chance that the veneer of perfect relations would crack and so the risk of an unscripted outcome was reduced. But to make it interesting and to get the people to sign up, the meeting between ruler and ruled had to have an element of risk. It was this that the spirit of carnival brought to the occasion because, although it was mainly contained within the arena itself, it could sometimes spill out into the crowd.

11. A wall painting of a fight in the crowd at the amphitheatre in Pompeii

We saw in chapter 1 that rioting was a tactic the people had at their disposal to exert pressure on the authorities whenever they felt their moral rights to food and work were not being met. But riots were not only about such high matters. The carnivalesque nature of the games and the violent streak in the popular culture meant that simple exuberance sometimes resulted in disorder. Riots often had a festive air and could represent simple acts of collective hooliganism.[123] They were not always political. Ammianus noted that riots were about both 'serious and trivial things'.[124] One of the laws refers to 'those who commonly call themselves "the lads"', who misbehave at the spectacles and 'in certain towns where there is unrest play to the gallery for the applause of the mob'.[125] A fight between the people of Nuceria and Pompeii, where many died, 'arose out of a trivial incident at a gladiatorial show ... During an exchange of taunts – characteristic of these disorderly country towns – abuse led to stone-throwing, and then swords were drawn.'[126] One of the complaints of the elite was that crowds were notoriously volatile. As Artemidorus says, 'the sea resembles a crowd because of its instability'.[127] But if a crowd is fickle, it is because it is making its own mind up and doing what it wants. The mob was not simply a tool to be manipulated by elite leaders. Crowds had their own local leaders within, who helped generate spontaneous and improvised demands from those in authority. Calling for benefits in this way helped the people keep their rulers on their toes. And in acting on whims, the crowd merely aped the whimsy of its rulers. The emperors were, after all, notoriously inconsistent in their decision-making and government. The emperors wanted the games to be a place where the people could go 'to drive away their cares' in a spirit of licensed fun.[128] The new mode of leadership in Roman society also necessitated an area where people could speak more freely and critically to those in power. This was achieved through the incorporation of carnivalesque elements into the games, which meant that: 'The language of the people in the circus is not offensive. The place excuses the transgression. Ready tolerance of their free speech makes the emperor popular.'[129] But the licence could not always contain the people's spirit.

By the end of the republic, Roman society needed to create a new urban vision of social relations and establish rituals to define it. New outlets for wealth were required to enable the vast profits of empire to be spent in a manner that was socially acceptable to the elite and could accommodate the moral economy of those below. This was no easy matter for a traditional society to achieve. Lavish expenditure on the games by the emperors enabled them to redefine their power in communal terms. The games therefore became a place where wealth could be spent without creating envy and discord. Mean emperors, who failed to spend generously, were akin to hoarders who rejected the social contract implicit in this new arrangement: food and entertainment in return for political legitimacy. By appealing to popular tastes in entertainment, the games created concord through a shared set of passions. The games redefined, repositioned and regulated pleasure, and shifted some of the aspects of carnival to new controlled sites. But whereas carnival celebrated difference by destroying hierarchy, the games celebrated unity by creating hierarchy.

The redefinition of the role of leadership within Roman society fundamentally altered the relationship between the non-elite and the state. Citizenship moved from playing a central role. Instead the defining relationship was that of client of the emperor. This was a gradual, steady shift, not an overnight revolution. Citizenship still counted for something – it made men eligible for benefits such as the corn dole. But such gifts, like the games, were no longer just a citizen's right: they had become a symbol of the reciprocal relationship that had been established between the people and their emperor. It was a claim to a wider, more penetrating form of leadership. The old system of politics was restructured so that it could shoulder a heavier burden of public meaning. The emperor, as leader, sought to send down roots into the lower levels of Roman society and engage the non-elite everywhere in a meaningful relationship with him. Carnivalesque games functioned to provide entertainment and social control in a new common culture. This served to reunite the classes after the elite and non-elite had drawn away from each other in the later republic. The games were not just a bit of fun: they expressed an urgent need to show that the new political system worked in practical and concrete ways. They articulated a desire for what the fractured society of the late republic most lacked: concord and effective central control. They created a focus for social harmony, a place where only one Roman culture existed.

The people were not passive in this process. They tried to influence and manage the elite by means of flattery, by showing appreciation and by the occasional display of anger, nudging them towards forms that would bring the people the most benefit. They acted as the non-elite had to in their daily lives. Both sides were active in the process, and not surprisingly it was largely the elite who set the direction, even if their aim was in part always to give the people something they wanted to have. Status was a relative concept and the elite needed the people. Spending money on public largesse was a social investment every bit as sensible as a financial one. The fact that the emperors asked for the people's consent to their rule shows they still had considerable legitimating power. Ignoring the people was not an option: as the mouse said to the lion in the fable, 'You once laughed at me because you didn't expect to get any return for your favour to me, but now you know that even mice can show their gratitude.'[130] In reality, the emperors expected such consent to be readily given, which made it hurt all the more when it was even partially withheld: during a food shortage Constantine was dejected by the feebleness of the applause that greeted him in the theatre in Constantinople, because 'he loved to be praised by the populace'.[131] It mattered to emperors on a personal level that the people liked them and the applause at the games acted as an opinion poll on their rule. By the end of the republic, the people were looking for just rule and a social solidarity that had been missing for too long. The imperial entertainments incorporated elements of popular fun to entice them back into harmony. In doing so, the popular culture managed to exert a powerful upward influence on the form of Roman government.

Imperial power rested in part on mass urban appeal. It was important to the emperors that they were seen to be actively supporting and enjoying popular causes. This ran the risk of creating tensions with the elite who saw themselves as worthier of imperial support and patronage. In reality, of course, the elite had lost political power under the emperors too. Like the people, they were reduced to the status of clients, however carefully they might try to hide that fact. The emperor needed to carry out a balancing act, not giving out his favour at will but carefully and systematically allocating patronage to each according to their status. Status was very much the watchword in this division of the imperial bounty. Need did not come into it. It was the residual worth of citizenship, not hunger, that qualified the recipient for the corn dole. Even the wealthiest could go and pick up their free bread if they so wished. But if the emperor was seen to err on the side of favouring one group over another, particularly in a way that threatened existing status divisions, the outcry could be considerable. Emperors who seemed to be overly zealous in courting popularity with the crowd, such as Nero, faced an elite literary backlash.

Nero's popularity was based, as Yavetz says, on meeting people's material needs, on providing elementary justice, on his common touch (*levitas popularis*) and on the fact that he humiliated arrogant aristocrats by making them appear in games before the people.[132] Dio Chrysostom explained his popularity as due to his extravagant generosity.[133] He may also have pleased the plebs with his visits to brothels and taverns because they showed he was one of them.[134] For a long time after he died, the plebs used to adorn his grave with spring and summer flowers and put effigies of him dressed in imperial robes in marketplaces.[135] Like some ancient Elvis, many people refused to believe he was dead and three false Neros appeared after his death.[136]

But 'Nero the Hero' is too simple a reading. He did, after all, enforce the execution of all 400 of Pedanius Secundus's slaves after his murder by one of them, even though the people reacted strongly and 'gathered in a great crowd and threatened the senate with torches and stones'. Despite these popular pressure tactics, Nero 'issued an edict admonishing the people, and lined the whole route along which the condemned were taken to execution with soldiers from the city garrison'.[137] He also became synonymous for some Christians with the Antichrist because of his persecutions and the fact that he personified the excesses of Roman rule. Dio tells us that there was much merrymaking when Nero died, and people wore the same freedmen caps of liberty they wore in the Saturnalia.[138] These various popular reactions to the image of Nero should warn us against seeing the people as responding in unison to imperial activities. The non-elite did not share a single agenda and they actively interpreted imperial behaviour according to their own individual priorities.

The key point is that the broad principles of popular entertainment were on display in the spectacles. These reflected a very different culture to that of the elite: one that showed rather than explored; that sought to intensify the characteristics of ordinary life; that thought with people and acts and things. The games tell us a good deal about what the people wanted because the sponsors gave them what they wanted in return for popularity. Underlying the provision of these entertainments was the fact that individuals wanted more than food and subsistence – they wanted their fair share of the good life. Poverty was not just about lacking cash; it was about not having enough status to observe the social decencies. The people were always out to claim a fair level of status for themselves. It was a kind of moral society that mirrored their moral view of the economy. Their main aim was always to secure subsistence, but that aim was also linked to a notion of there being a minimum level of subsistence status, without which life was not worth living. The elite owed them that bare minimum of luxury. Consuming valued cultural items, such as public shows, directly reflected one's own social and moral worth. Work may have been important to non-elite identity, but it was not the only factor. As Clarke says of non-elite funerary art, it shows that 'they wanted people to remember them living life to the fullest'.[139] Or, as one tombstone inscription put it, 'Eat, drink, play, follow me'.[140] Or, as one of the laws notes, to restrict the spectacles would cause too much unhappiness.[141]

The games were a re-enactment of Roman life: an image of how Romans saw themselves and how they wanted to be seen – brave, competitive, not beyond cheating, clever, ritualistic and, above all, winners. But we should remember that this was a public ritual funded by the powerful. It was, therefore, the transcript of a respectable performance, which provided an appearance of unanimity. Portraying society as a well-ordered, cohesive parade, based on a set of shared beliefs, was a way of emphasizing the vertical relationships in Roman society. We are justified in wondering whether these ceremonies were carried out by the elite as a kind of 'self-hypnosis' to convince themselves it was all true.[142] One of the reasons that public acts of defiance were stamped on so ferociously, such as those by the Christians in the empire's amphitheatres, was that they publicly contradicted the whole official story in the place where it should have been most clear. The crowd intent on the races in the circus, as described by Ammianus, suggests that the games did successfully integrate large sections of Roman society. But this was a carnivalesque act and may only have provided a temporary unity. As we shall see later, the popular culture could also be extremely resistant to elite attempts to control and restrain it.

4

Common Scents,
Common Senses

What had box-office appeal in Rome? Popular heroes triumphing over adversity by means of their own skill. The thrill of seeing people killed for your own fun. Above all, it was the total sensory experience of the games that won people over. What I want to do in this chapter is give an account of the sensory history of the Roman non-elite. Sensory history deals with the ways in which people experience the world through their senses. The senses act as the gateways to the mind and the body and so mediate between the individual and the social world. They are not, however, fixed. The ways in which different senses are experienced varies greatly both between and within cultures. What smells disgusting, for instance, is culturally influenced.[1] The Roman sensory experience was very different from ours. We cannot hope to re-create their experience in its entirety, but we can establish some of the different cultural meanings that the senses held for them. Above all, Roman sensory experience was related to social status. The non-elite mostly inhabited a very different sensory world from the elite. Moreover, the Romans saw the senses differently from us – not simply as signals which the body picks up, but as agents that acted upon the individual. The increase in sensory pleasure, which the wealth of empire allowed, created huge moral problems because it was seen as having a direct, harmful effect on the citizen body. The social tensions of the late republic were reflected in great anxiety about disorder in the sensory universe. We have seen how the games reflected a re-ordering of the role of leadership in Roman society. I want to show in this chapter that the games were the place where a new sensory discourse was developed that helped overcome social discord. In the games, the Romans used what they understood to be the affective properties of the senses to create a morally improving atmosphere, one which could help restore the health of the body politic and re-establish social harmony. The enterprise was in many ways successful. But by establishing a new sensory orthodoxy, the emperors opened up the possibility of a new vocabulary of resistance and rejection.

Lavish expenditure on ornamentation had always been one of the strategies the wealthy elite employed to differentiate themselves from the mass of society. As the grim assessment of the anonymous writer of the fourth century *On Military Matters* put it, 'the houses of the powerful were crammed full and their splendour enhanced to the destruction of the poor, the poorer classes of course being held down by force'.[2] Ostentatious decorative items were part of the shared language of elite culture, which, as Brown has shown, acted as a unifying force across the empire and, later, in the upper echelons of the Church.[3] During an early fifth-century religious controversy, one of the main protagonists, Cyril, bishop of Alexandria, showered what he called 'blessings' (or, as we might say, 'bribes') on the closest advisers of the emperor, Theodosius II, to ensure they would help keep him on the right side. Along with 1,080 lbs of gold, he gave the chamberlain, Romanus, 'four large rugs, four sofa covers, four tapestries, six covers for stools, two for thrones, six curtains, and two thrones of ivory'; and to the head of the imperial household, Chryseros, he donated 'six large carpets, four medium-sized ones, four large rugs, eight sofa covers, six table cloths, six large woven hangings, six small hangings, six covers for stools, twelve for thrones, four large curtains, four thrones of ivory, four stools of ivory' as well as 'six ostrich eggs'.[4]

Finery of this kind, though, provided more than a means of ostentatious display. External sensory influences were believed to have a direct impact on the individual receiver, which meant that exposing oneself to the right kind of sensations became a critical personal and moral issue. Smells, for example, were not seen as just a by-product of an object or person, they were 'effective agents in and of themselves'.[5] The boundaries of the body were thought to be permeable, enabling senses to penetrate and affect the individual in a variety of ways. Bad air, for example, could cause internal corruption if drawn into the body: a Roman was what he or she smelled. This affective view of the senses was seen especially in medicine. Treatments sought to manage the physical environment so as to restore harmony to the patient. So music might be used as a cure for madness because its sounds acted on the whole body to restore the humours to harmony. Caelius recommends sternutatories for the treatment of mania so that sufferers would sneeze out their imbalances. Additional remedies might include shaving the head to reduce the heat around the brain, as well as the application of a plaster compounded of such strong-smelling elements as nitrium, spurge, pepper and frankincense.[6] Oil of roses rubbed on to the head provided a calming medication for phrenitis.[7] Excessive visual stimulation, though, was thought to encourage apparitions and hallucinations that would lead the patient 'away from what is real'. Aretaeus therefore advises that there should be no paintings or bright colours in the rooms of phrenitis sufferers.[8] Victims of hysteria underwent treatments that involved the use of strong odours to coax the wandering womb back into its proper place. So a foetid fumigation placed under the woman's nose would repel the ascending uterus, whereas an aromatic applied to the vagina would attract it downwards. On a more popular level, the peasants of North Italy wore amber necklaces as amulets against swellings in the neck.[9]

The senses were an important way of communicating with and experiencing the gods.[10] Changes in sensory effects marked out the advent of the non-routine: so clothing was altered to hood the male head, veils were worn by women; processions gave visual aspect to the divine order and were accompanied by music and dance and spoken prayers, and shared meals established special relationships between the celebrants. Touching cult statues with the hand or a kiss was an important way to transfer divine power to the individual, condemned by the Christians as 'licking the sandals of a clay Juno'.[11] Various toilet-rituals centred on the washing, oiling, purifying and dressing of the cult statue itself. Sacrifice was characterized by the smells it emitted: incense, flowers, roasting meat, smoke. Wine was also sometimes poured on to the burning coals of incense to intensify the sensory experience. Such wondrous scents were thought to rub off on those who managed to establish a close relationship with the gods: 'Those humans whose lives demonstrated exceptional blessing themselves exhaled a wondrous scent, near to the divine as they were.'[12] In this way, the senses could admit spiritual qualities into the body, which could have a palpable moral effect. In the wrong hands, the senses could become a potent weapon to entice people away from righteousness: the heretic Arius 'composed songs to be sung by sailors, millers, and travellers, and others of the same kind, which he adapted to certain tunes . . . and thus seduced the unlearned by the attractiveness of his songs to his own impiety'.[13] Moreover, the sensory impressions that people gave out through their smell, touch or image conveyed their own inner moral state. At its most powerful, this revealed itself in the healing touch of the holy man. A woman who had suffered blood loss for twelve years was cured by Jesus simply by touching the hem of his clothes, but he was aware that 'virtue has gone out of me'.[14] The fact that the divine was sensed everywhere made contact with it an intensely physical experience. Demons could enter the body through a yawning mouth, and when stirred up by Daniel the Stylite, these spirits appeared like phantoms and 'a great howling arose and they flew round his face like a swarm of bats and with a whir of wings went out of the window'.[15] When the possessed spoke in tongues it was because they spoke the language of these devils.[16] One of main ways to influence the demonic powers was though the sounds of words. The *voces mysticae* of magical incantations represented this language of demons. Sharp, ringing noises, like those produced by tintinabula, could ward off demons, perhaps because it was believed that the tinkling of a brass pot was in fact the voice of a demon imprisoned within the metal.[17]

Life in Rome was a strongly sensuous experience. Given the potential impact of these sensations on health and morality it was vital for the elite that the senses be brought under control. By controlling their environment, they were able to display their power and also re-create status in doing so. So, as Wallace-Hadrill has shown, a hierarchy of colours operated in the domestic decoration of the wealthy: plain white was the cheapest colour, then yellow and red, blue was rare, and black used only in rooms of grandeur to create an area of high value, luxury and prestige.[18] Luxury goods acted to unite the rich in their shared appreciation of such refined goods. It showed they had taste. But such discrimination also served to create social distance between the owner and the poorer visitor. The elite distanced themselves from the senses by manipulating their social environment. They built houses with space to avoid the touch of crowds, extra rooms to provide quiet and privacy, with art to establish their claim to visual discernment and perfume to keep more common scents at bay. They built these houses in places like the Palatine Hill in Rome, which was better drained and cooler, the coolness serving to lessen the stench generated by the heat of summer. The elite re-ordered the sensory experiences of their houses and thereby redefined the sensory context in which their social relations took place. The senses became an important way for Romans to know their status and their worth.

The importance of controlling the senses for the elite extended to codes of comportment that would prevent any unwanted smells emanating from the body, smells that might reveal an inner lack of health and status. Flatulence was thought by some to be caused by demons.[19] Belching that had a foetid or fishy odour was considered by some doctors to be a sign of melancholy.[20] Similarly, flatulence was one of the warning signs of the imminent onset of mania.[21] The emperor Constantius II, when making his grand entry into Rome, made sure not to spit or wipe his nose, lest it should reduce his majesty.[22] People attending dinner parties would go to great lengths to maintain decorum. The emperor Claudius was said to have intended to issue an edict that allowed 'all people freedom to break wind at table if their stomachs were distended by flatulence', after hearing about someone whose modesty had nearly cost him his life.[23] Likewise, the nouveau riche Trimalchio knew of people who had 'died from being too polite and holding it in'. He is mocked in Petronius's account of his vulgar dinner party because he 'cannot imagine any torture like holding yourself in . . . the vapours go straight to the brain and make a disturbance throughout the body'.[24] It was supposedly typical of the emperor Heliogabalus's poor behaviour that he used to seat his guests on whoopy cushions so that they embarrassed themselves in front of him.[25]

Flatulence leads inevitably to faeces. Dung was fine when it was in its rightful place in the countryside, manuring crops. It could even be beneficial as an ingredient in certain folk remedies: for suppurating ulcers of the head, Pliny advises that they be rubbed with cat's dung.[26] But when filth got into the city, the shit really hit the fan. Artemidorus tells us that 'when human faeces are seen in the street, in the market, or in any public place, it indicates that the dreamer will be prevented from using the place in question'. The worst was to dream of defecating in a temple, the marketplace or a street, as this would signal 'the wrath of the gods, great indecorum and extraordinary loss'.[27] Public areas were places that were supposed to be undefiled. The Romans put a lot of effort into providing sewers, the famous *Cloaca Maxima*, to keep the symbolic centre of the Forum Romanum clean. Combined with public latrines, these had a significant impact on air quality, and were a feat of which Roman engineers were proud. As Frontinus notes, 'The results of the great number of reservoirs, works, fountains and water basins can be seen in the improved health of Rome . . . The city looks cleaner, and the causes of the unhealthy air which gave Rome a bad name amongst people in the past are now removed.'[28] Backwash from the Tiber could still sometimes inundate the monumental areas,[29] but on the whole the cloaca's concrete and masonry tunnels channelled Rome's refuse beneath the Fora, around the hills, away from the valleys of the Circus Maximus and the Campus Martius. As Hopkins notes, the Cloaca Maxima 'served a vital role in changing the physical space of central Rome and came to signify the power of the Romans who built it'.[30]

The elite had long-standing cultural prejudices about the city. The sprawling mass of Rome horrified many elite writers. It was the city where the masses wasted their days in idleness or imperially sponsored leisure. It was in the city that luxury and extravagance and devotion to pleasure made the bodies of young men 'so flabby and enervated that death seems likely to make no change in them'.[31] It was the city that had destroyed the traditional relationship between patron and client, splitting the people into the 'dirty plebs and worst slaves who are used to the Circus and the theatre' and the 'respectable part of the people attached to the great households'.[32] Rome's challenge to the traditional order of society was reflected in the way it created sensory disorder. Above all, it was full of shit: 'Along your route each open window may be a death-trap . . . So hope and pray, you poor man, that the local housewife drops nothing worse on your head than a bed pan full of slops.'[33] Nor was it just chamber pots that posed a hazard. Signs in doorways in Pompeii warn people against urinating there. Statues were convenient places to hide behind and relieve oneself.[34] A joke in the *Philogelos* tells how an egghead moved into a new house and having cleaned up in front of the door put up a notice saying 'Anyone who dumps excrement here will not get it back.'[35] The elite had latrines in their houses, where they performed in privacy, private that is in the sense that they were accompanied only by a slave to wipe them clean. The vulgar Trimalchio, by contrast, openly lectured his guests on how to shit well.[36]

The elite had long-standing political insecurities about the people. The growth of the great mass of the million-strong city of Rome exacerbated these fears. This volatile mass represented an ever-present danger to social stability and needed to be controlled by repression if necessary: 'You will not restrain the scum unless by terror.'[37] The people began to smell symbolically. Hence, it was all right to dream that a rich man defecated on one's head because that indicated that good fortune was on its way; but if the defecator was poor then great harm and humiliation would follow.[38] Ruling the people was the equivalent of sitting atop a dung-heap: so to dream of sleeping on a dunghill was good for the rich as it indicated forthcoming public office, 'since all common people carry and cast something on to the dunghill just as they also contribute and give something to their rulers'.[39] The poor came to be thought of as 'dung heaps'.[40] Medical treatment could be adjusted according to the social status of the patient. So Galen believed that the excrement of a boy could be externally applied for dangerous swellings in the throat, so long as the patient was not told and the treatment was reserved for people of no standing – they were no better than donkeys and so might be similarly treated.[41] The law held the low-born in similar sensory contempt, referring to those 'descended from servile muck', and in one case reserving the death penalty for those 'thrown by poverty into plebeian vileness and filth'.[42] The elite held the people in contempt because they had to work manually for their living. They were 'the unclean'.[43] The least respectable were those who catered for the sensual pleasure of others – fishmongers, butchers, cooks, poulterers, fishermen, perfumers, dancers and those who performed in cheap variety shows. Those engaged in occupations associated with dirt and stench were stigmatized, especially dyers, tanners and the men who shovelled-up the shit from the streets. Taken together, these sentiments formed the basis of an osmology, a system that differentiated between persons on the grounds of specific odours that were associated with them. It was common scents. More than that, the elite constructed a whole sensory classification that distinguished between their own proper use of the senses and the disordered usage of the people at large. Romans came to be organized into distinct categories according to certain sensual criteria. These groupings were then used as the basis for higher-status Romans to condemn the lower strata for their physicality and materiality.

In the minds of the elite, it was the city where the foulness of the people was most evident. The filth of the city was transposed on to the crowd: they became the *faex populi*, the shit of the people.[44] Craftsmen, shopkeepers and 'all that filth of the cities',[45] were seen as debased and debasing, degenerating both itself and those above it who came in contact with it. The people were the 'bilgewater of the city'.[46] Juvenal complains that it is the oriental influence that has degraded Rome with its foul-smelling and foreign-sounding pollutants: 'For years now the Syrian Orontes has poured its sewerage into our native Tiber – its lingo and manners, its flutes, its outlandish harps with their transverse strings, its native tambourines, and the whores who hang out round the race-course.'[47] The elite tried to distance themselves from the senses by introducing a notion of critical discernment that mediated between the input of the senses and their reaction to that. The people, by contrast, experienced their world directly. Theirs was a smellier, rougher, noisier place, largely because they were in no position to try and control their physical environment. The reality for the non-elite was that they inhabited a world of strong sensory experience. The streets of Rome were narrow, noisy, full of refuse, graffiti, animals and people. Above all, it was a world of proximity. As Martial complains, 'Novius is my neighbour. We can reach out of our windows and touch hands.'[48] Most lived in poor-quality housing. The non-elite may have had low sensitivity to privacy and low space expectations, but a shabby shack was not chique and drove people outdoors to live a life that contrasted with the more indoor life of the elite. On the streets, people became part of the throng of Rome.[49] Bustle of this kind invaded the personal body space of the wealthy, who responded by employing retinues and retainers to doughnut them and so re-establish distance between themselves and the crowd. The Romans had, as Fagan says, a 'propensity for violence' in situations of close social contact and in crowded situations like the baths often hit out or used slaves to clear a path.[50] The atmosphere of the city could be heavy with smoky kitchens and dust.[51] Certain localities were associated with particular smells, such as the area across the Tiber where tanners worked. Martial complains of the smell of a hide torn from a dog there.[52] Other streets were where the butchers congregated or the perfumers, each producing their own distinctive odours by which individuals could locate themselves within the urban environment. The effect of the sensory overload of the city was, in elite eyes, a paradoxical loss in colour, that left the rosy-cheeked country-dweller's face whitewashed.[53]

The noise of the non-elite urban environment, though probably lower than the modern level because of less traffic, startled contemporaries. Rome was a city that never slept and daytime traffic restrictions meant that carts trundled through streets throughout the night.[54] Hawkers had their own particular call to enable buyers to locate their wares and loudness was a useful quality for a street vendor's voice to have.[55] Seneca gives a famous description of living above some baths:

> If silence is as necessary as it seems for someone who wants seclusion to read and study, then I'm really in trouble. Here I am surrounded on all sides by a variety of noises. I live right over a public bath. Just imagine the whole range of voices which can irritate my ears. When the more muscular types are exercising and swinging about lead weights in their hands, and when they are straining themselves, or at least pretending to strain, I hear groans. And when they hold their breath for a while and let it out I hear hissing and very hoarse gasps. But when I have to put up with an unathletic fellow, one satisfied with a low-class rub-down, I hear the slap of a hand pummelling his shoulders (the sound varies somewhat depending on whether the hand is flat or cupped). Now if a ball player comes along and begins to count his score aloud I'm definitely finished. Imagine also a quarrelsome drunk, or sometimes a thief caught in the act, or a man who loves to sing in the bath. And then imagine people diving into the pool with a great splash of water. Besides these men whose voices are, if nothing else at least natural, imagine the hair plucker with his shrill and high-pitched voice continually shrieking in order to be noticed; he's never quiet except when he's plucking armpits and forcing his customer to shriek instead of him. I could wear myself out just listening to the variety of shouts among people selling drinks, sausages, pastries; each restaurant or snack bar has its own hawker with his own recognizable jingle.[56]

Most of the elite shared Seneca's view that a surround of silence reflected their own control of their social situation. Hence, some insisted on keeping slaves attending them at meals silent: 'A whip punishes any murmur and not even accidents – a cough, a sneeze, a hiccup – are let pass without a beating.'[57] But the non-elite did not attribute social significance to sounds of this type and so were quite capable of blocking out such background noise. Dio Chrysostom describes how the people went about their daily business oblivious to the hubbub that engulfed them:

> And we often see how even in the middle of a very great turmoil and crowd the individual is not hampered in carrying on his own occupation; but, on the contrary, the man who is playing the flute or teaching a pupil to play it devotes himself to that, often holding school in the very street, and the crowd does not distract him at all, nor the din made by the passers-by; and likewise the dancer, or dancing master, is engrossed in his work, being utterly heedless of those who are fighting and selling and doing other things; and so also with the harpist and the painter. But here is the most extreme case of all: the elementary teachers sit in the streets with their pupils, and nothing hinders them in this great throng from teaching and learning. And I remember once seeing, while walking through the Hippodrome, many people on one spot and each one doing something different: one playing the flute, another dancing, another doing a juggler's trick, another reading a poem aloud, another singing, and another telling some story or myth; and yet not a single one of them prevented anyone else from attending to his own business and doing the work that he had in hand.[58]

12. Mosaic showing itinerant musicians in the street

The elite used the senses as a means of social distinction. The non-elite were 'othered' by the establishment of a cordon sanitaire around high culture, which excluded the majority by means of a taste based on wealth. Elite taste was established by such means as using expensive paints to decorate their rooms or costly education to enable someone to read and appreciate literature. Connoisseurship was what countered, and served to transmute arbitrary choices in to becoming the dominant, legitimate culture. Taste became a means of social distinction, which was then itself used as evidence of the elite's cultural superiority. Yet the non-elite could be highly discriminating about things that mattered to them. They were active and vocally critical consumers of the games and shows. Actors who fell short of the required standard could expect a rough ride. But the elite always tried to move beyond the sensual. They continuously defined themselves by rejecting the low, dirty, noisy and malodorous. In many ways, it was the act of exclusion that constituted their identity.

We can see this in attitudes towards food. The rich ate highly spiced and perfumed cuisine, which had undergone various processes to transform and reshape the ingredients into more elaborate dishes, or incorporated luxury items, such as gold, to elevate the costs.[59] At meals where patrons and clients were both present, food was differentiated according to status, as Juvenal complains:

> he grumbles as he hands out the bread, although it's so hard you can scarcely break it, solidified lumps of mouldy dough that crack your teeth rather than let you bite them. But the loaf reserved for the master is snowy-white, fresh-baked from the finest flour. And remember please, to keep your hands to yourself, to show a proper respect for the bread basket. For if by chance you presume to reach for a slice, someone is bound to make you drop it at once, shouting, 'The impertinence! Keep to your own basket if you please, learn the colour of your bread!'

Even further down the scale came *panis cibarius*, a coarse bread reserved for slaves and peasants.[60]

The rigours of poverty meant that the poorest were often visibly stamped as such by their appearance. They had lice and sores, while beggars were 'unshorn and unwashed'.[61] The ragged children of the poor would sometimes appear at weddings, where they were paid to go away as people saw them as unlucky omens.[62] As Parkin notes, by doing this the children managed to 'exploit societal disgust by manipulating it to their own advantage'.[63] Many others were deaf from disease, shook, and had poor and pallid complexions.[64] Blindness seems to have been common. The astrologer Firmicus Maternus mentions it frequently in conjunction with extreme poverty: 'blindness and weakness of body together with wretched beggary'.[65] Such was the importance and vulnerability of sight for the non-elite, that in the astrologer Dorotheus's list of headings, the eyes were the only sensory organ to qualify for their own section. Perceptions of colour altered according to social status. When the elite used expensive red paint to decorate rooms it signalled refinery, but when a slave or a criminal saw a red fish in a dream, it portended tortures.[66] In many ways, it was the importance of visuality that characterized elite culture. They painted, created clean open spaces, vistas and grand buildings, and used texts to mediate and express their experience of the world

But, above all, it was a lower sense of touch and smell that the elite associated with the people. The elite used perfumes to ensure that they smelled differently and they washed away the dirt associated with manual work. To dream of having 'a handsome and well-shaped nose is auspicious for all men. For it is a sign of great sensitivity, foresight in one's affairs, and the acquaintance of good men.' By contrast, dreaming of having no nose signified 'hatred of prominent people'.[67] Smell became a term of rhetorical abuse, hence Mark Antony, treating with contempt Augustus's ancestry, claimed that his great-grandfather had at one time kept a perfumer's shop.[68] Although much of the elite's abuse of the people reflected their 'animalization' of the poor, it also has to be admitted that the non-elite probably did smell strongly. Living in close proximity, carrying out strenuous manual work in a hot climate was not conducive to preventing body odour. There was little escape for most from stench. The streets of Rome would have stunk most in the narrow, squalid slums inhabited by the masses. Many people's smell would have reflected their work, in a kind of order of the odours. A father advising his son on how to make a living emphasized that it was no good to be 'overcome with disgust at the type of merchandise which has to be relegated to the other side of the Tiber, or think that you should make any distinction between perfumes and hides: profit smells sweet, no matter from what goods it is derived'.[69] Garlic, which did not feature in elite cookery, was closely associated with poor food. This was a worry because the great strength of garlic was thought to exacerbate a hot-headed temperament.[70] The insecurity of poverty probably meant that many people carried coins in their mouth like the Greeks did, which gave their breath a metallic taint.[71] But bad breath was mostly caused by poor diet and even worse dental hygiene. The Roman joke book, the *Philogelos*, has numerous bad breath gags. In one a man with bad breath decided to kill himself, so he covered his face and was asphyxiated. In another, a man with bad breath goes to a doctor and complains that his uvula is lower than it should be: 'Phew!' gasped the doctor, as the man opened his mouth to show him; 'It's not your uvula that has gone down, it's your arsehole that has come up!'[72] Vulgar halitosis would not surprise the elite, given that a freedman, like one of Trimalchio's friends in the *Satyricon*, was 'always ready to pick a coin out of the shit with his teeth'.[73] But bad breath was also attributed to sexual misdemeanours.[74] The physical and the moral blurred so that immorality came to stink. Brothels became notorious for their foul odour, 'reeking with long-used coverlets', as did prostitutes who worked in 'filthy rooms' or stood 'naked in a stinking archway'.[75] The fact that prostitutes disrupted the social order by using their bodies in an alternative way to that sanctioned by the dominant culture meant that they were thought to smell like corrupted bodies themselves. Society linked unpleasant, dangerous groups with unpleasant, dangerous sensations.

The non-elite had a far more tactile, rough-hewn culture. Overcrowding meant personal space was limited and touching others was an unavoidable part of everyday life. Bed-sharing was probably commonplace. Being out in a crowd was a highly physical experience, full of jostling and shoving. People believed generally that touch could convey both healing power and the power of demons, and that cosmic forces affected them at birth. But just because it was a tactile culture did not make it in any way touchy-feely. Physical work took a heavy toll on the body. It coarsened the hands and, in the eyes of the elite, coarsened the morals too since it brought the labourer into contact with filth and dirt. Peasants developed hard, misshapen bodies under the deforming effects of severe skeletal stress.[76] The non-elite aged quickly, both the men, because of their crippling physical work that left their skin caloused and craggy, and the women, worn down by a never-ending cycle of childbirth and childcare. People could be quite touchy about this: one aristocrat running for election laughed at a peasant's rough hands and lost the election as a result.[77]

Touch acted as an important marker of social power. Society controlled those who had no control over their own boundaries of touch, primarily by means of beatings and floggings. As Saller points out, whipping was a highly potent form of symbolic behaviour, which created physical, social and psychological anguish. Beaten men were paraded about their city to exhibit their torn backs to the crowd, a shocking humiliation for anyone of standing.[78] The people approved of such physical punishments, perhaps because it seemed both relevant and appropriate to their tactile outlook. Libanius describes how the governor flogged some bakers for profiteering during a corn shortage: 'I heard the sound of the lash, so dear to the common people, who were all agog at the sight of the bleeding backs.'[79] The average slave's mind was portrayed as being 'constantly preoccupied with corporal punishment' past and future.[80] Exemption from beating was associated with Roman citizenship, even if the multiple floggings that St Paul endured show us that the reality often fell short of the ideal. Gaining exemption from physical punishment was a much sought-after privilege, particularly in the later empire when servile punishments spread up the social scale. Those who had no exemption bore the marks of their subordination for a long time. In Achilles Tatius's novel, the heroine Leucippe acquires the scars of hard agricultural slave labour: shackles, a shaven head, a filthy body and lash marks.[81] The deep psychological scars that this could leave are seen in a caricature of a wealthy ex-slave, which describes a man who pricks up his ears if someone passing just cracks a whip.[82]

Touch relayed moral and social information. Torture was a requirement for slaves when testifying in court because it ensured that the truth would out. Branding and tattooing helped to mark out the servile and the socially deviant for the benefit of all. Romans could read the skin of others for the pockmarks, brands and scars that were the tell-tale signs of low status. Popular heroes, such as the animal hunters in the games, took great pride in their scars, showing off their bites as if they were beauty marks.[83] But those who had been branded often sought to conceal the physical stigma of their servile status after they had been freed. Tattoos and brand marks on the faces of slaves could be cut out, burned and scarred over to conceal their original meaning. Similarly, former slaves tried to cover up old whip marks to try and raise their skin quality to a level more appropriate to their new status.[84] The public touch of the whip contrasted with the distance of private exile that was used as a punishment for the elite. Touch was seen as a less intellectual, more carnal sense that was closely associated with the animal-like world of the people. The elite used touch as a means to establish control over society and lack of touch to establish their own superiority.

Kissing was a special form of touch that was acceptable in elite circles, within strictly defined limits of comportment. The emperor Tiberius tried to ban the daily kiss at court receptions, complaining that kissing was unavoidable at Rome.[85] Kissing signalled respect between social equals and also a desire for some kind of transference of power between patron and client. This resulted in at least one outbreak of an infectious facial disorder among the leading citizens.[86] Indeed, one of the reasons some gave for Tiberius leaving Rome was his facial disfigurement with ulcers and plasters.[87] The empire saw a growing hierarchy of touch. It had been thought that to have to kiss the emperor's feet would be to live under tyranny.[88] Caligula revealed his tyrannical side by giving senators his foot to kiss but kissing stage actors himself every day.[89] But by the early second century Pliny was praising Trajan for requiring citizens to embrace his knees, while reserving kisses for senators and equals. Two centuries later, the ritual of the *adoratio purpurae* was being used to help convert the image of the emperor from first among equals, *princeps*, to absolute monarch, *dominus*. So the highest honour in the later empire was to be allowed to kiss the hem of the emperor's purple cloak, while lying prostrate on the floor. Being allowed to touch the divine, albeit obliquely through their clothing, showed clearly that the kisser was close to the centre of power. The relics of Christian saints were also believed to transfer their healing power to those lucky or blessed enough to be able to touch them. Some sought to take this a step further: one supplicant approached the relics of the true cross and bent down as if to kiss them, but then grabbed a piece in his teeth and ran off. The beggars at Aricia, on the Appian Way near Rome, waited there because a steep hill meant that passing coaches had to slow to a crawl. This gave them the opportunity to mob the wealthy travellers and almost coerce money from them. Given that a poor beggar would never normally be allowed to get near enough to the rich to kiss them, it is hard not to interpret the fact that they blew kisses after the coaches as they sped away down the other side of the hill as anything but irony.[90]

The quality and texture of an individual's clothing and soft furnishings indicated both status and their inner moral state. The rich were immediately distinguishable by sight: one woman's nice dress 'proclaimed her a lady'. By contrast, a miserly moneylender dressed badly to pretend that he was poor and so avoid his social obligations.[91] Dreaming of 'wearing a soft, costly garment is auspicious for both the rich and the poor' as it indicates 'continued prosperity for the rich and an improvement for the poor'. Indeed, 'it is always better to wear bright, clean, well-washed clothes than filthy, unwashed clothes'.[92] But the meanings of clothing mostly varied according to social status. So it was bad for slaves longing for freedom to dream of wearing new clothes because they last a long time, as would their servitude. But to dream of wearing a red robe was auspicious for slaves as only the free can wear such an item. Wearing white was bad news for artisans because it indicated unemployment, as artisans do not wear white clothes. Dreaming about wearing multicoloured or sea-purple clothing brought benefit for priests, musicians, actors and festival performers, but disturbance and danger for others.[93] Only those who lay outside the boundaries of normal life, such as religious officials and popular performers, would normally wear such strange clothing.

Clothing acted to invest social superiors with a mantle of authority and ensure the deference of the poor. A rough guide to the huge disparities in the cost and status of different textiles can be seen in the prices for fabrics in Diocletian's Edict on Maximum Prices (prices are in denarii per item or per pound of raw material):

Soldier's winter tunic	75
African cloak	500
Hooded Laodicean cloak	4,500
Dalmatian tunic	2,000
Wool from Tarentum	75
White silk	12,000
Purple silk	150,000

Cloth was an expensive item and it is not surprising that the destitute could not afford anything comfortable. As the seventh-century St John the Almsgiver bemoans, 'how many have only a rough blanket' so small that 'they cannot stretch out their legs but lie shivering, rolled up like a ball of thread?'[94] The non-elite had to be content with coarse fabric and poor-quality, ill-fitting footwear. Even items that should have provided some comfort, such as pillows, often tormented the skin by being full of fleas.[95] Most of the non-elite had few possessions and little decoration in their homes. Most peasants had earth floors, in contrast to the stone or mosaics of the elite. Carpets and rugs were a sign of honour, which is why Cyril used them to bribe members of the imperial household. But honour could bring its own difficulties: the toga, which only the Roman citizen could wear, was usually made of wool and was heavy, hot and uncomfortable. By contrast, the clothes of slaves were usually chosen solely on the basis of practicality: 'The foreman should chose the slaves' clothing with an eye to utility rather than fashion, and he should take care to protect them from the wind, cold, and rain with long-sleeved leather tunics, patchwork cloaks, or hooded capes.'[96] But when trying to sell slaves, some window-dressing might take place. In the *Aesop Romance*, a slave dealer clothed a good-looking musician he owned in 'a white robe, put light shoes on him, combed his hair, gave him a scarf for his shoulders, and put him on the selling block'; whereas the teacher he owned had spindly legs, so he dressed him in 'a long robe and high boots' to hide them.[97]

The fact that status was so caught up with what people looked like, meant they took great pains to manage their appearance. Rich ladies would dye their hair and shape it with curling irons. Ovid describes how this once went wrong and his girlfriend's hair fell out, meaning that 'Now Germany will send you her captured locks of hair and a conquered race will save you the embarrassment of baldness.'[98] Blond, barbarian wigs were unnecessary according to the Christian bishop Synesius of Cyrene's *Eulogy of Baldness*, itself a rejoinder to Dio Chrysostom's *In Praise of Hair*, because baldness 'brings innumerable benefits to both body and mind', whereas bushy hair brings troubles and 'likeness to beasts'. But most people realized that personal

13. Mosaic of a personification of winter in the kind of dark cloak worn by the poor

appearance revealed a lot about themselves. Many of the non-elite took to cheating as a way to create an impression of wealth and higher status. The high demand for status symbols created a thriving market in forgeries, cheap copies and imitation gems.[99] There were manuals in existence for making fake gemstones.[100] Magic books told people how to make bronze look like gold.[101] The non-elite used these methods to emulate the rich, but it was not simply a matter of their adopting an ersatz, second-rate imitation of elite culture. The purpose of such imitation was to establish status within their own social milieu, not to compete with the wealthy. It was therefore an active appropriation of elite symbols of status and taste for their own ends.

The non-elite could be distinguished by the kind of noises they made. Ammianus talks about how 'some of the multitude of the lowest condition' quarrel with one another in their dice games, 'making a disgusting sound by drawing back their breath into their nostrils'.[102] Sidonius also talks about the noise that gamblers made.[103] Once Horace had become a successful writer, he allegedly claimed that his father had been a freedman and tax-collector, when it was generally believed he had actually been a dealer in salted foods. So someone once attacked his low-class origins by jeering, 'How often have I seen your father wiping his nose with his fist?'[104] Such snorting and grunting was linked in elite minds with animal-like bad manners, arguments and sex.[105] We have seen how Dio Chrysostom censured the people of Tarsus for the snorting noises they commonly made, which was reminiscent of the bestial, immoral grunts that emanated from a brothel. He even compares such outrageous behaviour to that of a man who would point at everything with the *digitus infamis*, the finger used to make obscene gestures, or who walked about with his clothes drawn up as if wading in a pool. Tatian also complains that mime actors make snorting noises: 'They blow through their noses, use foul language, posture obscenely and perform sex acts on stage.' The bottom line was that such grunting noises sounded sexual and well-brought-up people did not make them.[106] By contrast, the non-elite found such noises funny. In one joke, a wag of a boatman, when asked where the wind was coming from, replied, 'From the beans and onions.'[107] In the *Satyricon*, the porter Corax confidently asserts, 'I'm no less a free man than you people', then farts loudly.[108] No wonder Horace called them the 'windy plebs'.[109] The people had rough mannerisms and found physical breaches of normal behaviour highly amusing. It was a kind of sensory subversion that confounded the serious, official culture by snorting and farting and then laughing about it. But we should not think that the non-elite did not have their own modes of comportment that established sensory standards. They did after all love going to the baths. Bathing was a way of making oneself smell like a Roman. And when 'someone dreamt that he lifted his clothes in front of his fellow members in an association to which he belonged and urinated upon each of them, he was expelled as being unworthy'.[110]

One other area where the non-elite could often be distinguished from the elite was by the way they spoke. The popular culture was primarily an oral culture, although many will probably have been able to write or recognize a few words if it was of practical benefit in their daily lives. Gossip and chat were central to their formation of group assessment and opinion. Arguing formed the cornerstone of how they protected their status and reputation and resolved conflicts. It was the elite who had created a separate, refined literary Latin in roughly the third century BCE, different from the popular Latin (which still labours under the pejorative-sounding term of 'vulgar Latin'). To read and write are to see the world in a certain way, and the Latin of high culture served to establish the basis of an elite learning, which differentiated it from the majority. It was act of exclusion. The non-elite were, however, not entirely cut off. One fuller showed his loyalty to his protecting deity, Minerva, by carving 'I sing of owls not arms and men' (*ululam ego cano non arma virumque*), in imitation of the famous first line of Virgil's *Aeneid*. Whether this amounted to more than knowing a phrase such as 'To be or not to be' is impossible to say, but other Virgilian graffiti have been found in a brothel, an iron-mongers and a gladiators' barracks.[111] Graffiti in Pompeii show, however, that the non-elite had little awareness of official codes of spelling or grammar. Jerome tells us that Latin changed constantly from area to area.[112] But most of the non-elite throughout the empire will not have spoken Latin or Greek. There were lots of provincial languages: Syriac, Coptic, Punic, Celtic and Hebrew, to name but a few. Rome itself was filled with the gabble of hundreds of different languages from all parts of the empire.[113] Those non-elite who did speak Latin found that their manner of speech revealed their social status and so opened them up to ridicule: 'You are not of our cloth, and so you make fun of the way we poor men talk.'[114] Using fables and proverbs had negative connotations for the elite because it was reminiscent of a servile past spent dealing with the mucky world of animals: 'You can spot a louse on someone else, but you can't see the tick on yourself.'[115] This does not mean that all of the elite talked posh. Certain emperors, for example, came from provincial back-grounds and were mocked for their accents or lack of education. There would always be a grey area between the most refined Latin and the everyday speech of the people. But for the most part, High Latin was closed off to the non-elite; not that they would have cared as it was irrelevant to their daily concerns.

This was not just a question of accent, but of tone. The non-elite had to be very wary when dealing directly with the powerful. They expressed subordination in their speech – hesitant, indirect and fal-tering. They used flattery to try and cajole their social superiors into giving them something of what they wanted. A 'wanted' poster from the village of Chenres in the area of Anthribite in Egypt gives a description of a fugitive. By trade he was a weaver but instead of showing the expected deference, 'he swaggers around as if he were someone important, chattering in a shrill voice'.[116] This was not how simple artisans were meant to behave. Normally, slaves could be spotted by their submissive shrugs of the shoulders, which made it a gesture for the elite orator to avoid: 'as a rule, it is unbecoming to raise or contract the shoulders. For it shortens the neck and produces a mean and slavish gesture, which is even suggestive of dishonesty when men assume an attitude of flattery, admiration or fear.'[117] Linguistic differences between the elite and non-elite also centred on content. Beggars may have had their own argot, a private language that served to exclude others in the same way that elite literary Latin did.[118] Speaking in a kind of code helped give the poor protection from the authorities. But for the most part the people spoke in a way that reflected the specialisms of their work and leisure. Carpenters talked woodwork, and butchers butchery. Their speech was full of proverbs as they used this common store of wisdom as a resource to place everyday problems into a wider context.[119] Then in the games they were brought together by their shared fascination with the details of horses and their drivers or the fight-statistics of gladiators.

Above all it was a question of style.[120] The people spoke in a way that reflected their cultural concerns. To some extent, popular speech had a functional aspect: it was a way of speaking that was not an end in itself like a literary form, but full of necessity and urgency. It could be an unstylized way of talking, characterized by directness rather than the rhetorical posturing of Cicero. There was little standardization and, as is most easily seen in the way Petronius mocks the way Trimalchio and his friends speak, their speech was full of what were in formal Latin errors of gender and syntax, faults of declension, and confusion about active and deponent verbs. Double negatives were commonplace: 'never do no one a good turn'.[121] Awkward consonants were allowed to drop away for ease of speech, so *scriptus* became *scritus*, *santus* replaced *sanctus*, *isse* was used for *ipse*. H's were also often dropped, so *hortus* became *ortus*. Words could be shortened, such as *anglus* for *angulus*, or lengthened if that made pronunciation easier, as with *techina* for *techna*. Certain different words were commonly used in popular Latin in contrast to literary words: *testa* for *caput* (head), *caballus* for *equus* (horse), *bucca* for *os* (mouth). Sentences tended to be short and simple, with no periods or subordinate clauses. Parenthetic statements were added on, as afterthoughts, reflecting a spontaneous manner of building up sentences: 'I gave the letter to a merchant to deliver to him, my master, the one who was in Athens, the one who loved this girl.'[122] But it was not simply a practical and unadorned style. Popular speech had its own forms of linguistic decoration and effect. Compound words were used for comic impact. Plautus is full of new words, often influenced by Greek, such as slang words like *colaphus*, meaning a clout round the head. Popular Latin loved diminutives as a way to stimulate the emotions. This was a culture where feelings were sited near the surface, not held down and controlled like those of the elite, and diminutives served both to endear and to mock. Exaggeration was central to getting the

message across, and so popular Latin had plenty of suffixes and pre-
fixes to emphasize ideas. Double adverbs were also really, really
popular, as were frequentative verbs – why *fugo*, run away, when you
can *fugito*, run like hell? The easiest way to achieve exaggeration and
to add colour to a sentence was to spice it up with some coarse, rude
swearing. Libanius complains of the rudeness that was expected of a
smith or a tanner.[123] The same sentiment is found in the traditional
English word for abusive swearing – Billingsgate – reflecting the view
of the kind of language that was thought to characterize the old
London fish market. Much more emphasis was placed on the physicality of the speaker: as Quintilian says, the great unwashed in their
dirty black clothes take special pleasure in the speaker who 'smacks
his hand, stamps the ground, slaps his thigh, breast and brow'.[124] This
was a physical, aggressive way of talking where forceful gestures were
key to being listened to. All of these tactics helped give the common
language an emotional intensity and immediacy, but also a range of
stylistic devices to impress and dominate the hearer.

The popular culture shared the view that the senses could directly
affect the world around them. This can be seen best in their magical
spells and curses. Magic worked by confounding the everyday senses,
playing with texture, colour and smell to subvert the normal sensory
world. A sense of their complexity can be seen in dream interpretation, where woollen garlands signify witchcraft and spells because
they are 'intricate and multicoloured'. A simple spell for a cough
involved writing in black ink on hyena parchment. A 'tested spell for
invisibility' took something more complicated: 'Take an eye of an ape
or of a corpse that has died a violent death and a peony plant', then
'rub them with oil of lily.' A request for divination used ritual noises
to invoke the spirits of the underworld: 'Wrap a naked boy in linen
from head to toe, then clap your hands. After making a ringing noise,
place the boy opposite the sun, and standing behind him say the
magic formula.'[125] Magic acted on the senses to put the strange in
everyday places, and the everyday in strange places. So a charm for
a direct vision of Apollo involves the supplicant being 'in a ground-
floor room without light, while you are crowned with a wreath of
marjoram and while wearing wolf-skin sandals'. It changed the form
of everyday objects by grinding and mixing, then textualized them by
incorporating them into a new written, authoritative form. By specifying in exact, minute detail the ways in which particular items were to
be used in the ritual, magic placed the individual in a new relationship
both to the outlandish and to objects they encountered in their
normal lives. An 'indispensable invisibility spell' directs: 'Take fat or
an eye of a night-owl and a ball of dung rolled by a beetle and oil of
an unripe olive and grind them all together until smooth, and smear

your whole body with it, and say to Helios, "I adjure you by your great name, BORKE PHOIOUR".'[126]

Magic worked to disorientate the senses – left/right, back/front, up/down – and confound sensory expectations. A spell to gain control of one's own shadow includes wheaten meal, ripe mulberries and a beet and tells the supplicant to 'go at the sixth hour toward the sun to a deserted place and girt with a palm fibre basket, put on your head a scarlet cord, behind your right ear the feather of a falcon and your left that of an ibis'. It also mashed up words into new verbal sounds that became the vital means by which communication with the other-worldly powers could be achieved. So, for a headache, it is directed to write ABRASAX on scarlet parchment, make it into a plaster and then place it on the side of the head. By combining the exotic, the bizarre and the mundane in unexpected ways, magic created an over-awing sensory experience. An initiation rite, it is unclear for what, creates total sensory disarray: 'On two bricks standing on their sides, build a fire with olive wood', and when the sun is up 'cut off the head of an unblemished, solid white cock', which must have been carried 'under your left arm.' When beheading the cock 'hold it down all by yourself. Throw the head into the river and drink up the blood, drain-ing it off into your right hand, and putting what's left of the body on the burning altar, then jump into the river. Immerse yourself in the clothes you have on, walk backwards out of the water, and, after changing into fresh garments, depart without turning around. After this, take bile from an owl, rub some of it over your eyes with the feather of an ibis', and then 'your initiation will be complete.'[127]

The popular culture rejoiced in the senses, revelling in such physi-cal fun as drink and sex. The elite placed much more emphasis on control of the senses by establishing distance between the individual and their sensory perceptions through mediators such as education, discernment and taste. It would be wrong, though, to say that the people were in no way discerning consumers. We have seen how knowledgeable they could be about their work and leisure pursuits, such as horse-racing. The pantomimes also reflect a highly refined sensory palate:

> There appeared on stage a young man representing the Trojan prince, Paris, gorgeously costumed in a cloak of foreign design which flowed down from his shoulders. On his head was a gold tiara. Next there appeared a radiantly fair young boy, whose long golden hair attracted everyone's eyes. He wore little golden wings and represented Mercury. He danced towards Paris and offered him the golden apple. By his gestures he informed him of Jupiter's command and then danced grace-fully out of sight.[128]

But it is probably fair to say that, for the most part, popular tastes leaned towards the hedonistic and materialistic. The people lived physical lives, focused largely on meeting material needs, so it is hardly surprising that their tastes were informed by the conditions of their subordination. Whatever decorative items they had, such as the small oil lamps that were cheap and very popular, tended to be practical in nature. Functionality was built into the art.

The growth of empire, wealth and urban centres like Rome did, however, increase the variety of sensory experiences that were available to at least a part of the non-elite. It also radically altered elite behaviour. Instead of sober, traditional restraint, the wealthy were in a position to spend vast sums on luxury, some of which fed down to the people. This created grave problems for the elite in that such sensations were assumed to have a direct and degrading moral impact. Actions which broke the proper sensory order were frowned upon. So dreaming of being anointed with oils was good only for women, not men.[129] Singing out of tune gave forewarning of unemployment and poverty. Luxury represented a total onslaught against the senses since it reflected a coalescence of various sensuous experiences. The baths were a place that pampered the ordinary people in a way that elite moralists found unacceptable. An increase in cleanliness came at the cost of a decrease in morals and manly vigour.[130] The sensory excess that the nouveaux riches indulged in at the baths was epitomized by Trimalchio: 'There we found Trimalchio again. His skin was glistening all over with perfumed oil. He was being rubbed down, not with ordinary linen, but with towels of the purest and softest wool ... He was then wrapped in a blazing scarlet robe, hoisted into a litter, and trundled off.'[131] Even his cushions were stuffed with purple wool and he had a slave whipped for binding his slightly bruised arm with white instead of purple cloth.[132] The new wealth that flowed into the capital city meant that to the traditional elite it seemed that, 'Everyone thinks himself impoverished and distressed unless the walls of his bathing area sparkle with marble, paintings and glass; or unless Thasian marble, once a rare sight even in a temple, lines the swimming pools (into which we dip bodies from which the sweat has been squeezed), and the water pours out of silver taps.' The wealthy were cooling their drinks with snow and using feather cushions.[133] Silver seemed to glisten everywhere – even slaves had silver mirrors.[134] The emperors themselves were the most extreme examples of sensuous excess. Nero supposedly used to fish with a golden net, drawn by silken cords of purple and scarlet.[135] All of this was, of course, hopelessly exaggerated, but reflects how a new sensory discourse had grown up to express concerns about the new social realities. It certainly cannot be applied to the non-elite, for whom the benefits of empire were modest and distinctly unevenly spread.

Roman society underwent enormous change during the later republic and early empire, which was reflected in a period of sensory confusion. The Romans were learning how to use their senses in an expanded fashion, but the tensions that this sensory rearrangement created were expressed as a perceived illness in the social body. The body of the average Roman man, whose legendary toughness had after all won the empire in the first place, seemed to moralistic elite writers to be softening under this sensuousness. The orator Quintilian believed that the indecent and effeminate music of the stage had greatly contributed to the destruction of the last remnants of virility.[136] The soft and effeminate notes of corrupting music could 'provoke immodest touches and lascivious tickling'.[137] The sensationalism of popular actors, with their splendid garments and masks, epitomized the poor example that the people were being given. Depilation had become more common among men, making their once hairy legs smooth and effeminate. Other 'metrosexuals' were wearing balsam and cinnamon to perfume themselves.[138] Spices and perfumes were associated with the decadent Greek and Persian East, which added to their moral connotations. 'Aesthetics were ethics', as Olson says, and the way a person smelled revealed both rank and moral character.[139]

Adornment had traditionally been seen as a female preoccupation that merely underlined their superficiality and triviality. Now the emperors themselves were dressing up in the wrong clothes at the wrong time. Nero wore the brightly coloured synthesis usually reserved for dinner parties and the Saturnalia in public.[140] Caligula 'did not wear what was either national, or properly civic, or peculiar to the male sex, or appropriate to mere mortals'. Instead he wore clothes that were 'richly embroidered and blazing with jewels' or sometimes 'all in silks and dressed like a woman'.[141] Likewise, Heliogabalus would wear a tunic 'made wholly of cloth of gold, or one made of purple, or a Persian one studded with jewels'. He even wore jewels on his shoes and 'wanted to wear a jewelled diadem as well in order to enhance his beauty and make his face look more like a woman's'.[142] Such vivid, no doubt exaggerated descriptions of the changes to the way certain emperors dressed reflected fears about gender instability in the more luxurious world of imperial Rome. By focusing on the individuals where power itself had become focused, elite writers translated discussions concerning societal change into personal, concrete and readily understood terms. Emperors personified wider societal anxieties by challenging traditional norms of sensory order.

Misuse of the senses, therefore, became part of the rhetoric of elite condemnation of each other's behaviour. Rather than simply reflecting social reality in the upper echelons of society, such attacks served as vehicles for discussing societal changes and the emperors' centrality to those developments. Moralistic writers hoped that stories of imperial misbehaviour would act as moral anchors in a society of turbulent cultural change, by fixing views about what was considered acceptable behaviour for normal people in a civilized society. But, as Corbeill has argued, accusations of acting effeminately may actually have reflected political stances adopted by certain members of the ruling elite.[143] Julius Caesar was often attacked for his effeminacy, but such attacks may not simply be rhetorical devices, they may reflect the fact that he did indeed wear more populist clothes as a way of aligning himself with modes of behaviour that were associated with the urban plebs not the elite. That is not the same as saying that he dressed like the non-elite. Rather that he dressed in a more sophisticated way, which was conspicuously different from traditional elite fashion and characterized populist policies that involved spending some of the fruits of empire on entertaining and feeding the plebs. We can suggest that some of the more populist elite were using the senses to advertise a political stance. So Cicero accuses Rullus of planning on becoming tribune of the people, 'to adopt another expression, another voice, another walk, and wear more worn-out clothing'.[144] Caesar rejected elite complaints of sensory misuse by stating simply, 'my soldiers can fight well even while wearing perfume'.[145]

When Caesar's successor, Octavian (later rebranded as Augustus), became sole ruler, he was faced with the problem of how to reintegrate a society fractured by decades of civil war and by cultural tensions emanating from the social transformation engendered by empire. I would argue that he and later emperors put the senses to work to help achieve this reconciliation, making use of their morally affective capabilities. Public space became a place for providing luxury for the people in a way that would leave them morally improved, the theory broadly being that if they *sensed* better they would *be* better. Every art combined to intoxicate the senses, but the focus was not just on the tactile and olfactory senses with which the non-elite were usually associated. The emperors sought to educate the people visually, so that they would take their pleasures in a more distanced, controlled manner. The elite, as we have seen, had always criticized the negative character of the popular culture for the bad effect it had on high culture, on the people themselves and on society as a whole. Providing state-sponsored luxury represented an attempt to cajole the people into a new, more disciplined mode of pleasure that would transform their culture itself. The games were an act of political urgency, because the political order itself had seemed to be breaking down. It was also a way of morally improving the urban popular culture without undermining elite power or status. But for the entertainments to appeal to the people they had to reflect some of their tastes. The games therefore represented a cultural alloy that fused together elite and popular values into a new form of political entertainment. It was an act of incorporation that left both recipient and host transformed.

Augustus realized that his new form of power would require a re-evaluation of the relationship between his government and urban space. Certain areas acquired a greater burden of moral symbolism, such as the area around the Ara Pacis, which visually re-created the harmony that Augustus had brought to the Roman world. It was a moral geography. But linked to this was a sensual geography that used sensory inputs to help reinforce the moral message. The Augustan building programme on the Campus Martius included gardens, the Ara Pacis itself, his mausoleum, the huge sundial and a spacious plaza. Over time, the public areas of Rome grew to represent about 25 per cent of the urban space.[146] But these spaces were not simply architectural. In the Colonnade of Livia stood a giant grapevine, whose shade cooled the crowds.[147] Animals and curiosities were also put on display to satisfy popular interest in the wonders of the world and the grotesque. Four elephants carved from highly polished obsidian stood in the Aedes Concordiae Augustae. The elephants – peace-loving, modest, monogamous, long-living, dutiful to their parents and adoring of their offspring – came to represent all that was good about the Augustan regime.[148] The great carved frieze around the precinct wall of the Ara Pacis reflected the flourishing Augustan state, in which all lived in harmony, just like the carved animals on the frieze. The Campus Martius, with its long, straight streets and clean lines of classical colonnades, contrasted with the jumbled mess of narrow alleyways in the popular areas of the city. Stone pavements separated the stroller from the filth beneath his feet. In Agrippa's baths, the internal space was radiant with glazed windows, polychrome marble and mosaics, which combined with the steam, heat and massages to generate a total sensory overload. Temples glistened with the varied hues of murals. Buildings were framed by gardens and parks, most of which were open to the public, while avenues of laurel and plane provided the shade that was synonymous with the elite life of leisure. Flowers and bushes made the air sweet-smelling,[149] and waterworks abounded – falls, ponds, fountains – all serving to cool the air and create a fresh, clean atmosphere.[150] The areas were filled with classical bronze and marble statues, depicting heroes and mythological scenes. When all of this decorative effort is taken together it can seem to us as something of a ragtag collection. But in Roman eyes it produced a thematic whole. It was total art, designed to morally uplift those who experienced it.

It is easy to focus on individual monuments in isolation, but the buildings were part of an overall effect. The Augustan building programme was, as Purcell says, designed to create 'a sense of decency and good order and good government, of responsibility, tidiness and justice'.[151] Or, as Wallace-Hadrill says, 'The Augustan reorganization of Rome created a city that was defined and knowable in a fundamentally different way.'[152] The purpose of various sensory effects was to distinguish between different social areas and make them morally fit for purpose. Augustus's urban plan owes much to creating views, space, geometry, light and smoothness. A hierarchy of colour and building materials marked out prestige areas. Stone and marble were particularly useful as markers of superior spatial importance. Counters in non-elite taverns often had surfaces made from marble fragments or of marble veneer to give the impression of status, and could also be the focus of the decorative scheme.[153] Stone had always been associated with wealth and Augustus's extensive use of masonry for monumental effect gave out a clear impression of power, as well as representing the solid stability and endurance that made his regime different from the political chaos of before. Its very smoothness symbolized the political concord that Augustus had established. At some point in the empire, a marble map of Rome, the *Forma Urbis Romae*, was placed symbolically on a wall in the Temple of Peace.[154] Stone was also associated with Greek temples, so helped create a feeling of a new, more sophisticated and permanent relationship with the gods. The use of Greek columns marked out certain spaces as sacred and prestigious. The empire itself brought access to new quarries: stones such as purple porphyry from Egypt, granite, honey-coloured alabaster, and Phoenician snow-white marble all became available. The range of marble hues increased, from Phrygian marble that was spotted with violet, to stone with a reddish-yellow tint and green veins. It all acted as a sensory reminder of the empire and its benefits. But the use of stone had greater significance that this. For centuries, stone had been noted for its ability to affect the senses directly and so create change in those exposed to its power. A poem ascribed to Orpheus, 'On Stones', describes their special properties. It notes that 'there is great power in herbs, but far greater in stones'.[155] Coral, for example, 'works even on dreams and it drives away apparitions by virtue of its repellent power'. If the stone was carved with divine images, coral could even affect moods and feelings: 'it is a powerful phylactery against the anger of one's master once the image of the figure of Hekate or of the Gorgon is carved into it. Anyone who wears

14. A classy cookshop in Pompeii decorated with marble and wall paintings

it will never succumb to spells, thunder, or lightning, nor be wounded by evil demons.'[156] By using masonry in specific settings, often carved with selected images, the imperial building programme sought to have a similar moral impact on the viewers.

Stone statues were erected almost everywhere. Augustus's right-hand man, Agrippa, set up waterworks with 300 bronze and marble statues, as well as 400 marble columns.[157] By the fourth century there were over 4,000 bronze statues of emperors in Rome, not to mention those carved of stone. Sculpture was smooth, colourful (in that it was often painted), hard, permanent, and oozed authority. Mounted high on a plinth, a classical statue was in stark contrast with the low, rough, penetrable body of the popular grotesque. A statue personified moral qualities, establishing a permanent record of favourable attributes, in the same way that stone inscriptions sought to create a fixed record of the past. When imperial statues were put up, there was an accompanying ritual to celebrate the act, as when in 403 CE a statue to Eudoxia, wife of the emperor Arcadius, was erected in Constantinople with a ceremony involving 'noise and public spectacles of dancers and mimes, as was then customary at the dedication of imperial images'.[158] A statue was not a lifeless thing; it was made of special matter that could exude a moral force, and was an integral part of the ritual life of the city.

Yet stone also meant luxury, particularly when it was marble. This was morally problematic for traditionalists in the elite. Pliny moans about the luxury of statues and the move from temples of terracotta to Greek marble.[159] Seneca complains of 'walls glistening with large and expensive circular pieces of marble, with Alexandrian blocks contrasting with stone from Numidia'.[160] But it was a question of moral purpose. Private luxury, which helped no one and served only to degrade the individual, was strongly denounced. The Augustan programme, though, created a sensory world that acted upon the viewer to produce a social benefit. Augustus's claim to have found Rome in brick and left it in marble was much more than simply an architectural boast.[161] It represented the creation of a more diffuse and penetrating form of government, which used an intensified sensory experience for political ends.

Architecture was seen by many, but few are likely to have understood the many nuances of detail that each monument contained. More important for the non-elite viewer was the overall sensory impact of material and colour, its place in the wider spatial context and its ongoing use in the ritual life of the city. Imperial building programmes were not just about images, undoubtedly important though these were. I want now to look at the games in the arena and the circus to show how the emperors created a carefully orchestrated overall sensory experience, which was designed to have a morally improving effect on the spectator.

Vespasian built the Colosseum from blocks of Travertine stone from the quarries of Albulae near Tibur, modern Tivoli, but, in a politically significant act, also re-used the marble from Nero's Golden Palace which had stood on the site. The halls were ornamented with statues, stucco decoration and brightly coloured plaster. The crowd were seated according to status. This created a hierarchy of clothing and colour, from the pure white togas of the citizens to the darker tunics of the poor in the highest seats. A religious ceremony preceded the games with the presiding magistrate leading in the garb of a general at a triumph, wearing a gold-braided purple toga and a tunic embroidered with palms, holding an ivory sceptre with an eagle's head, and with a bejewelled wreath of golden oak leaves resting on his head. The procession was accompanied by musicians, statues of gods and pictures of the emperor and his family. Any breach of etiquette was an excuse for the whole day's races to be repeated, a ruse which Claudius had earlier tried to put a stop to. The crowd rose and cheered. The trumpets sounded to start the contests.[162] The senses guided the social flow of the performance: the crowd knew when to do what, what was about to happen and how to feel because of the sensory triggers implanted into the proceedings. The senses helped to structure the social encounter and in doing so were integral to reproducing social relationships. They were not just an incidental reflection of social practice.

Smell, as we have seen, was an important way for a Roman to know his or her status and worth. It was also a way of communicating with and experiencing the gods. The games began with a sacrifice. Sacrifice was characterized by the smell it created, with burning incense, flowers, the roasting of the sacrificial meat and the smoke of the fire.[163] At the imperial cult, then, it was fitting that worshippers should burn incense because it established the appropriate divine odours. It was right that when Romans met the emperor, his representatives and his images, they should sense his divinity, not in some vague way, but as an awe-inspiring and overpowering encounter. When the emperor Caracalla entered Alexandria in 215 CE the city prepared a ticker-tape parade for him: 'musical instruments of all sorts were set up everywhere ... clouds of perfume and incense provided a sweet-smelling odour in the streets, and the emperor was honoured with torch-light processions and with showers of flowers'[164] The emperors adopted the smells associated with sacrifice to enhance their aura of authority and divinity and thereby earn the respect, admiration and awe of the spectator.

Light was manipulated to add to the impact. Special effects were part of the spectacle.[165] Fireworks could be used.[166] As part of the preliminaries to the Saturnalia, Domitian had a circle of lights lowered into the amphitheatre at dusk, turning night into day.[167] Caligula held night-time performances and lit up the whole city, which only served to underline his immorality to moralists. Nero's quinquennial feasts lasted all night long and objections to the immorality that might result were met with the reply that the light would be too bright to allow indiscretion.[168] And Nero's nocturnal chariot races were illuminated by the pitch-covered bodies of burning Christians. In 32 CE, Sejanus had the spectators of the festival of the Floralia escorted home by 5,000 slaves bearing torches.[169] Other visual effects included a Neronian star-spangled, purple awning in the amphitheatre.[170] That the Romans cared about light can be seen from disputes that arose over access to light: 'Many quarrel over windows and openings for light, and they bring one another to court.'[171] Romans' own descriptions of their buildings tend to focus on their light, brilliance and splendour, rather than purely architectural features. One of the main purposes of mosaics was to create a shimmering lustre that gave visual texture to the area where they lay. At the games, awnings were provided to help control the distribution of light within the ampitheatre. Their popularity is attested to by the fact that adverts for shows often emphasize that awnings will be available.[172] The benefits were partly practical, in that they kept spectators out of the scorching heat of the daytime sun, but also symbolic in that they created the shade that was associated with a life of leisure. Within the sensory scheme of the amphitheatre, awnings served to spotlight the stage so that all the action took place in the bright heat of the arena. The best fights were those where the combatants did not run away into the corners but where the 'butchery was done in the middle where the ampitheatre can see it'.[173] The sand itself, the *harena*, helped establish visual focus by means of its glittering mobility.

The empire brought an explosion of colour into the Roman world. The first century saw a decisive expansion in the number of colour terms, with over seventy words in use, including sixteen reds, eight blues and ten greens.[174] Pliny complains that painting was by the first century thought worthless if it was not executed in a multitude of costly and exotic pigments.[175] At one of Julius Caesar's games, the gladiators appeared wearing silver armour, and at one of Nero's, amber.[176] There was colour even in death, with gold-braided carpets and pictures covering the funeral pyres of emperors.[177] The colour, size and sound of exotic animals imported into the arena over-turned the normal sensory rules of sight, movement and sound. Lions had decorated, gilded manes, sheep appeared with purple and scarlet fleeces, and at Gordian the First's games 300 vermilion ostriches strutted across the sand.[178] Carefully coordinated contrasts were created, with a bull fighting an elephant a common pairing. Inversion and variety were popular themes. Condemned criminals entered dressed in gold tunics, purple cloaks and gold crowns, which then spontaneously combusted. The brightly coloured pagan clothes that St Perpetua's Christians were made to wear mocked the dire position the condemned found themselves in.[179] Transformation scenes turned the arena into a forest of trees, or a ship that broke up to release animals that started fighting each other, or the ground opened and up came a wood and fragrant fountains from which monsters emerged.[180] The people liked broad brushstrokes of bright colours, and the spectacles created an exaggeration of the pleasure of looking to suit this taste. It magnified surface appearance and worked on the senses, all of which the traditional elite saw as superficial and sensational.

The games resounded with orchestrated noise. Musical accompaniment came from horns and trumpets, or in Carinus's games from a hundred flutes.[181] The screams of victims rang out, which would not, as Cicero says, provide an effective training for the ear 'in the endurance of pain and death'.[182] When 100 lions were slain at Probus's games, their roars were like thunder.[183] Cowards were driven on by whips and hot irons, and 'there was noise everywhere produced by the equipment of death; here a sword was being sharpened, there someone was heating metal plates, here rods were produced, there whips ... The trumpets were blaring with their funereal sound ... everywhere there were wounds, moans, gore; you could only see danger.'[184] In the circus, the horses were encouraged by men shouting or waving cloths, torches, flutes and ribbons.[185] When the emperor entered a loud, formal acclamation greeted him. Such acclamations acted as an audible register of popular support for the regime and it mattered greatly to the emperors to be cheered by the people. It gave them popular legitimacy. It is for this reason that chanting played such a pervasive role in numerous aspects of public life in the empire.[186] Within this framework of orchestrated noise, the crowd could still be spontaneous and noisy. Crescendos of cries arose according to the action of the arena. The carnival authority of the games allowed the crowd to question the emperors with immunity, and chants could sometimes spring up in protest against a war or food shortages or against an unpopular official.[187]

The crowd enjoyed an intense verbal and physical participation, waving, shouting and clapping. Every sensory experience became exaggerated: staring at the fights or the chariots, jumping up at moments of excitement, screaming in support or swearing loudly in fury at some piece of cheating. The thunderous applause of the winners echoed across Rome and could be heard well beyond the city walls.[188] Such physical participation meant that the air could easily start to grow stale. Water was sprinkled to reduce the dust that was thrown up by contests and to cool the air. Perfume was sprayed on to the crowd to freshen the atmosphere. Fresh sand was spread in the arena to cover the blood-spattered traces of the previous combat and create a clean slate for the next fight. Cushions were sold to the public to make the experience more comfortable.[189] The comfort of the crowd contrasted with the tough treatment of those in the arena. The public punishments involved extremes of touch: wounding, whipping, being torn by the teeth of wild beasts. Men who volunteered to become gladiators had to agree that they could be burned, beaten and cut with iron, symbolizing their transition from freedom to constraint.[190]

Touch was part of the physicality of the experience. Citizens had to wear the heavy toga to the games but this may not have been seen as an inconvenience. Numerous funerary busts and statues of freed slaves, who had been successful enough in later life to afford such things, depict them proudly wearing their togas. Citizenship was perhaps more important to these freedmen than the freeborn, but they probably present a more intense expression of the general feeling. The toga, like many symbolic items, was supremely impractical: expensive, hard to fold correctly, difficult to keep white. But when worn properly, the folds of the cloth created an extended area of personal space, symbolic of the freedom the individual enjoyed. The inner fold, the *sinus*, became an extension of the self and a metaphor for the individual's heart and affection. The toga was white but the cost of cleaning and age meant that a hierarchy of whiteness will have operated, a threadbare greyness acting to show the lower status of the wearer. It was a sign of Commodus's madness that he once required spectators to wear the dark cloak that was usually worn by mourners at funerals.[191] Discomfort could be an acceptable part of the experience as it was associated with feelings of self-worth. Even though the toga was a hot and heavy woollen garment, Domitian was seen as strange for letting people come barefoot to the games and allowing senators to wear parasol hats instead of being bareheaded.[192]

Cloth played a role in shaping the order of events and expressing the emotions of the crowd. The fold of the toga was waved to indicate that mercy should be given to a fallen gladiator or that a spectator thought a chariot race should start again: 'Quirites, toss your togas in signal from every side! See, they call them back!'[193] Races were started by the drop of a white handkerchief, the *mappa*, supposedly because Nero had once kept the crowd waiting until he had finished having his lunch, something he signalled by throwing out his napkin from the imperial box. In 88 CE, imperial servants in rich costume waited on the toga-clad audience, indicating sartorially that they were worthy of such an honour.[194] Fabrics were used to communicate imperial news: at the Judaean triumph of Vespasian and Titus, three- or four-storey-high scaffolding held tapestries embroidered with gold and ivory ornaments, on which pictures of the whole course of the war were depicted, like an ancient Bayeaux tapestry:

A rich country was seen being devastated, whole hosts of the foe fleeing, falling or surrendering, huge walls collapsing under the blows of battering engines; strong fortresses being stormed, the round walls of populous towns being mounted, the army pouring in and spreading murder, and the defenceless begging for mercy, temples being forced, houses collapsing over their occupants heads, and, after much misery, streams of water, not finding the fields or slaking thirst, but pouring through the burning streets.

Decoration was not simply about finery and embellishment; it could be used to play an active role in informing the people about recent events, literally spinning the news into a pro-imperial form.[195] We should not assume that people were sceptical about these scenes. Many may have had a literal way of reading such images and believed in the veracity of the depictions of art. When a tribune wanted to convince his audience that Lucullus was indulging in excessive luxury, he showed them paintings of his Tusculan villa. In a similar way, ship-wrecked men trying to beg for money may have carried pictures of themselves swimming to land from a wreck.[196] Equally, we should not assume that people automatically believed these images: we have seen repeated examples of popular scepticism applied to situations where it helped their interests to be wary.

The spectacles established a space where the people could be orga-nized into a disciplined ritual, where they publicly affirmed their loyalty and obedience to the ruling regime. Important imperial ideas were anchored in concrete forms that played on the senses to achieve their effect. The games combined a cross-social desire for political stability after the ravages of the late republic, with an image of the emperor that emphasized his power. It showed how the emperors wanted to be seen: magnanimous, in control, but also popular. The constant repetition of these images in the games, the number of which increased steadily during the empire, grounded all politics in the terms of this imperial iconography. Repetition created habit and helped reduce the need for hard repression. Symbols emphasized imperial power, but by educating people in the new political realities made it less likely that such power would have to be used. Being a spectator taught Romans the etiquette for proper conduct in public: enthusiastic and vigorously supportive, but at the same time obedient and under control. The metaphor of the emperor as father helped define the form that such obedience should take, and also justified the threat and use of corrective punishment. By using such all-encompassing imagery, Augustus also widened the scope of impe-rial government to include all of society.

The emperors created a new sensual literacy to help them achieve these goals. The enjoyment of the luxuries of empire was made avail-able to all in a way that appealed in the direct, sensational way favoured by the people. Pleasure could be expressed in an overtly emotional way but only within the confines of an ordered and regu-lated environment. This fusion of the sensual and the moral overcame some of the traditional objections to the non-elite having access to leisure and luxury. The games would not corrupt the people because they manipulated sensory values to maintain social hierarchy and create social consensus. This fusion was also reflected in elite literary descriptions of the games, many of the more extreme (and not necessarily entirely true) examples of which I have used in this chapter. In the same way that the games presented a visualization of the new alloy of moral luxury, so written descriptions in histories such as Suetonius's *Lives* and the *Scriptores Historiae Augustae* presented a florid and overblown textual account. Texts such as these represented an explosion of literary sensuousness that paralleled the wider cultural shift in that direction. They came to focus on the extremes of imperial largesse as a way of highlighting concerns that this new luxury was tipping over into immoral excess. These were traditional concerns of the elite. But, in reality, exaggerated stories such as these show clearly that luxury had now become an acceptable part of the political mainstream. It was now normal for sensuous luxury to provide the backdrop for the meeting between the emperor and his people, whatever misgivings the literary elite might still have had.

The popular culture experienced the world directly through its senses. Elite culture, though, was distanced by elite learning and education. Unlike the carnival, the games divided the spectator from the spectacle. The treatment of victims in the games encouraged the crowd to distance themselves from deviant others and feel a strong sense of communal solidarity. The building itself dominated the skyline and so created a communal focal point for harmony. Of course, communal solidarity is the not the same thing as equality. Being part of the crowd was to be granted membership in a hierarchical club. Even though the Colosseum was built on the site of Nero's unpopular Golden Palace, effectively making it a people's palace, the seating was arranged to reflect the social hierarchy. This seating plan replaced earlier scrumming and scrimmaging, where people would have to fight to get a good spot at the gladiatorial combats, although seats were still close enough together that the knees of people behind could probably stick into one's back as they did at the circus.[197] By placing their imperial box as a focal point, the emperors established distance between themselves and the people. They became something to go and look at as part of the spectacle, rather than being one of the crowd. The games carefully defined the sensory context in which their meetings with the people took place, over-awing their 'clients' and maintaining an appropriate distance strictly according to rank. The lofty columns and shimmering marbles, lackeys in livery, decorative features such as eagles, jewels and purple coverlets, all dazzled with their splendour. By making themselves focal points, the emperors effectively objectivized their own bodies, making them the targets of a distanced form of contemplation. And by establishing hierarchies of space, the emperors created an 'ascent in privilege', to adopt Wallace-Hadrill's phrase.[198] Going to see the emperor at the games was like going to see a patron: waiting, hoping for gifts, being over-awed by the sensory experience, being kept at bay. The crowd were unified by this shared reality.

The games represented a visual drama of society's hierarchy and the moral values on which elite authority rested. The contests in the circus and arena also offered living tableaux of the virtues that subordinates would do well to copy. It is always tempting to see the provision of these entertainments as purely a matter of state control: allowing the people to let off steam and diverting them from the real problems they faced. But the care with which the games were crafted shows that this would be too simple a reading. The games had to be skilfully manufactured to generate consent. They had to give people what they wanted to get them to agree to take part. From the elite point of view, it was perhaps better to have some control and encourage the elements of the popular culture that seemed best – honour and resilience, the traditional virtues of the Roman yeoman soldier – than to risk losing control entirely. It is important to recognize that elite authority was always a matter of compromise, cooption and intimidation as much as outright force. There was a limit to imperial power and it took charisma, persuasion and habit to keep the people buying into the system.

If the emperors used a new sensory language to communicate with the people at the games, the non-elite adopted it to talk back. They used the senses to manipulate those in authority, in the same way that they managed the powerful in their daily lives. Acclamations were an ideological device to deny the existence of any tensions between the emperor and his subjects. That is what the emperors wanted so the people gave them, for the most part, positive feedback by turning up, cheering and shaking their togas, providing a clapometer for imperial performance. The elite eagerly waited to see what kind of reception they received and boasted among themselves afterwards.[199] The Magerius mosaic in North Africa shows that being able to give the crowd what it wanted and be acclaimed was the pinnacle of public life, with the giver of the games boasting: 'this is wealth, this is power'.[200] But by denying the usual ritual affirmation the people retained an important critical voice. Collective action such as chanting and clapping in unison, shouted complaints and mocking jokes, gossip and rumour-mongering, violence and rioting, all could have a powerful impact on the giver of the games. To be sure, this was not a card that could be overplayed, but when it was it generally worked.[201]

The people went along with the ritual most of the time because it served them to do so. Flattery and sycophancy were the currency of despotism. Dio claims that the masses were naturally sycophantic and always flattering.[202] In reality it was the safest way to speak to the powerful, verbally re-enacting power relations. Such deferential behaviour became the norm for all towards the emperor. The advent of autocracy under the emperors therefore changed the sound of speech, so that the speech of the flatterer seemed to be literally perfumed and effeminate.[203] Pliny describes in his oleaginous Panegyric to Trajan that when the emperor was known to be appearing the people would gather to shout acclamations and hope for largesse in return. They even taught their children the formula to chant.[204] Pliny sees this purely as an act of adulation but it is just as possible to see it as an act of flattery, whereby people actively sought to massage the imperial ego in the hope of getting material benefits in return. The elite were aware that acclamation could be used as a political tactic. Germanicus rebuked the Alexandrians for their tumultuous welcome and threatened to reduce his number of public appearances if they did not calm down.[205] If the people were as fickle as they were often accused of being by the elite, it was because they had learned how to go with the wind.[206] As the empire became more sophisticated so the people's response had adapted to the changed realities of dealing with power.

The late republic had given the people ample experience of the elite's political ineptness. The early emperors therefore had to press their claims for legitimacy and competency hard. The games put forward such a message, but we should not assume that they were received as such. The crowd was made up of sophisticated and creative consumers who produced their own range of meanings. The text's message was not set in stone even if the text itself was. The audience was actively able to interpret events in the games in ways that were at odds with the intended message. There were many ways to watch the games. Some ignored the messages completely and used the games to look at women. Others became excessive consumers. Such fans created a highly discriminatory and knowledgeable community. They indulged in what Fiske calls 'producerly activity', making their own texts over and above the original text.[207] In their endless talk about the races, these fans rewrote what could, should and would have been, using the horse-racing as a cultural resource from which to fashion a multitude of new cultural texts. They worshipped their popular heroes and gossiped about them. They used magical charms to try and actively affect the outcome of the races. All of this helped to create new identities within the non-elite group.

By the sixth century in Constantinople, clothing had become a way for groups within the circus to fabricate an alternative identity based around their membership of one of the factions. Procopius describes how these mainly young men wore extravagant clothes with special sleeves on their tunics that billowed out when they waved their arms. They combined this theatrical display with synchronized clapping and chanting to maximize their group effect. Interestingly, they also wore their hair long, except in the front where, mullet-style, they cut it short across the forehead, and grew Persian-style beards and moustaches. They called this the 'Hunnic' look.[208] The popularity of barbarian styles can also be seen in laws dating from Rome, a few years after the sack of the city in 410 CE by the Visigoths, which banned people from having long hair or wearing animal skins in the city. Clearly, the authorities were touchy about such things when the city had been damaged by real barbarians.[209] It appears that some urban young men were adopting styles of dress and appearance that were associated with non-Romans and then using membership of close-knit groups, such as the factions, as a way of expressing a strong sense of group identity. The relative freedom of expression granted to the crowd in the circus also gave them opportunities to express discontent as and when they felt like it. It is impossible to be certain about any of these conclusions because we have no information about who these young men were. But it is clear that they used combined sensory effects to establish a powerful collective presence in a space that had become an important political arena.

The emperors' power was such that it enabled them to force their fantasies and fictions on the world. But the popular culture carried on subverting these messages. The emperors tried to keep purple as an exclusive colour for themselves, though its use remained widespread.[210] People ignored the seating code and wore colourful dress.[211] They scratched graffiti into the stone to reclaim the surface for the popular culture. The seats in Aphrodisias were littered with gameboards, phalluses and abuse: 'Bad years for the Greens'.[212] It shows that public buildings should be understood not only at an imperial level but also from the user's point of view. Ovid shows that elite authors could also delight in the unofficial culture. He subverts the Augustan ideology of moral rebirth and uses the circus as a place to have an affair. The new sensory language of the emperors becomes the language of sensuousness:

> Don't neglect the horse races if you're looking for a place to meet your girlfriend. A circus crowded with people offers many advantages. You don't have to use a secret sign language here or be content with a slight nod to acknowledge each other's presence. Sit right next to your

girlfriend – no one will stop you – and squeeze up beside her as closely as possible. It's really easy to do. The narrowness of the seats forces you to squeeze together . . . Perhaps a speck of dust will settle on her breast (it often happens); be sure to brush it off with your hand. Even if there is no speck of dust, pretend – and keep brushing off nothing! Take advantage of every opportunity. If her skirt is trailing along the ground, pick up the edge and at once you'll receive a reward for your careful concern because you'll be able to look at her legs and she won't mind . . . Many men have found it useful to bring along a cushion which they can offer. And fan her with the racing programme. These little touches win over female hearts.[213]

We have seen in the Tavern of the Seven Sages how comic the popular culture found it to see the high culture expressed in coarse terms. The non-elite used images of philosophers discussing bowel movements as a way to subvert the elite's view of them as filth. Similarly, in popular riots, the crowd used excrement to express their own disdain at their treatment by the authorities. Vitellius and the consul Bibulus were both pelted with dung.[214] During riots in Antioch in 387, Theodosius's statues were pulled down, smashed and covered in muck, then dragged through the streets.

But such riots represented temporary revolts against authority. Other more radical approaches appropriated the language of the senses to reject Rome outright. Christians embraced the non-sensual to express their opposition to the Roman style of doing things. 'I should speak against the pleasures of the five senses', explains Lactantius, 'all of which should be overcome by virtue because they are vicious and deadly.' The animal world gave a pointer for how to treat the senses: 'they use their senses for the necessity of their nature'. So they see to protect themselves, and use their taste and smell to find food. Above all, 'they reject things which are useless'. Tellingly, Lactantius's choice to illustrate uselessness in the human environment is the folly that was the games: 'What else does the circus contain but levity, vanity, and madness?' The spectators are carried away with 'mad excitement' so that the spectators themselves become the spectacle 'when they begin to shout, go wild with excitement, and jump up from their seats. Therefore all spectacles should be avoided.'[215]

Many Christians went a lot further than the gentle philosophizing of Lactantius. A fifth-century peasant monk in Egypt, Shenute, wrote a letter to a landowner called Saturnus, complaining that he was stealing peasants' property, including their cattle and carts, was forcing them to work for him for nothing, and was making widows, old men and women buy meat from a calf 'which is nothing but bones and worthless stuff' for twice its value. He goes on to attack the bath tax they had to pay: 'We don't want to wash – we have no bread to eat; we have no care for anything of that sort when our children are starving and naked.' As he says, those who are forced to build them 'do not wash in baths'. Holy men began to use stench as a measure of their ascetic devotion: Simeon Stylites rejected bathing and 'so powerful and bad was the stench that not even half way up the ladder could one ascend except with distress. Some of his disciples who forced themselves to go up to him could not ascend until after they had put on their noses incense and fragrant ointment.'[216] St Theodore of Sykeon emerged after two years in a cave, and 'his head was covered with sores and pus, his hair was matted and an indescribable number of worms were lodged in it; his bones were all but through the flesh and the stench was such that no one could stand near him.'[217] Holy men such as these rejected the sensory world of Rome and its concomitant sensuality in favour of the 'odour of sanctity'. As Clement of Alexandria says of the Christian gnostic, he:

> is far from surrendering himself to the mob-government which tyrannizes the theatres ... he repudiates these spectacular pleasures and the other refinements of luxury, such as costly perfumes which flatter the sense of smell, or combinations of meats and the attractions of various wines which entice the palate, or fragrant wreaths of various flowers which enfeeble the soul though the senses.[218]

Monks rejected the sensory world of Rome and subverted it to create a new sensory language. They left the city to rejoice in smell, threadbare clothing and poor food, and thereby win divine favour. But Basil warns his monks that just because they now wore the clothes of the poor, that did not mean they could behave badly by playing around, shouting or become 'accustomed to hitting and to being hit'.[219] Monks were expected to exercise a high degree of personal control. A new sensory order was created, but in the Christian world the senses continued to play an important role in the creation, explanation and transmission of power. Touch, in particular, allowed the divine to pass through its human conduits into the bodies of the ill: when touched with mere face cloths that had touched St Paul 'their diseases left them and the evil spirits came out of them'.[220] Rome, meanwhile, that 'unclean' and 'most lamentable city, full of revelry', was left to await its foretold destruction. At that day of judgement, it would be 'reduced to ashes'; and its daughter, 'drunk and clothed in gold and luxury', would become a mere slave bride and 'oft shall thy mistress cut off thy flowing hair'.[221]

5

Popular Resistance

In the 348th Aesop fable, the wolf, who was governor, proposes to the ass that they should share everything equally. But the ass is having none of it and simply points out that this has never happened before. For, as the moral states, 'The very persons who appear to make just disposition of the laws do not abide by their own laws and decisions.' The astrologer Firmicus Maternus similarly notes that 'often by general consent we see penalties inflicted on innocent people'.[1] Not that the people could do much about such injustice. As Kelly observes, the poor 'had little hope of redress against a powerful defendant. They rarely even bothered to litigate.'[2] Even if they had complained, there were limits to the ability of the Roman government to deal with petitions. If emperors dealt thoroughly with one, then they merely excluded others through lack of time. The rebel Calgacus lists the complaints of the oppressed Britons: conscription, over-taxation, the exaction of tribute, forced labour and overweening Roman arrogance, 'whose oppression you have in vain tried to escape by obedience and submission'.[3] Tacitus's account of this defiant speech showed that the Romans themselves recognized that alternative visions of their power were possible. Given such misrule, it is no surprise to find that some people throughout the empire did resist Roman authority and government. Like the hare who is ruled justly by the lion, 'they prayed for this day always, when even the strong would fear the weak'.[4] Many of the social conflicts that blew up between the elite and non-elite gained their spark from frictions generated by attempts by the people to defy elite power. This chapter looks at some of the ways the people went about that resistance.

It is important to realize that resistance does not always have to be of the heroic, 'I'm Spartacus' kind. As Scott has shown in his studies of peasants in South East Asia, popular dissent covers a vast range of acts and thoughts.[5] There is a sliding scale of resistance, ranging from the occasional drama of open rebellion to the oblique and passive opposition of everyday life. Such small-scale defiance can take many forms and is not always confrontational, involving tactics such as evasion to avoid elite domination. Outright rebellion was extremely rare in the Roman world. Even open political discussion was a luxury for most during the republic and all under the empire. We must be careful not to dramatize social relations into a model which sees Roman society as involved in a constant class conflict. By far the most common course to steer lay somewhere between outright opposition or collusion. Such dissent as did occur was mostly delivered in a subtle, measured way. Resistance for the most part represented an accumulation of tiny, individual acts that served to counter the facts of non-elite subordination. Mostly these acts were indirect and delivered anonymously to protect the individual from reprisals. But it all constituted part of the popular mode of politics in the Roman world. It was how they went about getting what they could out of the system, even if it reflected a largely negative politics of maintaining what little they had and stopping the elite from getting their hands on any more. Many acts of popular resistance can be interpreted as negotiating techniques between the people and those in power. They constantly probed to see what they could get away with, thereby chipping away at the boundaries of elite domination. In doing so, the popular culture sought to create new spaces of their own, which were free from elite control and influence. In the same way that the elite had established areas of Roman culture that were effectively closed off from the people, such as fine cuisine and high literature, so the people tried to establish fields of interest which the elite did not understand. Fans in the games, house churches, private languages such as a beggars' patois, all served to exclude the elite. But anything that was not under elite control represented a potential threat, and the authorities took various measures to try to suppress such dissent.

Given that Roman Italy was one of the great slave-owning societies in history, it is not surprising to find that slaves carried out many acts of resistance. As Hopkins says, hostility between slave-owners and slaves 'lay just below the surface of Roman civilization like an unexploded volcano'.[6] A Roman proverb held that there were as many enemies as there were slaves – *quot servi tot hostes*. But slave rebellions were rare and, with the exception of Spartacus's revolt, easily crushed. By the time of the empire the slave system was too well-oiled to face serious, large-scale threats. Slave resistance coalesced around small acts of lying, cheating, pretending to be ill and going slow. Columella describes how country slaves would claim to have sown more seed than they had actually used, steal, shirk and fiddle the books. 'Lazy and sleepy' city slaves would try and lounge around the town, enjoying the many leisure pursuits the urban environment had to offer.[7] Seneca warns owners to 'guard against their thieving hands'.[8] These tactics were not just resistance for its own sake. Theft obviously helped slaves to supplement their meagre rations, while shirking helped to reduce the amount of work that they would be expected to perform under normal conditions. It probably also benefited slaves to appear to be dull because it stopped them from having to meet higher performance expectations. Pantomalus, the slave in *The Complainer*, claims that 'we are not as miserable and dull-witted as certain people think'.[9] Others may have used their natural wit to improve their position: Aesop is always outwitting his master in the *Aesop Romance* by taking things literally:

> 'Where were you born?' asked his master.
>   'In my mother's belly', replies Aesop.
>   'No, in what place were you born?' tries the master again.
>   'My mother didn't tell me whether it was the bedroom or the dining room.'[10]

One of the sayings of Publius Syrus was that 'the clever slave has a share in power', which was of course meant as a warning to slave-owners to be on their guard.[11]

Cowardice could be a useful tactic for a slave in that it would prevent him or her being placed in any position of danger. Another was to appeal to the master's soft side, if he had one. One of the irritations of owning slaves was that it meant relying on people who were always breaking down in tears.[12] Such crying could have been an actual expression of anguish or distress, or it could have been a tactic to try and avoid an unpleasant task or punishment. Owners denied the humanity of their slaves, animalizing them in the process.[13] By breaking down in tears, the slave could try to reverse this process and assert their humanity, showing masters the effects of their brutal treatment. In reality, this was probably a tactic that was only likely to benefit some domestic slaves, who were in a position to have some kind of relationship with their master. But like the ass, to which slaves were compared, the slave could have a nasty kick. Slaves could collude to annoy their masters in the manner of Aesop.[14] They could also run away, in effect robbing their masters of a valuable asset.

Masters created a stereotypical image of the slave as impudent, gossiping, lazy, deceitful, light-fingered and unscrupulous.[15] This contrasted with the image of the ideal slave, who was loyal, industrious, diligent and thrifty.[16] St Paul's exhortation to slaves to obey their masters 'with fear and trembling and in singleness of heart' suggests that some, if not most, were failing to meet this ideal.[17] Passive resistance actually reinforced the owners' view of the slave as being work-shy and untrustworthy. Masters' paranoia led them to imagine that slaves were leading alternative lives away from their gaze. In *The Complainer*, the slave Pantomalus describes how, 'Nature created nothing better than night. This is our day; we do everything then.' They bathe with the other slaves and slave girls. 'Isn't this a free life?' he asks, 'I grasp naked one who the master is hardly allowed to see clothed', all of which illicit fun is carried out with 'Enough light supplied to be sufficient, but not to give us away.'[18] But if the masters had an image of the good and bad slave, so slaves created an image of the good and bad master. As Aesop lectures his master, 'If you are good to your slaves, no one is going to run away from what is good to what is bad and condemn himself to vagrancy with the prospect of hunger and fear to face.'[19]

Gossip was an effective way for the slaves and clients of the wealthy to try and actively alter their masters' and patrons' behaviour. Gossip about maltreatment was a way to reject its injustice and advertise that fact to a wider audience. It sought to deny the master the status of a good man and reduce his standing in the community. Advice given to Cicero on electioneering warns that gossip often emanates from households, so that even slaves should be treated with great consideration in the run-up to an election. Martial similarly describes how clients and slaves love to gossip and delight in revealing their masters' secrets more than stealing or drinking his best Falernian wine.[20] Needless to say, such gossip could be slanderous. If a rich man dreamed of having more than two ears, it signified 'much talk about him', good if the ears were shapely, bad if deformed, but if they were the ears of wild animals it meant 'a plot against him that will arise from slander'.[21] Misers were despised because they failed to deliver the expected reciprocity of the rich and gossip sought to deprive them in turn of the social status they would otherwise enjoy. The non-elite were forced to gossip between themselves because speaking openly could be dangerous. The innocent remarks of slaves at a dinner party in Spain were reported as treasonable.[22] People had to watch what they said. Hence, dreaming of being unable to speak signalled unemployment and poverty, 'for poverty destroys a person's freedom of speech'.[23] Fables themselves were supposedly invented to enable a slave to express 'in a disguised form sentiments which he dared not say aloud for fear of punishment'.[24] In the run-up to a slave revolt in Sicily, the slaves, 'crushed by their physical hardship and mistreated, almost beyond reason, with frequent beatings, could no longer patiently endure. When they had the opportunity to do so, they met together and talked about a revolt.'[25] Patiently enduring even the most excessive mistreatment was probably the norm for most slaves. But when they decided they had nothing left to lose and to do something about their plight, it was hushed discussions in clandestine meetings that gave them the means to devise a plan.

Trickster tales, like those of the *Aesop Romance*, allowed the downtrodden to enjoy situations where the little man won, albeit temporarily. The trickster hero was a clever mischief-maker, who overturned the normal world where the master was in charge. Such a symbolic levelling provided a kind of psychic revenge against the rich, which was in itself a kind of empowerment, a way of coping with the situation. Imagining alternative, better worlds also released the idea of utopia into the collective consciousness of slaves. The anonymous Aesop fables taught how to deal with oppression in a more practical way. They appealed to 'rustics and the uneducated'.[26] Here we find less of the panache of the hero of the *Aesop Romance*, and more of the passive resistance that probably characterized most acts of daily defiance. Fables rejected the authorities' claim to deliver justice: so the swallow grieves after her brood are eaten by a snake in a court-house, because she has 'been wronged here in this place where those who are wronged find help'.[27] Other fables emphasized that it was often better the devil you knew: in one a jackdaw, kept as a pet on a piece of string, tries to escape but the string gets caught and, as he lies dying, says, 'Poor fool! I couldn't bear servitude to man but I've robbed myself of life itself.' Similarly, 'servants long for their old masters only when they get a taste of new ones'.[28] The fables are full of implied dissatisfaction. So the fox whose young have been eaten by an eagle, 'stood and cursed his enemy from a distance, which is the only resort of those who are weak and impotent'. They are full of resignation. When the wild doves are caught by fowlers using tame doves, the wild ones complain they should have warned them; but the tame ones reply, 'it's better for us to look out for our masters than to do a favour to our own kind'.[29] It is 'better to be a servant in safety than to be a master in peril', and doing anything that could upset those in authority is risky: 'men who annoy those more powerful than themselves pay the penalty for their bad judgement'; far better not to oppose the powerful but 'bend like the reed in the wind'. It is only when one has the luxury of being in a position like the kid on a rooftop that it is safe to abuse the wolf.[30]

Scepticism towards authorities was part of everyday non-elite life and consciousness. The hope and fatalism expressed in the *Aesop Romance* and fables were in reality two sides of the same coin of poverty. The lowest slaves did have aspirations – to freedom and higher status – and went to great lengths to achieve these goals when they could. But few were in a position to do so and many resorted to running away. This in itself was an act of hope as well as desperation, trying to flee and set up a new life, perhaps pretending to be free.[31] Simply asserting one's self-worth was a way to resist the dehumanizing effect of the dominant culture. Former slaves felt the urge to establish their identity in death and set up numerous stone memorials. Associations were often founded as burial clubs, presumably because many of the non-elite thought a proper funeral was worth saving for. Cicero's election advice tells him that the most important thing is to remember people's names since 'nothing is so popular or pleasing'. It all helped to resist the anonymity to which society mostly condemned the non-elite.

It was not just slaves who resisted the powerful. The poor often hated the rich.[32] As Reymond says of fourth-century Egypt, 'it seems evident that the great majority of Egypt's people hated not only their Roman oppressors, but the traitorous gods who are represented on the temple walls as supporting the tyrant power, and the craven priesthood which served them.'[33] But the people could rarely risk outright confrontation as individuals: as Epictetus warns, 'If there is a requisition and a soldier seizes your donkey, let it go. Don't resist and don't grumble. If you do, you will be beaten and you will still lose your donkey.'[34] Grumbling might not have achieved much, but it did release frustrations and helped maintain an alternative identity to the rulers. After the crushing defeats suffered by the Jews in their revolts of the first and early second centuries, such a quietistic approach became more popular: 'You go into the country and you meet a bailiff; you come back to town and bump into a tax-collector; you go home and find your sons and daughters starving.'[35] Many of the same tactics adopted by the servile population were used by the free non-elite to help them avoid elite claims on their labour or surplus produce.

Humour was a useful weapon in debunking the claims of the authorities and discussing dangerous issues. Humour was especially useful in this task because it fed off the emperor's need to display that he was one of the people and could take a joke as such. Humour acted as a kind of managed disrespect. Quintillian warns aspiring orators to avoid 'those coarse jibes so common on the lips of the rabble, when the ambiguity of words is turned to the service of abuse'.[36] So jokes were told about the alleged illegitimacy of

Augustus, or the fact that Julius Caesar acted as the passive sexual partner when a young man.[37] The piss-pots that stood outside fullers' shops were called 'Vespasians' because he had introduced an unpopular tax on them.[38] When Vindex rose in revolt against Nero, he mocked him by insulting the emperor's musicianship.[39] These small-scale acts changed little but they did express statements of defiance against the regime.

Wives were expected to be meekly obedient. Most were in a weak position to resist such expectations. Yet there are examples of wives who seem to have worn the toga in the relationship with their husbands. One astrologer forecasts that 'the wife will be adulterous and attack her husband with all kinds of injuries'.[40] Marital problems were common and show that some women resisted the destructive effects of their unsatisfactory relationships. Galen remembers how his mother was 'so bad-tempered that she would sometimes bite her maids; she was perpetually shouting and fighting with my father'.[41] It was a commonplace of astrology that women could be troublesome. Some men were forecast to endure 'a marriage with unending conflict'; others that 'they will have trouble with slave women over sexual problems'; and then are those who are weak in body and are 'sluggish, epileptic, liable to wounds from weapons, sickly, the type whom women always attack and who have trouble with women'.[42] A handbook on the interpretation of twitches asserts that, 'If your left knee jumps, it means changes and trouble from women.'[43] Jokes in the *Philogelos* also rely on marital strife and nagging wives for their humour: 'A misogynist paid his last respects at the tomb of his dead wife. When someone asked him, "Who has gained their everlasting rest?", he replied, "Me, now that I'm rid of her."'[44] The proximity of non-elite living conditions can only have exacerbated such marital tensions and arguments.

Society placed a huge burden on women to ensure that the large number of offspring needed to overcome the shockingly high mortality rates was delivered. This often left women trapped in a cycle of childbirth and childcare that only death brought to a stop. Not surprisingly, some women bridled at this suppression. We have seen how hysteria offered women a socially acceptable way of expressing such tensions. Working in bars, singing and dancing all went against what was usually considered decent for a woman. Sallust complains that Catiline's friend Sempronia danced and sang better than an honest woman should.[45] Prostitution provided a socially unacceptable way of escaping from the Roman household and its norms of behaviour. The prostitute adopted an inverted lifestyle, living in public. The elite condemned them as 'base women who . . . ought to appear in public at their best behaviour, but who actually misbehave the most in the streets'.[46] They wore male dress to symbolize this active, public role. But the decision to become a prostitute can be seen as reflecting a positive choice, one resistant to society's norms, which offered a more male identity. To be sure, most women forced into prostitution probably did so out of the direst necessity. But alternative motivations were possible.

Some seem to have used their sexuality to express alternative lifestyles to society's norm. Some slaves hung around 'the Campus, the Circus, and the theatres', where they grew accustomed to 'gambling, cookshops, and brothels'.[47] Dyson describes this as a 'community of low-life types whose social life centered on the brothel in much the same way that the social life of the elite was focused on the curia or the basilica'.[48] Some seem to have focused their sexual desires on one gender. So there were 'shrewish women who never couple sexually with men or, if they do, do not conceive'; or women who 'make love unchastely to other women'. Similarly, certain men were 'sterile, not able to engender children, never enjoy conjugal life, and always prefer intercourse with boys'. Some men went so far as to actively adopt female fashions: 'They twist their hair in ringlets' and 'soften their whole body with various cosmetics; pull out their body hair and wear clothes in the likeness of women; they walk softly on their tip-toes.'[49] These *cinaedi* came to represent everything that 'a real man must not be'.[50] Even if it can be argued that such effeminate men 'ultimately supported the ideological system by constituting a necessary negative',[51] the appearance of this new type of male represented a structural shift in the shape of aesthetic taste among some sections of society. Here was a new pattern of sexual consumption, one which relied on camp to express resistance to and difference from the overbearing societal norms of sexual behaviour. These were individuals who seem to have had an alternative sense of shame to the dominant culture. They flaunted their sexual differences openly and publicly, an act which trampled on traditional decencies. It suggests that once a member of such a group, deviancy came to be regarded as such only in regard to normality – there was no shame within the deviant group itself.

The people could also take collective action to resist elite misrule. Food was the most common cause for protest and the reason for the 'usual popular protests'.[52] Often it was fear of hunger rather than hunger itself that made the urban poor riot.[53] This was rebellion with the emphasis very much on the belly. Such actions tended to be spontaneous and aimed at immediate social superiors. But these riots were often in accord with the concept of the moral economy we saw in the first chapter. Those in the crowd were always concerned that social bonds would break down in times of shortage and that the elite would try and evade their social responsibilities. They used violence tactically in the pursuit of clear material objectives. Resistance was strongest when it seemed that the elite were withdrawing their traditional support. So an angry crowd burned down the consul Symmachus's house for saying that he would rather use his wine for quenching lime-kilns than sell it at popular prices.[54] The rich were condemned for deserting the city when grain and oil ran short.[55] The crowd used rioting as a bargaining chip to help force the elite to meet the obligations of the perceived moral economy. The elite partly justified their own superiority by reference to their benevolent patronage so, by forcing them to deliver on this promised reciprocity, the people were able to hold them to account. The elite response was mostly placatory. Emperors tried to force local elites into acting to calm situations down.[56] But such riots had limited aims. They cannot be seen as part of any wider, organized protest movement. In many ways, such occasional violence actually reinforced existing hierarchical structures because it forcibly re-established the status quo. This was conservative rioting.

Other collective actions served to express public opinion with no material aim. The crowd at the games once complained about Severus's war by clapping in unison and chanting 'How long will we wage war?', but then they shouted 'That's enough' and turned their attention back to races.[57] They had no intention of pushing such an issue to the next, more dangerous level of rioting. Debt, though, was worth fighting against. Josephus recounts how during the Jewish revolt of 66 CE, the temple in Jerusalem was occupied because 'they were keen to destroy the bonds of the money lenders and to bring debt-recovery to an end'. The political attractions of burning debt records to the rebels were that it would 'win over a mass of debtors to themselves and set the poor against the rich, from whom they would now have nothing to fear'.[58] This popular action obviously took place in a time of great social tension in a relatively newly conquered, rebellious province. The Acts of the Apostles give a good impression of the degree to which the crowd could be a force to be reckoned with elsewhere in the Eastern empire at roughly that time. Written from a non-elite viewpoint, the Acts describe the twelve disciples and Paul preaching the Gospel across the East and then Rome after Jesus's death.[59] His message led to a breakdown of public order in six different places.

At one point, the disciples Peter and John, described as 'uneducated and ordinary men', were taken before the temple leaders and told to keep quiet. The leaders, 'when they saw the boldness of Peter and John and realized that they were uneducated and ordinary men, were amazed'. This kind of bold, direct speech was not what the elite expected of the common man. Deference was the norm, but they found no way to punish them 'because of the people'.[60] Paul caused riots in Ephesus because his message threatened the local religious centre of Artemis and the livelihoods associated with that cult. The Ephesians rushed to the theatre and spent two hours shouting, 'Great is Artemis of the Ephesians'.[61] He upset some of the locals at Philippi by driving out the spirit from a slave-girl that allowed her to predict the future. Her owners, aggrieved at losing their cash-cow, took him before the magistrates and accused him of 'throwing our city into an uproar'. The crowd joined in the attack against Paul and the magistrates ordered him to be stripped and beaten. Paul was in fact flogged on several occasions despite being a Roman citizen and so supposedly immune from such punishment.[62] The crowd in Lystra stoned Paul and left him for dead outside the city. In Thessalonica, Paul and his followers are described as 'These people who have been turning the world upside down', who are all 'acting contrary to the decrees of the emperor, saying that there is another king named Jesus.'[63] Throughout all of this, the local elites are portrayed as powerful, with extensive powers to arrest and punish by beating and execution, but also perennially concerned about public disorder. They are petrified about the Roman authorities getting involved. So the magistrates in Philippi apologized for the flogging after finding out that Paul was a Roman citizen. Equally, the senior Roman administrators are keen to let the local elites police themselves and not interfere. Hence Gallio, the Proconsul of Achaia, washes his hands of the matter: 'If you Jews were making a complaint about some misdemeanour or serious crime, it would be reasonable for me to listen to you. But since it involves questions about words and names and your own law, settle the matter yourselves. I do not wish to be a judge of these matters.'[64] The crowd were a volatile but powerful force in local politics and the local rulers were keen to appease them. To be sure, the Acts probably do not describe a normal period in Roman provincial life, but they do give a clear indication of how the non-elite could employ strong, autonomous actions to affect local political outcomes.

Direct individual action was considerably more dangerous as it exposed the perpetrator to identification and the full rigours of the Roman law. Running away was a less risky option, in particular because poor communications and lack of an integrated police force made detection difficult. We saw in the first chapter that the Oracles of Astrampsychus imply that a majority of runaways succeeded in making their escape. But it was not only slaves who resorted to flight. Some Christians fled temporarily into the countryside or other towns to avoid persecution, exploiting the Christian network to stay with other believers until the trouble had blown over. Tactical withdrawal meant that 'the man who flees will fight again'.[65] Peasants often ran away to escape from crushing debt and taxes. They also used the threat of flight to try and pressure the authorities into reducing their burdens. An inscription from an imperial estate in North Africa, the *Saltus Burunitanus*, describes how farmers complained of abuse and beatings at the hand of imperial procurators, even though that was where they were 'both born and raised and from the time of our ancestors as peasants have kept faith with the imperial account'. This loyal-sounding message is tinted with the threat that if things do not improve, 'we will become fugitives from your imperial estate'.[66]

Many of those who fled became brigands. The leader of one of these gangs, Bulla Felix, told the authorities how to put a stop to banditry: 'Tell your masters that if they want to stop brigandage, they must feed their slaves.'[67] Not all outlaws were runaway slaves; some were pressed into service, others were attracted by the loot, while others were only too pleased to exchange a 'life of drudgery to join a group which was almost as powerful as the state'.[68] Many were happy to abandon the Roman Empire altogether, preferring 'to endure a poor freedom among the barbarians rather than the harried condition of a taxpayer among the Romans'.[69] Priscus, on a diplomatic mission to the court of Attila the Hun, met a Greek merchant who had been captured but who now chose to live with them, preferring it to the Roman Empire where you had to pay for justice.[70] The writer of the anonymous *On Military Matters* complains that corrupt provincial governors are 'all the more burdensome in that injustice proceeds from the very persons from whom a remedy should have been expected'.[71] The author had written to the emperor in the fourth or fifth century to suggest various ways he might improve the empire's situation. He warns that tax and injustice are driving the poor to crime: 'the poor were driven by their afflictions into various criminal enterprises, and losing sight of all respect for the law, all feelings of loyalty, they entrusted their revenge to crime. For they often inflicted the most severe injuries on the empire, laying waste the fields, breaking the peace with outbursts of brigandage, stirring up animosities.'

It is tempting to see these outlaws as what Hobsbawm called 'social bandits', Robin Hood figures who turn the injustice of the normal world on its head and form an egalitarian community to resist the corruption of the regime. As Grünewald says, the social bandit has 'become the favourite of those who would impute to the lower social classes . . . a hidden potential dynamism in the shape of some awareness of the way in which they were repressed and an active desire for violent and directed change'.[72] As he shows, it is more likely that bandits were used as an elite literary convention to highlight the poor governance of certain bad or corrupt officials and emperors. Yet the bandit stories do still use popular themes of injustice, poverty and corruption to exert pressure on poor-quality rulers. They threw the elite's own standards of governance back in their faces when they fell short. Bandit stories may also have evoked some vicarious admiration from the people, even if banditry in practice posed a major threat to them when they travelled.

The most extreme form of resistance was outright rebellion. The stated causes of these revolts did not vary much from those listed by Calgacus earlier. In a Gallic revolt, 'at public gatherings and private meetings they began to deliver rebellious harangues about the unremitting taxation, the burden of debt, the brutality and arrogance of their governors'.[73] Revolts tended to happen in provinces that had been relatively recently conquered. As Dyson says, revolts came as a result of 'extreme tensions placed on a native society in the process of rapid acculturation'. Often these social tensions were accompanied by 'deep group psychological malaise such as "millenarian" religious manifestations'.[74] Local religious traditions, such as Druidism, could also be used to give a boost to local morale in a way that the Romans found hard to interpret.[75]

Their military might meant that the Romans dealt easily with most uprisings. Religious ideas expressed dissent of a different kind. Notions of religious experience changed during the early empire. Broadly, there was a slow move away from traditional religion based on dealing correctly with and exploiting divine power, which helped to maintain personal and community identity, to a focus on religious experience and individual ethical progress. The healing cult of Asclepius, for example, brought the individual into a close relationship with a god. Mithraism focused on purification, instruction and discipline, and involved seven grades of progress on the long journey towards rebirth. Mysteries such as the symbolic rebirth in the taurobolium, where an initiate into the cult of Cybele was drenched in the blood of a bull sacrificed over him, all established a special relationship between the believer and the god. Christianity was a movement that came from the rebellious province of Judaea. It appealed to many of the non-elite by means of its optimistic message of an imminent and just new order. It represented a popular movement in which everyone was understood to be an active participant and have equal worth as a human being. Eastern cults such as Isis, Cybele, Mithras and Christianity all created spaces for non-elite subjectivities alternate to that of the official state religion. Cult imagery could serve as a weapon of cultural resistance to the official religion. These cults seem to have provided a particularly useful way for women to circumvent their subordination, allowing them to focus on individual feelings in a setting outside of the constraints of the family and home.

Non-Roman initiate cults, such as Christianity, could be used to express dissenting religious ideas. They provided a way for peripheral Romans to use local cults and secret rites to express resistance to Roman rule.[76] Religions such as Christianity showed that the people were capable of imagining a new social order. Clearly, this was a potentially threatening message and for Christianity to survive it needed to create a new social space where it had greater freedom to express itself. It achieved this partly by establishing a belief in a hidden order of things known only to the initiated few. It expressed this hidden transcript in ways that meant the underlying meanings were not immediately obvious to the authorities. Verbal ambiguity in the form of parables meant that the powerful would not understand them, yet their message was left clear to those in the know. Parables acted as a one-way mirror, showing outsiders only what they expected to see, but letting those within see clearly the truth beyond. Many Christian beliefs stood in stark opposition to the traditional Roman take on such issues. Roman religion was public and political, whereas Christianity, in theory at least, was collectivist, ethical, millenarian, and called for the redistribution and sharing of property.[77] It offered a world-turned-upside-down view of the future, where there was equality instead of hierarchy, charity not greed, continence not sex and simplicity versus sensuality. This was, to begin with at least, 'a revolutionary movement', targeted at the underdog, which rejected elite values and claims.[78]

15. A scene depicting a ritual of the cult of Isis

Christianity provided an alternative social order as well as a critique of the existing social order. Christian groups were 'of one heart and soul and no one claimed private ownership of any possessions but everything they owned was held in common'. 'There was not a needy person among them, for as many owned lands or houses sold them', and the proceeds were then distributed to each as had need.[79] By focusing on reciprocity and mutualism, it bypassed traditional patronage relationships and catered for non-elite needs. Christianity also offered an alternative symbolic order. The Christians steadfastly refused to sacrifice to the emperor. For the Romans, this was a complete rejection of the symbolic ideal of their society. We should, of course, be careful not to assume that expressing dissent was the focus of Christianity. For many Christians, sacrificing to the emperor simply contradicted their beliefs. Any differences Christians had with Roman beliefs may have been of secondary importance to them. Tertullian was happy to 'pray for the emperors, for their ministers and those in authority, for the preservation of society and for peace'.[80] But, whatever their motivation, the fact was that the Christians were living in the Roman Empire and many of their actions were perceived as rejectionist. This perception was often based on too literal an interpretation of the Christian message: as Justin complains, 'Hearing that we expect a kingdom, you really conclude that it must be a kingdom in the human sense.'[81] But sometimes Christians went out of their way to become martyrs, in a full-scale assault on Roman norms and authority. Most of these martyrs came from the non-elite. It was highly significant that these acts took place in the arena where Roman imperial society and its values were so clearly on display. The martyrs inverted the image of the gladiator to create an alternative popular hero. But these acts were rare. Far more Christians picked up their certificate to show they had sacrificed to the emperor than were martyred. That is not to downplay the harshness of the persecution that many Christians suffered for their beliefs at the hands of Roman officials, simply to emphasize that Christian writers had a vested interest in exaggerating these events.

Martyr acts and the reading of martyr acts to congregations across the empire created a group united in opposition to the state, even if the state was largely oblivious of and indifferent to it. The Romans mostly played back by refusing to kill them: in Lucian's *Peregrinus*, Peregrinus is imprisoned for being a Christian and brought before the governor, 'who being aware of Peregrinus's lunacy and that he would welcome death for the reputation he would acquire for it, released him as not being even worthy of punishment'.[82] Other religious radicals sought a far less dramatic way to reject Roman society. The early monks simply withdrew from it. In reality, though, such an anachoresis (the same word used of those who fled from taxes and oppression) was never simple. A variety of methods offered themselves: to withdraw as an individual, like St Anthony, to live in a cave or on a column, like Simon the Stylite, or up a tree, as a dendrite; or to live as part of a community of other monks. Jesus had provided the model for an individual to reject family and property as the primary concerns of life, in favour of a relationship with the kingdom of heaven and a new family of brothers and sisters in faith. It became possible to abandon one's social identity in a way that was previously only available to the insane. We saw in the second chapter, how ascetics adopted some of the symbols of madness to reject the seemingly sane world they inhabited and so encounter the divine more intensely. That this represented a social death was reflected in the fact that monks' cells were sometimes designed to resemble tombs.

Monks did not withdraw from society simply to express their dissent. They went seeking to explore the divine and the limits of human identity. But by doing so they dissolved social categories and relationships, which implicitly rejected the social world they came from. Monks were mostly of lower-class origins. Their withdrawal could be interpreted as a reaction against society's male roles and the norms of behaviour that were expected in the performance of those roles. It was a way of leaving behind the exhausting, hyper-competitive world of peasant life. Hermitage provided a good opportunity for non-elite women to escape from the endless grind of rearing children. But although they tried to leave behind the secular and sacred world of the Romans, they acquired a powerful urban role with the non-elite, acting as arbiters, healers and prophets to all. Holy men became popular heroes. In part, this was because they dramatized what it was like to live a normal life, expressing non-elite concerns about their physical and mental health in an intensified form. Ascetic labours were in some exaggerated way analogous to the back-breaking toil of peasant life: hence, someone counted Simon the Stylite touching his toes 1,244 times in bowing to God – it was work worth doing and worth counting (although he gave up counting in the end). These were men who had earned their religious power, not like a magician of traditional popular religion. Such easy access to power came in the later empire to be seen as a drawback, implying a diminished effectiveness. The hermit became, to use Brown's phrase, the 'utterly self-dependent, autarkic man'.[83] Free of the ties of patronage, tax and demons, and blessed with some of the freedom of speech traditionally granted to philosophers, the holy man epitomized everything the non-elite dreamed about being.

By the second century, wealth and power were concentrating steadily into the hands of a smaller and smaller group. The elite effectively had it sewn up. The people therefore needed heroes who could make active, positive interventions with a moral purpose on their behalf. The non-elite needed a new form of patronage in this new order. The rise of a spiritual elite paralleled the emergence of a sharper social elite. Holy men acquired a range of social functions: care for the sick, the poor and the oppressed within the cities. Theodore of Sykeon was a saint who 'puts demons to flight, who gives healing to the sick, a father to orphans, a food-supply to the poor, a covering to the homeless'.[84] But as Whitby warns, there is no simple social explanation for the rise of holy men. This was a complex and diverse phenomenon and cannot be seen purely as a function of popular demands. The writers of *Saints' Lives* had a vested interest in exaggerating their importance and popularity. But it is also true that they came to be hassled almost continuously for the social services they could provide, as the people sought out new ways of coping with a society whose traditional structures were failing to meet their needs.[85] In the end, the empire solved the problem that the creation of a new kind of religious space had created by colonizing that space itself. After Constantine's conversion, Christianity could become an expression of Romanness, not of social rejection. Similarly, the authorities solved the problem of asceticism by slowly bringing it under their control by the simple and traditional expedient of becoming its patron.

Some extreme views were incapable of assimilation. Apocalyptic literature looked forward to the end of Rome, when justice would be restored and revenge taken.[86] The Sibylline Oracles prophesy a time when 'implacable wrath shall fall upon the men of Latium'; a time when 'law and justice shall come from the starry heaven upon men' and 'lawlessness, blame, envy, anger and madness shall depart. Poverty and penury shall flee from men in those days, with murder and accursed strife and grievous wrangling, theft by night and every ill.' It will be payback time for Rome: 'For all the wealth that Rome took from Asia in tribute, three times as much shall Asia take from Rome, repaying her her own cursed arrogance: and for all the men who were taken from Asia to go and dwell in Italy, twenty times so many men of Italy shall serve in Asia as penniless slaves.'[87] This burning sense of indignation and thirst for vengeance often linked the Roman regime with the defiled and corrupt body of the prostitute, as in the biblical identification of the whore of Babylon with Rome, the city where 'the throne of Satan is located'.[88] Egypt had a long tradition of resisting foreign rule, having been conquered previously by the Greeks under Alexander the Great. One third-century papyrus prophesies, 'and it will go badly for the rich. Their arrogance will be cast down and their goods confiscated and delivered over to others ... And the poor will be exalted and the rich humbled.'[89] The Oracle of the Potter looked forward to a golden age when a good demon will come as a source of evil to the Greeks and reduce the 'upstart city by the sea' (that is to say, Alexandria) to a 'place where fishermen dry their nets'.[90] Resistance literature of this kind often adopted the cultural tools that Rome had provided but subverted them for its own purposes. What was to be resisted was present in the resistance to it. So, for some of the oppressed, Nero became the embodiment of Roman wickedness and his return would signal disaster for Rome.[91] Was all this just the impotent fury of the oppressed? It does at least show they could do something to resist Roman domination. And even if it were true that such writing suffers from problems of 'gross illiteracy, mental confusion, and repetitiveness inseparable from this kind of popular literature', such texts represented highly imaginative alternative visions of the social order, which managed to transform a dreadful situation into an imminent success.[92] The elite also seem to have been spooked by some of these predictions of doom, which were obviously quite common. Tiberius was so disturbed by a popular prophecy of the coming end of the empire that he had various spurious Sibylline oracles destroyed.[93]

How do we square these various degrees and forms of resistance and opposition with the official view? According to Veyne, 'the people loved their sovereign and right-thinking persons praised submission as the duty of every loyal subject'; 'evidence of this love was to be found everywhere: festivals and ceremonies, the Emperor's portrait displayed in all the shops, popular imagery'.[94] As Statius puts it: 'countless voices are raised to heaven cheering on the emperor's festival; with loving enthusiasm they acclaim their master'.[95] It is certainly true that the imperial image dominated social life: on coins and statues, through the imperial cult, and with poorly executed pictures of the emperor to be found on 'money-changers' tables, in stalls, in shops, hanging in the eaves, in entrance halls, in windows – in fact everywhere'.[96] Laws were passed to restrain excessive adulation of the imperial images displayed at contests.[97] People apparently loved their emperor so much that 'All men pay taxes to you with greater pleasure than some people would collect them from others.' And why shouldn't they, since 'all the common masses in the empire need have no fear of the powerful man among them; they can have recourse to you ... The present state of affairs is both pleasing and advantageous to rich and poor alike and there is no better way to live.'[98] But should we take all this at face value given what we know about popular scepticism elsewhere?

It is undoubtedly true to say that the idea of the emperor was a powerful one in Roman society, even if the majority of the population

16. Mosaic showing the wide-eyed excitement of the crowd at the circus

might not even have been able to name the current incumbent. The emperor was not only, to quote Millar's famous phrase, 'what the emperor did', because he became an image too – an accumulation of past acts by others, what emperors had done in the past and were expected to do in the future.[99] The emperors encouraged the people to believe in their divinity, but in doing so they created an image that could itself be used against them. It could become a weapon of the weak, to use Scott's words.[100] Once an ideal had been established, every emperor could be judged against it. And knowing what the attributes of an ideal emperor were gave ordinary Romans a way of thinking about the degree to which the reality fell short. Of course, thinking about it is not the same as talking about it, let alone doing something about it. Even elite writers had to be careful to couch their criticisms of the abuse of imperial power by locating them in discussions of reigns of previous dynasties. Hence, Tacitus and Suetonius, under Trajan and Hadrian, write about the Julio-Claudians and Flavians of earlier generations. The emperor could display his absolute power by flouting any of society's laws and norms with impunity. But if his actions undermined his claims to deliver the justice and liberty advertised on things such as his coins and buildings and in the imperial cult, then people would realize that the reality was falling short and judge the regime accordingly. Hence, when Hadrian said to a woman hassling him for a hearing that he did not have the time, she replied simply, 'Then don't be emperor.' The fact that this seems to have been a popular story, with various versions over the centuries, shows that this was a common approach to those in power: try and turn the official rhetoric back on the powerful to compel them to live up to their own propaganda.[101]

The popular demand for just rule found its clearest expression in their attitude towards imperial images. The emperor's image had become the ultimate place for protection and justice. The people tried to make use of this allowance to express their views: one woman followed a senator hurling abuse, while holding a picture of the emperor for protection.[102] Imperial images became the focus of riots. During a tax riot, 'seeing the many images on painted panels, they committed blasphemy by throwing stones at them, and jeered at them as they were smashed'; the statues of the emperor and empress were then thrown down and dragged through city and, 'as is usual on such occasions, the enraged multitude uttered every insult which passion could suggest'.[103] During riots imperial statues were often pulled down, smashed and mired with filth, flogged then dragged through the streets.[104] On Caligula's death, the people of Rome tore down his statues.[105] The fact that people so keenly tore them down suggests that they had disliked them when Caligula had been alive. If it had just been a ritual act of showing allegiance to the new regime, this kind of statue-destruction would have happened on all emperors' deaths. Instead it suggests that people conducted the same kind of flattery towards imperial statues that they had to employ to their superiors in their daily lives. Occasionally, the mask slipped and people may have used indirect means to express their views on the regime: so Caracalla convicted those who urinated near his statues and portraits.[106]

Such symbolic actions were sometimes replaced with direct and indirect vocal attacks. In the *Acts of the Pagan Martyrs*, Heliodorus complains that wheat is being sold at four times the fair price and that the emperor is getting the money; at least 'That is what we have heard.' The emperor says, 'You ought not to have circulated the story without being certain of it. Executioner!' It is clear that people used gossip and rumour to express critical judgements about the regime, but that these rarely reached imperial ears. As Heliodorus says, 'To whom can we speak, if no one will listen?'[107] This was a problem for the regime because they needed information both as a protection against plots but also as feedback to see what current public opinion was saying. The laws claimed that all who spoke against the emperor were foolish, insane or malicious or 'riotous with drunkenness'; but also that they were not to be persecuted. The emperors wanted to hear everything 'with all details unchanged'.[108] Ammianus describes the emperor Gallus wandering disguised in the streets and inns of Antioch asking people what they thought of him.[109] This suggests that it was an acceptable topic of conversation, although not one without risks. Epictetus tells how 'In Rome, reckless men are trapped by soldiers in the following manner. A soldier in civilian clothing sits down beside you and begins to vilify the emperor. Then, as if you had received from him a pledge of good faith just because he began the abuse, you too say what's on your mind – and the next moment you are handcuffed and led away.'[110] For the most part people limited their dissent to 'idle grumblings',[111] or some anonymous graffiti: 'The accountant of Nero Augustus is poison'.[112] But, as O'Neill argues, it seems that 'a widespread popular culture of discussion' existed which was at times political.[113]

The image of the emperor clearly played a powerful role in Roman society. A wide range of Romans displayed a religious loyalty to the emperor which 'far transcends mere political obedience'.[114] The cult of the emperor also gave provincial members of the empire a way of rationalizing their subjection. It was no disgrace to be conquered by and then be subject to a god. But other readings are possible and, in the light of popular scepticism and resistance literature, cannot be entirely dismissed. The government was an autocratic regime that tried to produce loyalty among its members by creating a charismatic aura about its leaders. The rituals and symbols of spectacles and the imperial cult established new traditions which displayed imperial power, helped enforce domination and constructed community. They dramatized the aspirations of the regime: to be leaders of a well-ordered, moral and contented society. There can be no doubt that these rituals did generate considerable legitimacy and expressed widely held views: the emperors had, after all, brought peace and relative prosperity. But even if they did produce legitimacy, public rituals were also just a statement of domination based on compliance. Public statements of loyalty were what mattered to the regime. Acclamations and sacrifices and panegyrics all served to flatter the regime. The endless repetition of the same rituals and the superfluity of imperial iconography also generated scepticism. Why should the popular culture which was so sceptical towards the authorities in its fables, suddenly fall for the emperors' story? We need to be careful here about transposing modern political attitudes back on to the Roman people. It would be wrong to see the non-elite as being cynical towards their leaders in the modern sense.[115] But, equally, we should be wary of accepting the transcript of public acts, performed before the powerful, as straightforward evidence of the people's loyalty and belief in the goodness of Roman government.

The neat, social order that was expressed in the imperial spectacles was far from evident in Roman life. The empire fell well short of its own claims of justice and good governance. It is tempting to think that the further the government fell short of its own self-proclaimed standards, the more it needed to turn up the volume of its public statements that everything was all right. So when we look at late Roman law and the 'the ferociously moral world of the fourth-century imperial constitutions',[116] we might well be seeing an attempt to cover up declining standards of rule. We have seen that Romans were capable of being critical of their emperors in private. Stories of transgression, such as martyrs and their public punishments, became part of the currency of resistance. Public acts of defiance were far more dangerous and so most had to hide behind a cloak of anonymity via the crowd. Only radical individuals such as Christian martyrs were prepared to challenge the official picture of society openly. This was particularly threatening to a regime that relied on public statements of loyalty to generate its legitimacy.

The regime obliged people to flatter it. The rich had to write increasingly florid panegyrics, prostrate themselves at the emperor's feet and, if they were lucky, kiss the hem of his cloak. The poor had to acclaim and cheer the benevolence of his reign. But it would hardly be surprising if such a regime also made people fake it. We know that many Christians during the persecutions swallowed their beliefs and sacrificed to the emperor. Public dissimulation of this kind became part of the experience of being Roman: it was how they dealt with power. Horace's slave, Davus, took advantage of the Saturnalia to criticize his master for running off from his clients in order to suck up to his own patron Maecenas: 'The truth is that you, who give orders to me, are yourself someone else's miserable slave, and you dance like a wooden puppet on strings that another controls.'[117] Flattery expressed both deference and social distance but also worked on a sense of shared values. It tried to make the emperors feel that they ought to help their people. There was no escaping from the political reality that power had become heavily concentrated into the hands of one man. Flattery was a way of dealing with that reality of power relations. Both sides got caught in an act: the emperor, like Constantius II, forced to sit motionless and bejewelled like a divine emperor should; the people forced obediently to cheer. Most participated in these public acts. They went along to get along. The vicious punishments of the spectacles served as a reminder of what happened to the aberrant. Politics for the people became a largely theatrical exercise, with spectacles that provided a 'safe' area for political expression. But it did serve to get them what they needed – patronage in the form of entertainment and handouts. And, from the emperor's point of view, the new politics generated civil obedience in a far more effective way than the use of pure military force ever could.

The elite tried to engineer social consent by creating an image of a just order. The emperor set himself up as father to all. In doing so the regime gave the non-elite a means to judge their government, in those, to use de Certeau's words, 'ingenious ways in which the weak make use of the strong'.[118] Reputation was important to the rich, and being good to the people was the way to get a good reputation. It was the only way the people had some control over the elite. It shows that the people possessed standards of approval and condemnation of elite behaviour, however vague such notions may have been. But ideas of the 'good rich' created a framework for stability, because it provided a socially acceptable outlet for criticism. Gossip formed a public opinion that judged leaders against shared norms of good governance.

Most acts of resistance were minor skirmishes along the border between ruler and ruled. Stories and jokes about the emperors' excesses relied on a shared language of power. By using the conceptual system of the emperors, they served to create not destroy community. Most resistance was small-scale and mundane, with no grander purpose. The sources give an impression of a largely passive popular culture, which occasionally erupted into violence. Resistance was more active and ongoing than that. To the extent that dissent did not publicly challenge the regime, it was largely tolerated. People learned to read between the lines and reinterpret things as criticisms, which is why so many lines in the theatre were actively reconstructed by the audience into criticisms.

Did the non-elite believe the emperors' imagery? The rejection by certain religious groups shows that some did not. They saw through what they regarded as imperial propaganda and mythology. Most people's views probably lay somewhere between total belief and scepticism, their attitude changing according to circumstance. They acted obediently for most of the time and actively participated in the acclamations at the games. But they retained some of the scepticism for authority that the people had always shown. Corruption worked both ways. In the same way that Roman government moved to a system where money bought access, so the people conformed so long as their leaders continued to buy their support. Just because the people were mostly deferential did not mean they were not still constantly calculating and weighing up their self-interest. Poverty and dependence had always entailed a requirement to present different social faces. The people massaged the elite's egos with flattery and respect, and so long as the rich paid their dues, they received loyalty and social recognition in return. The fable of the 'The Monkey King' told the people all they needed to know:[119] a liar and an honest man were travelling together and reached the land of the monkeys. The chief monkey ordered them to be held for questioning so he could see what they would say about him. He ordered the other monkeys to line up to his left and right and had a throne prepared for himself. He 'had them take their places just the way he had once seen the emperor do'. He then asked the travellers, 'Who am I?' The liar said, 'You are the emperor' and those 'with you are your courtiers, your officers, your drill masters, and your soldiers.' Flattered, the monkey rewarded him. The honest man thought that he would do even better if he told the truth, so he said, 'You are in truth a monkey and all these like you are still monkeys.' He was 'immediately ordered to be torn to pieces by tooth and nail'. The moral states that 'evil men who love falsehood and wrongdoing destroy honesty and truth', but more subversive readings are not hard to find.

Conclusion: Towards a Christian Popular Culture

In the ancient sanctuary of Quirinus in Rome 'stood two ancient myrtle trees, one named "The Patrician" and the other "The Plebeian". And when the Patricians were in the ascendant, their myrtle grew strong and flourished, spreading its branches abroad, while The Plebeian stood shrivelled and shrunken.' But after the Social War of 91–87 BCE, 'the noble tree declined whereas the popular tree lifted up its head and grew strong'.[1] After bearing the brunt of the challenges of completing it, the conquest of the Mediterranean world brought undoubted benefits for the ordinary Roman citizen. The huge growth of the city of Rome established a more differentiated economy that gave opportunities away from agriculture. The introduction of the corn-dole reduced (but did not eliminate) the urban plebs' need to work. Augustus brought peace, itself no mean benefit after decades of civil war. Fewer military demands were therefore placed on the people's manpower, reducing the negative knock-on effects of poverty, debt and dispossession that hurt many families whose menfolk spent long periods abroad. If they did enter the army they were better paid. Hundreds of thousands left to settle in new colonies.[2] It all served to reduce the risk that life held for the plebs. They enjoyed splendid games, which offered a chance for fame and fortune for the lucky few: the charioteer Diocles earned over 35 million sesterces in the course of his career. The importation of about 2 million slaves, who ranked well beneath the citizenry, may also have brought a significant psychological benefit to the plebs in a society where status mattered so much.

Of course, the fact that perhaps a quarter of the Italian population were slaves makes any interpretation of Roman popular culture based solely on the citizens of Rome misleading. Most of the non-elite throughout Italy and the wider empire had far less reason to thank Rome for what it had given them. The existence of the kinds of resistance we glimpsed in the last chapter makes a simple reading of Roman popular culture impossible. The popular culture was a complex entity that encompassed a wide range of different subcultures. There were numerous local variations in behaviour and belief, as well as refined gradations in status within the non-elite themselves. It could never speak with a single voice. What united the people was the shared experience of being weak in a hierarchical power structure. They had to find ways to deal with the similar range of problems that assailed them; they had to cope with the unique physical and psychological pressures that life in the Roman world placed on them; and they had to learn how to manage the powerful in their society.

Woolf rightly says that the symbolic centre of the Roman cultural system was a 'set of manners, tastes, sensibilities and ideals that were the common property of an aristocracy that was increasingly dispersed across the empire'.[3] The popular culture reflected a far less coherent set of beliefs and behaviours. Their manners were rough and rooted in the practical necessities of making a living; their tastes were simple and unrefined; their sensibilities were coarse and rough-hewn; their ideals were a simple and straightforward demand for good government and justice. In the same way that we do not expect the elite to be all alike even though they shared a common learning, we should not be surprised to find the non-elite as a diverse and disparate bunch. What differentiated the majority of them from the elite was their lack of power. They were economically weak, which meant that most had to do hard physical work to earn a living; they lacked the resources to help them cope with the higher level of psychological pressures they faced; and their low status meant they were always on the defensive in their dealings with the authorities.

But we should be careful not to create a chasm between the classes. Elite versus subaltern is too simple a divide. The popular culture had no single politics. Many, probably most, held a largely conservative outlook that was in broad social harmony with the elite. There were plenty of loyal slaves who concurred with the dominant culture, if not perhaps as readily as their masters might fantasize about: 'For us there are daily weddings and birthdays, spoofs and parties, and revelries with the maidservants. Because of this, not all slaves wish to flee; because of this, some of us do not want to be set free.'[4] Likewise, many of the non-elite throughout the empire were no doubt happy to accept the emperors' claims to leadership, if only to help them make sense of their own low place in society. Many people responded to the ritualized inequality of pageantry with raucous enthusiasm, taking advantage of the opportunity to identify themselves vicariously with the elite and bask in the grandeur of their society. If others withheld their consent, they still passively accepted the status quo. Most of these same people also probably resisted elite domination at some point in their daily lives. Some of this resistance was radical and extreme, but for the most part was small-scale and ineffectual. No simple dichotomy between the people who resisted and those who collaborated can be drawn. People exhibited a whole spectrum of different attitudes towards the authorities.

The flow of culture between the classes was two-way. Even if elite literary culture was almost entirely cut off from non-elite access, the popular culture held a fascination for many of the wealthy. They loved the thrill of breaking social ranks, of populism and enjoying themselves in a less refined way. The imperial political settlement also created a need for a new space where the classes could meet in a spirit of harmony. That meant new cultural forms were established which fused together many of the elements of popular and elite cultures, serving to draw together all social groups into a more binding social contract. Roman culture did not just trickle down from the elite to their social inferiors. Popular attitudes also moved upwards into the system of government.

The success of this strategy almost certainly varied considerably across the empire and across different social groups. The urban plebs in Rome did well and, for that reason, the 'poor of the city do not seem to have developed a counter-culture'.[5] But most were held in place by the simple need to make a living and by the threat of violence. Imperial ideology did not necessarily create an acceptance of Roman rule among the vanquished. Many in the provinces may have accepted the inevitable, but that does not mean they believed in the natural order of justice of the imperial regime. Again, though, we must be careful about seeing it as a simple matter of resistance or hegemony. Being ruled by Rome was a complex experience that created ambiguity in the articulation of that experience. Among the Jews, for example, apocalyptic visions appeared alongside continual appeasement and collaboration. As time went on, and the possibility of further rebellion receded, attitudes hardened and Rome came to be conventionally referred to as 'the evil empire'.[6] This is perhaps the opposite of what we might expect – that people would just get used to it.

Romanization was not just a matter of either becoming Roman or resisting it. Provincials built a bricolage of cultural forms, actively selecting from a variety of cultural sources to create their own identity. Elite culture was a resource for them to use as they saw fit. These new personal identities were 'driven by their own self-esteem', and aimed at their peers and their own households.[7] Carrying on local traditions cannot automatically be seen, therefore, as an act of resistance, nor was it regarded as such. The Romans actively encouraged localism so long as it had peaceful intent. That in itself gave provincials room for manoeuvre, allowing them to maintain a quietistic, cooperative front while grumbling behind the scenes. The Romans were probably indifferent to such complaints. Tacitus shows us they were well aware that their subordinates complained, even if they could only conceive of such complaints though the prism of Roman priorities. Mutterings of discontent were at the low end of dissent, well short of failing to comply, let alone publicly rejecting Rome's right to rule.

The problem in interpreting any imperial imagery or event is that it represents the public transcript of an autocratic regime. In public people put on a respectable performance to give the appearance of unanimity. Society was portrayed as a well-ordered procession, itself redolent of social cohesion and collective belief. Many imperial ceremonies may have acted as 'self-hypnosis', to convince the rulers themselves that it was all true.[8] It is impossible to say how much and how many of the non-elite believed it. When we read that taverns closed in mourning on the death of emperors and that 'all over the city, expressions of grief are displayed', it is tempting to believe that the people held the emperors in genuine affection.[9] That these expressions of grief were 'combined with festivals' suggests that the people still felt able to enjoy themselves. And the fact that the emperors used secret police and disguises to try and find out what people were really thinking suggests that there was another more critical popular discourse too. And popular enthusiasm seems at odds with the hard-nosed scepticism that they otherwise displayed towards their rulers: 'A change in ruler is just a change in master for the poor'; and, as the donkey in the fable says, 'what does it matter to me whose slave I am so long as I carry only one pack at a time'.[10] Most had limited expectations: 'Few men desire liberty; most are content with masters who are just.'[11]

Imperial authority among the people was based symbolically on lavish display and public ceremonial and ritual. Protests such as food riots were just part of the game of patron–client relations. But public acts of defiance like those of the Christian martyrs contradicted the whole system and had to be stamped on. The emperors dramatized their rule and thereby exaggerated their authority. Speaking truth to this kind of power is impossible within the constraints of personal safety. Flattery became the norm. Such public rituals of deference are less important in our society, but in the Roman world they were part of the act that the powerful required from the weak. The ritual use of a deferential language of politics reduced risk in that it kept social superiors at bay and helped nudge them into benevolent action. Conformity acted as manipulation in the pursuit of scarce resources. Fake smiles and humble shrugs were part of the arsenal of humility the weak could deploy against the strong. The elite were doubtless aware of what was going on but related it, not to cunning and nous, but to the natural, sycophantic characteristics of social inferiors.

The people developed a range of discourses to cope with the threats posed in dealing with a dangerous power structure. To be sure, consent was one option: agreeing with the official story and giving the authorities wholehearted support. Flattery was a safe form of public expression that allowed some room for manoeuvre by appealing to claims the elite had themselves made about the quality of their rule. Anonymity created an almost risk-free means of forming public opinion though means such as jokes, songs, rumour and gossip. Private languages among social groups such as slaves were entirely inaccessible to the elite and, regrettably, must remain so to us. Truth became what Scott calls a 'hidden transcript', that could only ever safely be expressed in a disguised form.[12] Disguising meaning through forms such as fables and parables effectively shut off the intended meaning from those who did not understand the hidden subtext, but still managed to bring alternative views out into the public realm for those who did. Creative interpretation of intended meanings in texts such as plays allowed subversive readings to be expressed. Together, these hidden discourses created a critique of power behind its back and represented an 'infrapolitics of the powerless', however ineffectual we might consider such a politics to have been.[13]

It is all too easy to see the popular culture as a static, monolithic mass. In reality, the same forces that affected Roman society as a whole can be seen to have had a powerful impact on the people. As the empire matured, a sharper distinction between the classes arose that saw wealth and power concentrate into the hands of a few. In the later empire, a more vertical society replaced the old ideal of the empire as commonwealth of citizens. It is tempting see this as unremittingly disastrous for the non-elite. The change in legal definition in the second and third centuries towards a divide between the more honourable and the humbler (*honestiores* and *humiliores*), and the more powerful and the weaker (*potentiores* and *tenuiores*) in the fourth and fifth, can be seen as reflective of a widening divide and greater antagonism between the classes. The free poor became subject to servile penalties such as torture, beatings and being condemned to the beasts. But the distinction was always blurred in practice and for most of the non-elite the law had always been a no-go area.[14] Citizenship was devalued to the point where, in 212 CE, the emperor Caracalla gave it to all freeborn people in the empire. But then, as St Paul had earlier found out during his ministry, the benefits of citizenship were often arbitrarily applied. The third-century crisis brought barbarian invasions and civil wars, yet if there was 'an age of anxiety' it is hard to pin down. The post-crisis need to maintain a larger army saw a shift towards a harder, bigger government whose purpose was to raise a higher level of taxes. As Kelly shows, buying access to government became the norm.[15] We might see that as corruption but this new approach simply replaced a system based more on patronage. The non-elite had never had much access to government. The economic decline that was once thought to have set in during the later empire now seems less certain, and if by 400 CE 'the inhabitants of the average town were a distinctly shabby lot', it is not clear that they were ever anything but.[16] Higher taxation and the colonate, which tied tenants to their land, may have undermined the stability of peasant income and reduced their ability to respond to fluctuations in harvest yields, but evidence for this is thin. As Brown says, 'the expanded presence of the Roman state did not necessarily bring as much misery upon its subjects as we had once thought'.[17]

One of the ways the popular culture did lose out in the later empire was from a marked decline in the provision of public amenities and entertainments. This breakdown in the traditional patronage system created a need for a new way for the people to extract support from the wealthy. Christian almsgiving may have seen some increase in the transference of wealth to those at the bottom of the social pile. But this may simply be a trick of the rhetoric since, as Brown says, 'Late antiquity witnessed the transition from one model of society, in which the poor were largely invisible, to another, in which they came to play a vivid imaginative role.'[18] What it does show is that despite an increase in the angle of the social hierarchy, some desire for social solidarity still existed. This could have a meaningful impact on the needy. Pope Cornelius, in the third century, was helping over 1,500 of the poor and widows.[19] If we assume that the Christian population at Rome was about 3–5 per cent of the total population of one million, then 1,500 represents 3–5 per cent of the entire Christian population being fed at the Church's expense. This was a not inconsiderable benefit given the limited resources for poor relief that had previously been available. In the East, a whole array of philanthropic institutions developed in the late fourth and early fifth centuries for orphans and foundlings, and for the destitute, sick and old.[20] 'The sick' became a recognizable body like 'the poor', which almost certainly does not indicate any actual increase in illness, but a shift to a society where this group became worthy of attention and resources. Indeed, poor relief and healthcare were doubtless part of Christianity's appeal to the non-elite.

The people became passionate about religious ideas. A famous quote of Gregory, fifth-century bishop of Nyssa, neatly captures this new found democritization of theology: 'If you ask about your change, you get some philosophizing about the Begotten and the unbegotten. If you ask how much a loaf of bread costs, the answer is "the Father is greater and the Son inferior". And if you say, "is the bath ready?", the reply is that the Son is from nothing.'[21] As Brown says, 'persons of the lower and "middling" classes, who found it difficult enough to support themselves in normal conditions, now entered with gusto and in increasing numbers into the high enterprise of religion'.[22] Of course, it might be that the people simply became much more interested in *Christian* ideas, rather than religion per se. Religion had always been a critical component of the popular culture, framing and informing most aspects of the non-elite's life. It had also always provided a living for a whole host of pedlars of religious wares, be they magicians, diviners or soothsayers. But it is certainly true that the people recognized that a newly Christian empire would require them to show interest in new forms of leadership and in new ways of exercising power, if they were to maintain even the little that they did get out of the system. Christianity offered itself as a new patron to the poor and, through the cult of the saints, established a lifelong patronage system that mirrored the benefits of secular patronage. The feast day of the patron saint became a focus for both religious devotion and amusement. Bishops started to provide communal feasts.[23] All this was an extremely popular development and Prudentius describes the crowds streaming out of Rome into the countryside to the shrine of Hippolytus: 'The love of their religion masses Latins and strangers together in one body ... The majestic city disgorges her Romans in a stream; with equal ardour patricians and the plebeian host are jumbled together, shoulder to shoulder, for the faith banishes distinctions of birth.'[24] Brown argues that the elite were not lapsing to pressure from below by providing such attractions, nor were they absorbing leaderless masses by offering watered-down superstition. He suggests:

> We must also redefine 'popular'. Let me suggest that we take seriously its late-Roman meaning: the ability of the few to mobilize the support of the many. We are in a world where the great are seldom presented in art without an admiring crowd. One of the most interesting features of late antiquity, indeed, is the capacity of its elites to strike roots that worked themselves downwards into deeper layers of the populace than

had apparently been true in the classical Roman Empire. So much of what we call the 'democratization of culture' in late antiquity is democratization from on top.[25]

By giving alms, the Church was establishing a claim to leadership among the people. But, while it is undoubtedly the case that the elite were the more active of the two sides, the people did have some influence in this process. The non-elite used their tried-and-tested methods of patron-management to encourage these new leaders in their almsgiving. By giving their enthusiastic support, the people did their part to establish a new moral economy at a time when the old system had broken down. Most wanted to be integrated into whatever new system of power relations was evolving in late Roman society, as it was one of the few methods they had of alleviating the material conditions of their life. As such, what the new religious leadership gave them was in some sense an articulation of popular desires. It was one side of an exchange of gifts where, in return for enthusiastic support, the Church sought to provide what the people wanted.

What the people most ardently desired was social concord and for power to be exercised in a clean and untainted way. Above all, they needed patrons that worked. Baynes notes that, 'One of the outstanding features of early Byzantine asceticism is its passion for social justice and its championship of the poor and oppressed.'[26] Saints and holy men became the protectors of the oppressed, local heroes whose importance can be seen in the fierce fighting that often broke out for control of their remains.[27] They personified Christian tenets in a way that was accessible to all. Their popularity rested on the fact that saints met many of the popular needs. The holy man's actions gained the force of charisma because they tapped in to the hidden agenda of the subordinate. They articulated the unarticulated desires of the people. They performed almost routine miracles: healing physical defects, exorcizing demons, calming storms, putting out fires, relieving droughts and helping in difficult tasks, all of which emphasized the practical benefits that this new leadership could bring. They also brought help in the difficult area of social relations: dealing with troublesome neighbours and officials, taking on the elite on the people's behalf. These holy men also embodied many of the popular virtues: protecting their rights and status jealously, often outwitting the powerful with their natural wit. Like the people, they distrusted distant authorities. Yet this was a conservative revolution. The holy man was less a resistance fighter than a plain-speaker who sought to hold the powerful to their own claims of good government. He set out to restore order, no more; not trying to change the system but just trying to get it to work.

This process did not only represent a Christianization of the popular but also a popularization of the Christian. The Christian message was shaped to conform more to popular tastes. This was a vitally important task because the Christian mission was to get out among the people and win them over as converts. In the event, Christianity was easily incorporated within the popular culture because it had originally grown from it. It was in many ways the elite who struggled with a religion that urged its members to 'sell all they have' and preached that a rich man had less chance of making it into heaven than a camel had of passing through the eye of a needle. The kingdom of heaven resembled the world-turned-upside-down of popular festivals, a world where the meek will inherit the earth and those who hunger and thirst for righteousness will be filled. Early Christian writings sometimes had images of inversion, such as apples growing in the sea and fish living in the trees.[28] Christianity also offered alternatives to the traditional round of festivals, where entertainment and piety were mixed in the same way as had been done for pagan holidays. Music and hymns sought to use popular songs to win over the people, although the heretic Arius seems to have been more skilful than most: he wrote popular theological ballads set to catchy tunes for use by sailors, millers and travellers.[29] The magic of miracles was often based on the typically lower-class sense, that of touch. Success was achieved not via contemplation but by physical contact. In the same way, relics became a tangible source of power. Augustine recorded almost seventy miracles in just two years at Hippo in North Africa,[30] and this almost profligate use of the miraculous was itself something that would always appeal to the popular taste for the sensational. Popular religion had always favoured the fabulous and the fantastic. Doctrine was also translated into material terms. The afterlife was represented as an extreme version of the people's physical fears and aspirations: their sin was weighed before a court, with the heaven and hell that awaited them a black-and-white, concrete expression of abundant food, hierarchy and order, or agonizing tortures and chaos. The re-use of old pagan sites merely added to the appeal of Christianity. Pope Gregory the Great, in 601 CE, advised bishop Augustine in England that 'the temples of the idols in that country should on no account be destroyed'. Instead they were to be converted into churches: 'since they have a custom of sacrificing many oxen to devils, let some other solemnity be substituted in its place'.[31]

The tales of the heroic deeds of martyrs and the miracles of saints aimed to appeal to the popular taste. To be sure, these tales were not written only for the people – they were written for all – but they incorporated many of the elements of popular entertainment to ensure that they had broad cross-social appeal. Texts such as these were read out loud on saints' days and at festivals, in part because 'It is the custom of peasants to venerate more zealously those of God's saints whose feats are read aloud to them.'[32] Their content is melodramatic and repetitive. Chronological and geographical details are treated casually, with the emphasis being on translating divine power into an impressive and awe-inspiring catalogue of the tangible benefits that conversion and faith could be expected to bring. The central tenets of the religion were personified into the heroes and villains themselves, so that the listeners could fully grasp the magnitude of God's power and indeed the demonic powers that could assail them at any time. Likewise, sermons were filled with easily assimilated stories and concrete examples taken from daily life. Simple and direct, not aiming at originality, this was a new literature aimed at a largely illiterate audience. The clergy, who increasingly came from the wealthier sections of society, used vernacular and widely shared views to make themselves understood by their non-elite flocks. The clergy therefore occupied a bi-cultural position, versed in elite culture but addressing the ordinary folk in an accessible, colloquial style, often using simple imagery in order to reach the illiterate. The vernacular of sermons circumvented illiteracy in the same way as did images and songs. Such cultural adaptation to the common people was necessary for the Church to achieve its mission. The result was that the clergy's desire to reach out to and connect with the people had the effect of narrowing the gap between the great and little traditions. It helped to reconnect the popular and elite cultures after a period when society had become more steeply stratified and power more concentrated into the hands of the few.

The cult of the saints came to mirror the secular system of patronage, but with a holy man providing protection through the course of life. Here were leaders who offered to act as honest go-betweens between the people and a dependable and just divine authority. It was everything the people had always wanted. That is not to say that holy men were always at one with the people. It was assumed that the people would need the guidance and leadership of the Church. Part of the role of the patron was to enforce correct theology where necessary. The holy man's persona of independent loner made it easier for him to maintain the necessary distance to fulfil that role. We should also remember that the *Lives* written about these saints were part of the new leadership's hard sell. Hagiographical texts present an idealized picture of this relationship between saints and their public. We would also do well to recall the distrust that the people generally had for those in authority and the scepticism they showed towards traditional religious practitioners. It was, after all, this very scepticism that forced the writers of the *Lives* to work so hard to promote their case. But, overall, the support of holy men brought benefits to the people. The change in power relations in the late empire had denied the non-elite of many of its traditional sources of patronage, and, by actively encouraging the new spiritual elite, the people managed to adopt new patrons who were well-attuned to their needs. The average person, the middling sort, 'had always shown impressive ingenuity in the search for some form of social "safety-net" against impoverishment', and now they worked it so that they got it from the Church.[33]

Once Christianity had become the dominant religion, the problems of dealing with the popular became more pressing. The attainment of the popularity the Church had fought so hard to establish for itself brought concerns that religious debate would degenerate into a dangerous free-for-all. Theological democracy was not a concept that sat easily with the hierarchical structure of ecclesiastical authority. The Church therefore attempted to control theology and orthodoxy. The emperor Marcian went so far as to try to ban public theological debate in 452 CE.[34] Holy men came to be seen as too great a power not to be assimilated into the organization of the Church. The accounts of the lives of these saints sought to reclaim their divine authority for the Church, emphasizing their orthodoxy and playing down their resistance to ecclesiastical control. It was portrayed as natural for the holy man to be the active and willing partner of orthodoxy. But the people continued to have a mind of their own about religious matters and refused simply to follow the bidding of their new Church leadership. The proliferation of what from the Church's view were heretical teachings and ideas show that no simple consensus was established. Many, for example, were persuaded by the heretical teachings of Arius. This was a development which left Church leaders at a loss to explain in religious terms. Gregory of Nyssa was unsure what this evil should be called, 'inflammation of the brain or madness, or some sort of epidemic disease which deranges reasoning'.[35] But the Church leadership's inability to comprehend a popular need for diversity of religious expression does not alter the fact that diverse religious ideas continued to flourish in the Christian world.

When a man gave St John the Almsgiver all the gold he possessed, some 7½ pounds in weight, in order to protect his son, his ship and its cargo, we can understand that he would have been less than happy when his son died and then all his goods were lost in a shipwreck off the lighthouse at Pharos. The *Life* is forced to account for such a failure on the part of the holy man, so it recounts how the man received, not a refund, but a vision in a dream that his son had in fact been saved, 'For had he lived he would have turned out a most pernicious and unclean fellow.'[36] Such failures show how hard Christian leaders had to work to win the people over and then keep them. There were always religious alternatives available, which offered to provide people with the practical help they needed, whether it was from magicians or soothsayers or pagan priests. The *Lives* do their best to emphasize the dangers of dabbling in the occult: one man, who hadn't waited for St Theodore's prayer, ran to a 'woman who used magic' and taking an amulet from her hung it on his sick brother with the result that he died immediately.[37] But, despite the Church's vigorous efforts, the people continued to use religious symbols eclectically – from magic, paganism and Christianity – picking and choosing according to what they thought worked best. Augustine complains how, 'When children suffer from a headache, wicked and faithless mothers have recourse to sacrilegious amulets and incantations.'[38] Given the deep-rooted belief in the power of magic to influence the supernatural, it was always going to be tough for Christianity to persuade most people that it held a monopoly on religious power. Other Christians resisted Church control by throwing raucous parties on the feast days of their patron saints. Bishop Caesarius of Arles complains that the locals were having sex on a Sunday.[39] We should also remember that the late empire was not just an age of Christian faith; many still prayed exclusively to the old pagan gods and were probably largely indifferent to this new Christian populism.

A description of religious life in the melting-pot that was the city of Alexandria, attributed to the emperor Hadrian in the early second century but probably written in the late fourth century, gives some idea of the eclecticism that could exist:

> The land of Egypt . . . I have found to be wholly light-minded, unstable, and blown about by every breath of rumour. Those who worship Serapis are, in fact, Christians, and those who call themselves bishops of Christ are, in fact, devotees of Serapis. There is no chief of the Jewish synagogue, no Samaritan, no Christian presbyter, who is not also an astrologer, a soothsayer, or an anointer. Even the Patriarch himself, when he comes to Egypt, is forced by some to worship Serapis, by others to worship Christ.[40]

What Hadrian saw as light-minded instability can also be seen as the people actively making up and changing their own minds as they saw fit, spreading their risk by consulting various religious sources, and pressuring even senior religious officials to accommodate their needs.

The later Roman Empire had seen power relations redefined in response to the third-century crisis. The imperial government had reorganized itself, and the popular culture could only react as best it could to this change in the structure of society. The crisis had exposed the old system as obsolete and robbed it of legitimacy. A new way was needed to rationalize the structure of Roman society and justify the emperors' claims to its leadership. The Christian Church provided some of this much-needed legitimacy. The intensification of the public performance of government was another way that the authorities got their message across loud and clear. The people largely consented to this settlement but it made elite ideology work hard to produce its desired legitimacy. And whatever new ideology was created, the popular culture always found ways to manipulate, debunk and resist it. The popular culture never simply reproduced the dominant ideology. The people actively selected from a range of cultural resources available to them to establish identities that suited their own social ends. It is probably impossible to say whether the non-elite's lot generally improved or worsened over the course of the empire, but, whatever social changes did take place, the people were always quick to respond: thinking on their feet, trying to keep sane, managing the powerful as best they could, defending their interests vigorously when necessary, all the time making the most of whatever hand luck had dealt them.

Notes

In the interests of accessibility I have used the most easily available translation where possible. If a text can be found with other similar documents of interest in one of the number of useful sourcebooks that are now available, I have quoted it from that source. I have included some of the key Latin terms and phrases in the notes for the more specialist reader. Teubner editions have been used unless otherwise stated.

Introduction: Elite and Popular Cultures

1 See Burke, P., *Popular Culture in Early Modern Europe*, Temple Smith, 1978, prologue. This remains the model study of historical popular culture. For a discussion of the theory of popular culture as it relates to the ancient world, see Toner, J. P., *Leisure and Ancient Rome*, Cambridge: Polity, 1995, pp. 65–7, and Meggitt, J. J., *Paul, Poverty and Survival*, Edinburgh: T&T Clark, 1998, pp. 12–18.
2 Tac. *Ann.* 14.42–5.
3 Horsfall argues that a 'nexus between theatre, song and memory was at the heart of popular culture', in *The Culture of the Roman Plebs*, Duckworth, 2003, p. 17. I would agree with the review of Goldberg, S. M., in *JRS* 94 (2004): 202–3, that H.'s work is 'under-theorized', but it is also a pleasure to read and is a mine of interesting and useful information. I suspect, if I may, that H. would be only too happy to be called 'under-theorized'.
4 Horsfall, ibid., has a useful appendix on the culture of the soldier, 'The Legionary as his own Historian', pp. 103–15.

5 Hoggart, R., *The Uses of Literacy: aspects of working class life*, Chatto and Windus, 1957.
6 All of these figures are no more than approximate estimates; see Scheidel, W., 'Demography', in W. Scheidel, I. Morris and R. Saller (eds), *The Cambridge Economic History of the Greco-Roman World*, Cambridge: Cambridge University Press, 2007, pp. 38–86; and Parkin, A. R., 'Poverty in the Early Roman Empire: ancient and modern conceptions and constructs', unpublished PhD dissertation, Cambridge University, 2001, summarized in Parkin, A. R., '"You do him no service": an exploration of pagan almsgiving', in M. Atkins and R. Osborne, *Poverty in the Roman World*, Cambridge: Cambridge University Press, 2006, pp. 60–82. In her thesis, P. notes, pp. 26–7, that there three types of poverty: structural or endemic, which includes most of the disabled, sick, maimed, widows and the elderly, who comprise 5–10 per cent of the population; conjectural or epidemic poverty includes those who are at subsistence level and so are highly vulnerable to any changes in income, and covers another 20 per cent; occasional episodic poverty covers those who are hit by events such as famine and accounts for another 40 per cent of the total population. The grand total of 70 per cent poor is obviously a maximum. As P. also discusses, poverty can be seen as both a relative and an absolute concept.
7 See Brown, P., *Power and Persuasion in Late Antiquity: towards a Christian empire*, Madison, Wisc.: University of Wisconsin Press, 1992.
8 See Kelly, C., *Ruling the Later Roman Empire*, Belknap, 2004, p. 31.
9 Val. Max. 2.6.17, *quidquid enim in excelso fastigio positum est, humili et trita consuetudine, quo sit venerabilius, vacuum esse convenit.*
10 Hopkins, K., *Conquerors and Slaves*, Cambridge: Cambridge University Press, 1978, p. 68, implies a figure of 42 per cent of the urban population being comprised of slaves in 28 BCE, which seems too high.
11 Herodian 7.6.4.
12 Wallace-Hadrill, A., *Rome's Cultural Revolution*, Cambridge: Cambridge University Press, 2008, p. 454.
13 Millar, F., 'The World of the Golden Ass', *JRS* 71 (1981): 63–75, p. 63.
14 For an overview of the available sources and how they relate to the ancient non-elite, see Meggitt, *Paul, Poverty and Survival*, pp. 18–39.
15 See, for example, Garnsey, P., *Food and Society in Classical Antiquity*, Cambridge: Cambridge University Press, 1999.
16 See Wallace-Hadrill, *Rome's Cultural Revolution*, pp. 315–55.

Chapter 1   Problem-solving

1 Purcell and Horden suggest that 'decision-making under uncertainty' characterizes the whole Mediterranean micro-ecology. See Horden, P., and Purcell, N., *The Corrupting Sea: a study of Mediterranean history*, Oxford: Blackwell, 2000, p. 522.

2   Brown, P., *Poverty and Leadership in the Later Roman Empire*, Hanover, NH: University Press of New England, 2002, p. 15.
3   Ibid., p. 14.
4   Gallant, T. W., *Risk and Survival in Ancient Greece: reconstructing the rural domestic economy*, Cambridge: Polity, 1991, p. ix.
5   Eidinow, E., *Oracles, Curses, and Risk among the Ancient Greeks*, Oxford: Oxford University Press, 2007, p. 5.
6   For the classic paper, see Markowitz, H. M., 'Portfolio Selection', *Journal of Finance* 7 (1952): 77–91.
7   *Aesop Romance* 59.
8   Tac. *Ann.* 3.54; see Kaster, R. A., *Emotion, Restraint, and Community in Ancient Rome*, Oxford: Oxford University Press, 2005, n.99 to p. 56.
9   See Wirszubski, C., '*Audaces*: a study in political phraseology', *JRS* 51 (1961): 12–22, pp. 17–18.
10   See Horden and Purcell, *The Corrupting Sea*, p. 152.
11   See Foster, G. M., 'Peasant Society and the Image of Limited Good', *American Anthropologist* 67 (1965): 293–315.
12   Eidinow, *Oracles, Curses, and Risk*, p. 7.
13   Easterlin, R. A., 'Does economic growth improve the human lot?', in P. A. David and M. W. Reder (eds), *Nations and Households in Economic Growth: essays in honor of Moses Abramovitz*, New York: Academic Press, 1974, pp. 89–125.
14   Aug. *In Psalm* 99.4, quoted in Getty, M. M., *The Life of the North Africans as Revealed in the Sermons of Saint Augustine*, Washington, DC: Catholic University of America, 1931, p. 3; cf. Aesop 13 for fishermen hauling in a net 'which was so heavy that they began to dance for joy', in Daly, L. W. (ed.), *Aesop without Morals: the famous fables and a life of Aesop*, New York: T. Yoseloff, 1961. All translations of the fables and the *Aesop Romance* are based on this text.
15   Famine appears to have been a fairly rare occurrence but food crises happened as often as perhaps every four years. See Garnsey, P., *Famine and Food Supply in the Graeco-Roman world: responses to risk and crisis*, Cambridge: Cambridge University Press, 1988, pp. 198–206. On famine foods, see Garnsey, *Food and Society in Classical Antiquity*, pp. 36–41.
16   Sen. *Contr.* 10.4.
17   Lucian *Dialogue of the Courtesans* 6.1.
18   Firm. Mat. 3.3.4. All translations are based on that of Bram, J. R., *Ancient Astrology, Theory and Practice: Matheseos Libri VIII by Firmicus Maternus*, Park Ridge, New Jersey: Noyes Press, 1975.
19   Aesop 53.
20   See esp. Parkin, *Poverty*, ch. 4.
21   *P. Oxy.* 1895, quoted in the excellent collection of Shelton, J., *As the Romans Did: a sourcebook in Roman social history*, Oxford: Oxford University Press, 1998, p. 30.
22   *P. Bour.* 25, quoted in ibid., p. 35.
23   Lucian *The Dream or Lucian's Career* 1.

24   *Dig.* 7.7.6.1 has children working by five. See Bradley, K., *Discovering the Roman Family: studies in Roman social history*, Oxford: Oxford University Press, 1991, pp. 114–16.
25   *CIL* 6.9213.
26   Aug. *Serm.* 32.25, quoted in Getty, *The Life of the North Africans*, p. 8.
27   Aug. *Serm.* 57.2.
28   *P. Oxy.* 744 quoted in Shelton, *As the Romans Did*, p. 28.
29   On exposure in general, see Boswell, J., *The Kindness of Strangers: the abandonment of children in Western Europe from late antiquity to the Renaissance*, Allen Lane, 1989.
30   Sen. *Contr.* 10.4.16.
31   Ibid., *omine infausto*; Dorotheus of Sidon *Carmen Astrologicum* 1.7.20, in Pingree, D. (ed.), *Dorothei Sidonii Carmen Astrologicum: interpretationem Arabicam in linguam Anglicam versam una cum Dorothei fragmentis et Graecis et Latinis*, Leipzig: Teubner, 1976. Dorotheus wrote in the first century CE, but his text survives from an eighth-century Arabic translation of a sixth-century Middle Persian translation, so the text is not without its problems. See Pingree for discussion (in Latin) and critical apparatus.
32   Firm. Mat. 7.2.10.
33   Ibid., 7.2.22.
34   Ibid., 8.16.2.
35   Ibid., 7.2 on charts of exposed infants: 7.2.9, 11, 12, 13, 20, 21 are all 'devoured by dogs'.
36   Musonius Rufus *Reliquiae* 15B.
37   *Philogelos* 24. in Baldwin, B., *The Philogelos or Laughter-lover*, Amsterdam: J. C. Gieben, 1983. All translations are based on this text.
38   Art. 2.68.
39   Plin. *Ep.* 7.22 *amat studia ut solent pauperes*.
40   Aug. *Serm.* 38.6, in Getty, *The Life of the North Africans*, p. 13.
41   For the central role that work played in creating non-elite personal identity, see Joshel, S. R., *Work, Identity, and Legal Status at Rome: a study of the occupational inscriptions*, Norman, OK: University of Oklahoma Press, 1992.
42   Lucian *Fugitives* 12–13.
43   Aesop 97 and 116.
44   SHA *Firm., Sat., Proc. & Bon.* 8 Loeb translation with minor changes.
45   For subsistence wheat equivalent figures, see Hopkins, *Conquerors and Slaves*, p. 56 n.79. Note that the modius in the Edict is the military modius, which equates to about 10 kg. The standard modius was smaller at about 6.5 kg.
46   On the corn dole of 5 standard modii per month, see Duncan-Jones, R., *The Economy of the Roman Empire: quantitative studies*, Cambridge: Cambridge University Press, 1982, p. 146. For an interesting attempt to compare the standard of living of labourers in the Roman empire with that of labourers in Europe and Asia in the Middle Ages and early modern period, see Allen, R. C., 'How prosperous were the

Romans? Evidence from Diocletian's Price Edict (301 AD)', Oxford: Oxford University Department of Economics, *Working Paper Number 363*, 2007. For an attempt to apply this to Roman Egypt, see Scheidel, W., 'Real wages in Roman Egypt: a contribution to recent work on pre-modern living standards', *Princeton/Stanford Working Papers in Classics*, 2008 .

47 For an introduction to Roman mortality tables, see Kelly, C., *The Roman Empire: a very short introduction*, Oxford: Oxford University Press, 2006, pp. 102–9.

48 *CIL* 3.3572, quoted in Shelton, *As the Romans Did*, p. 290, with minor changes.

49 Treggiari, S., 'Lower Class Women in the Roman Economy', *Florilegium* 1 (1979): 65–86.

50 *Ant. Fluch.* V, quoted in Kraemer, R. S. (ed.), *Maenads, Martyrs, Matrons, Monastics: a sourcebook on women's religions in the Greco-Roman world*, Philadelphia, PA: Fortress, 1988, p. 108.

51 Aesop 228.

52 Ibid., 40.

53 Juv. 3.254.

54 See Combet-Farnoux, B., *Mercure romain: le culte public de Mercure et la fonction mercantile à Rome, de la République archaïque à l'époque augustéenne*, Rome: École française de Rome, 1980, pp. 79–80.

55 Cic. *de Off.* 1.150.

56 *Or.* 1.109 and 42.24–5, quoted in Kelly, *Ruling the Later Roman Empire*, pp. 165–6.

57 Juv. 14.200–5 *pares quod uendere possis pluris dimidio, nec te fastidia mercis ullius subeant ablegandae Tiberim ultra, neu credas ponendum aliquid discriminis inter unguenta et corium: lucri bonus est odor ex re qualibet.*

58 Hopkins, *Conquerors and Slaves*, p. 22.

59 Greg. Nyss. *Against Usury*, in *Gregorii Nysseri Opera* 9.195–207 (= *PG* 46.433–52), with discussion and translation in McCambley, C., 'Against those who practise usury by Gregory of Nyssa', *Greek Orthodox Theological Review* 36 (1991): 287–302, with minor changes; this quote at pp. 300–1.

60 *CTh* 13.1.18 *crescentis in dies singulos pecuniae accessione laetantur.*

61 *Dig.* 13.4.3 pr. *pecuniarum quoque licet videatur una et eadem potestas ubique esse, tamem aliis locis facilius et levibus usuris inveniuntur, aliis difficilius et gravibus usuris.*

62 Still the best account of ancient interest rates is Billeter, G., *Geschichte des Zinsfusses im griechisch-römischen Altertum bis auf Justinian*, Leipzig: Teubner, 1898. A more accessible overview can be found in Homer, S., and Sylla, R., *A History of Interest Rates*, New Brunswick, NJ: Rutgers University Press, 1991. For 12 per cent as the 'routine in the majority of debt agreements', see Holman, S. R., '"You speculate on the misery of the poor": usury as civic injustice in Basil of Caesarea's second homily on Psalm 14', in Hopwood, K. (ed.), *Organised Crime in Antiquity*, Duckworth, 1999, pp. 207–28, n.4 to p. 208; on the

calculation of Roman interest, see Horsfall, *The Culture of the Roman Plebs*, pp. 12, 18–19.

63   Cic., *Att.* 5.21.12; *P. Tebt.* 110.

64   MacMullen, R., *Roman Social Relations, 50 B.C. to A.D. 284*, New Haven, CT: Yale University Press, 1974, p. 52.

65   *CTh* 2.33.1.

66   *P. Lond.* 1915 Loeb translation with minor changes, quoted in Holman, 'You speculate on the misery of the poor', p. 207.

67   Pub. Syr. 585 *qui debet limen creditoris non amat.*

68   Basil of Caesarea *Homily 2 on Psalm 14*. See Holman, 'You speculate on the misery of the poor', p. 214.

69   Aesop 171.

70   Chaniotis, A., 'Illness and cures in the Greek propitiatory inscriptions and dedications of Lydia and Phrygia', in P. J. van der Eijk, H. F. J. Horstmanshoff and P. H. Schrijvers (eds), *Ancient Medicine in its Sociocultural Context*, 2 vols, Amsterdam: Rodopi, 1995, pp. 323–44, p. 325.

71   Greg. Nyss., ibid.

72   Ibid.

73   Josephus *BJ* 2.425–7; on tax remissions, see Duncan-Jones, R., *Money and Government in the Roman Empire*, Cambridge: Cambridge University Press, 1994, pp. 59–61.

74   *P. Tebt.* 2.331 salt is conjecture.

75   Art. 4.70.

76   Quoted by Versnel, in 'Punish those who rejoice in our misery: on curse tablets and Schadenfreude', in D. R. Jordan, H. Montgomery and E. Thomassen (eds), *The World of Ancient Magic*, Bergen: Norwegian Institute at Athens, 1999, pp. 125–62, p. 128.

77   *Aesop Romance* 28.

78   For the 'highly localized', self-help justice in Apuleius's Metamorphoses, see Millar, 'The world of the Golden Ass', pp. 71–2.

79   *CIL* 4.4993, 4.10231 and 4.5251.

80   See MacMullen, *Roman Social Relations*, n.30 to p. 66, for references to various stonings.

81   Bücheler, F. (ed.), *Carmina Latina Epigraphica*, Leipzig: Teubner, 1895–7, no. 95, quoted in Abbott, F. F., *The Common People of Ancient Rome: studies of Roman life and literature*, Routledge, 1912, p. 87.

82   Apul. *Met.* 2.27.

83   Pet. *Sat.* 45.

84   Alciphron *Ep.* 2.3, quoted at Shaw, B., 'Our daily bread', *Social History of Medicine* 2 (1989): 205–13, p. 205, with minor changes.

85   *Querolus* 74, quoted in Mathisen, R. W., *People, Personal Expression, and Social Relations in Late Antiquity*, 2 vols, Ann Arbor, MI: University of Michigan Press, 2003, vol. 1, pp. 62–4, with minor changes. *illud autem nostrae felicitatis caput, quod zelotypi non sumus. furta omnes facimus, fraudem tamen nemo patitur, quoniam totum hoc mutuum est. dominos autem observamus atque excludimus, nam inter servos et ancillas una coniugatio est.*

86   Aesop 103.

87   *CIL* 4.3948.
88   Aug. *Serm.* 302.16; *In Psalm* 61.16, in Getty, *The Life of the North Africans*, p. 14.
89   Aesop 166.
90   Mart. 1.11 and 26.
91   Ibid., 12.57; cf. Philostr. *VA* 4.10.
92   *Life of St Daniel the Stylite* 89.
93   Aug. *Serm.* 41.7, in Getty, *The Life of the North Africans*, p. 95.
94   Doroth. Sidon. *Carmen Astrolog.* 5.35.76–8.
95   Ibid., 5.35.103.
96   Ibid., 5.35.136–7.
97   *Philogelos* 108; cf. 106.
98   *CTh* 7.13.10.
99   *TAMV.* 1.509, quoted in Chaniotis, 'Illness and cures in the Greek propitiatory inscriptions', p. 325.
100   On gambling, see Toner, *Leisure and Ancient Rome*, pp. 89–101. Also, the man who had the misfortune to be one of my PhD examiners, Purcell, N., 'Literate games: Roman urban society and the game of alea', *Past & Present* 147 (1995): 3–37.
101   *Dig.* 11.5.
102   Amm. Marc. 14.6.25–6.
103   *PGM* 7.423–8, in Betz, H. D. (ed.), *The Greek Magical Papyri in Translation, including the Demotic Spells*, Chicago, IL: University of Chicago Press, 1992. All translations of the magical papyri are based on this text.
104   Firm. Mat. 8.25.3 'will become famous players at dice'.
105   Amm. Marc. 28.4.21.
106   *CIL* 4.429.
107   Bücheler, *Carmina Latina Epigraphica*, no. 53 *pudentis hominis frugi cum magna fide*.
108   Ibid., 765 *castitas fides caritas pietas obsequium*.
109   Cic. *de Off.* 1.150 *qui in odia hominum incurrunt, ut portitorum, ut faeneratorum*.
110   Salv. *de Gub. Dei* 5.18 *quot curiales tot tyranni*.
111   Dio 54.21.
112   Luke 12:58–9; cf. Matt. 5:25–6.
113   Aesop 438.
114   Ibid., 378.
115   Babrius 67.
116   Apul. *Met.* 9.35 *verecundia*.
117   Firm. Mat. 2.10.5.
118   Levinson, S. C., and Brown, P., *Politeness: some universals in language usage*, Cambridge: Cambridge University Press, 1987, p. 186; on deference among elite Romans, see Lendon, J. E., *Empire of Honour: the art of government in the Roman world*, Oxford: Clarendon Press, 1997, pp. 58–63.
119   Tac. *Ann.* 1.7.1; on the need to present social faces in Roman literature, see Oliensis, E., *Horace and the Rhetoric of Authority*, Cambridge: Cambridge University Press, 1998.

120   Lucian *Timon the Misanthrope* 5, in Costa, C. D. N., *Lucian: selected dialogues*, Oxford: Oxford University Press, 2005.
121   Art. 5.38.
122   *Aesop Romance* 47.
123   Dio 72.32.1.
124   Parkin, *Poverty*, p. 119.
125   Sen. *de Const. Sap.* 13 *non placebit sibi, si illum mendicus coluerit.*
126   Art. 4.14.
127   Tac. *Ann.* 6.13; 12.43.
128   Cic. *Cat.* 4.17.
129   For the best recent coverage of this contentious topic, see Mouritsen, H., *Plebs and Politics in the Late Roman Republic*, Cambridge: Cambridge University Press, 2001. Millar argues for a more positive contribution in *The Crowd in Rome in the Late Republic*, Ann Arbor, MI: University of Michigan Press, 1998. Either way, the rights finally went in 14 CE.
130   Julian *Misopogon* 368C.
131   Thompson, E. P., 'The moral economy of the English crowd in the eighteenth century', *Past & Present* 50 (1971): 76–136.
132   Cameron, A., *Circus Factions: blues and greens at Rome and Byzantium*, Oxford: Clarendon Press, 1976, pp. 170–92; quote at p. 175.
133   Amm. Marc. 15.7.2–3 *prima igitur causa seditionis in eum concitandae vilissima fuit et levis.*
134   Philostr. *VA* 1.16.4.
135   On the theory of proverbs, see Obelkevich, J., 'Proverbs and social history', in P. Burke and R. Porter (eds), *The Social History of Language*, Cambridge: Cambridge University Press, 1987, pp. 43–72; for an impressively thorough analysis of the Roman tradition, see Morgan, T., *Popular Morality in the Early Roman Empire*, Cambridge: Cambridge University Press, 2007.
136   Cic. *de Off.* 1.97; *Tusc.* 1.37; Sen. *Ep. Mor.* 108.8–9.
137   Morgan, *Popular Morality*, p. 51.
138   Ibid., p. 82.
139   Ibid., p.14.
140   Veyne, P, 'La "plèbe moyenne" sous le Haut-Empire romain', *Annales (ESC)* 6 (2000): 1169–99.
141   Eidinow, *Oracles*, p. 6.
142   *CTh* 9.16.1–2.
143   Art. 2.69.
144   Gell. 9.4 *tenuit nos non idoneae scripturae taedium nihil ad ornandum iuvandumque usum vitae pertinentis.*
145   Apul. *Apol.* 56; Minuc. Felix *Oct.* 2.4 *ut vulgus superstitiosus solet.*
146   Plin. *NH* 28.28.
147   Maximus of Tyre *Diss.* 26.
148   Rüpke, R., *Religion of the Romans*, trans. R. Gordon, Cambridge: Polity, 2007, pp. 154–73.
149   See Green, C. M. C., *Roman Religion and the Cult of Diana at Aricia*, Cambridge: Cambridge University Press, 2007.

150   Betz, *The Greek Magical Papyri*, p. xlvii.
151   Lucian *Lover of Lies or The Sceptic* 7, in Costa, *Lucian.*
152   Ps.-Callisthenes *Alexander Romance* 12.
153   Liban. *Or.* 1.249.
154   Eidinow, *Oracles, Curses, and Risk*, p. 231.
155   Betz, *Greek Magical Papyri*, p. xlviii.
156   Yavetz, Z., *Plebs and Princeps*, Oxford: Clarendon Press, 1969, p. 134.
157   Lucian *False Prophet* 12.
158   Paul. Aegin. Appendix to Book 5, *On Feigned Diseases and their Detection.*
159   Aesop 56 and 161.
160   Art. 5.94.
161   *Philogelos* 187 and 201; cf. 202.
162   Aesop 170.
163   Pet. *Sat.* 43 *numquam autem recte faciet, qui cito credit, utique homo negotians.*
164   Tert. *Apol.* 40.1–2.
165   Bücheler, *Carmina Latina Epigraphica*, no. 225.
166   Ibid., no. 1495.
167   Ibid., nos 856 and 143.
168   See Rüpke, *Religion of the Romans*, pp. 84–5.
169   Pet. *Sat.* 71; see Clarke, J. R., *Art in the Lives of Ordinary Romans: visual representation and non-elite viewers in Italy, 100 B.C. – A.D. 315*, Berkeley, CA: University of California Press, 2003, pp. 185–7.
170   The dice oracle and alphabet oracle can be found in Horsley, G. H. R., and Mitchell, S. (eds), *The Inscriptions of Central Pisidia*, Bonn: Habelt, 2000; pp. 22–38 for the dice oracle; pp. 161–4 for the alphabet oracle. See also Graf, F., 'Rolling the dice for an answer', in Johnston, S. I., and Struck, P. T. (eds), *Mantikê: studies in ancient divination*, Leiden: Brill, 2005, pp. 51–97.
171   Dodds, E. R., *Pagan and Christian in an Age of Anxiety: some aspects of religious experience from Marcus Aurelius to Constantine*, Cambridge: Cambridge University Press, 1965, p. 57.
172   Corsten, T., 'Ein neues Buchstabenorakel aus Kibyra', *Epigraphica Anatolica* 28 (1997): 41–9.
173   To be more exact, it would have been possible to probability weight the outcomes as astragals have unequal probabilities of landing on each side (see n.22 to p. 91 of my *Leisure and Ancient Rome*), but this is not an exact science and it will not make much difference as the favourable and unfavourable responses are fairly evenly spread.
174   The oracles can be found in translation in the excellent collection Hansen, *Anthology of Ancient Greek Popular Literature*. See also Klingshirn, W., 'The *Sortes Sangallenses*', in Johnston and Struck, *Mantikê*, pp. 99–128; and Hoogendijk, F. A. J., and Clarysse, W., 'De Sortes van Astrampsychus: een orakelboek uit de oudheid bewerkt voor het middelbaar onderwijs', *Kleio* 11 (1981): 53–99.
175   Hansen, *Anthology of Ancient Greek Popular Literature*, p. 289.

176 Klingshirn, '*Sortes Sangallenses*', p. 112.
177 Tac. *Hist.* 1.4.
178 Hansen, *Anthology of Ancient Greek Popular Literature*, p. 288.
179 See Kelly, *The Roman Empire*, p. 105.
180 *CIL* 11.600 quoted in MacMullen, *Roman Social Relations*, p. 44, with minor alterations to his free translation.
181 Lucian *Timon the Misanthrope* 29.
182 Aesop 466.

Chapter 2 Mental Health

1 I want to thank Justin Meggitt for giving me the idea for this chapter by talking me through his article 'The madness of King Jesus: why was Jesus put to death, but his followers were not?', *Journal for the Study of the New Testament* 29 (2007): 379–413.
2 Dodds, *Pagan and Christian*, p. 36. 'Anxiety is hopelessly vague', according to R. Lane Fox in *JRS* 76 (1986): 304–5, where he reviews Smith, R. C., and Lounibos, J. (eds), *Pagan and Christian Anxiety: a response to E. R. Dodds*, University Press of America, 1984. See also Brown, P., *Religion and Society in the Age of Saint Augustine*, Faber and Faber, 1972, pp. 74–93.
3 The *Diagnostic and Statistical Manual of Mental Disorders*, 4th edn, Washington, DC: American Psychiatric Association, 1994. There is also a later text-revised (TR) edition, which has an updated bibliography. A new edition is expected in 2012. Ch. 5 of ICD-10, the *International Statistical Classification of Diseases and Related Health Problems*, 3 vols, Geneva: World Health Organisation, 1992–4, also covers mental illness but in far less detail.
4 Aneshensel, C. S., and Phelan, J. C. (eds), *Handbook of the Sociology of Mental Health*, Kluwer Academic, 1999, pp. 25, 132–3. On the UK, see Goldberg, D., and Huxley, P., *Common Mental Disorders: a bio-social model*, Routledge, 1992.
5 See Foucault, M., *Madness and Civilization: a history of insanity in the Age of Reason*, trans. R. Howard, Routledge, 1971; Laing, R. D., *The Divided Self: an existential study in sanity and madness*, Harmondsworth: Penguin, 1977; and Szasz, T. S., *The Myth of Mental Illness: foundations of a theory of personal conduct*, Paladin, 1972. For a spirited counter-argument, see Roth, M., and Kroll, J., *The Reality of Mental Illness*, Cambridge: Cambridge University Press, 1986.
6 See Cockerham, W. C., *Sociology of Mental Disorder*, Prentice Hall, 2000, p. 2.
7 Aneshensel and Phelan, *Handbook of the Sociology of Mental Health*, p. xi.
8 See Rogler, L. H., 'Making sense of historical changes in the Diagnostic and Statistical Manual of Mental Disorders: five propositions', *Journal of Health and Social Behavior* 38 (1997): 9–20.

9 Aneshensel and Phelan, *Handbook of the Sociology of Mental Health*, p. 23; Karem. E. G., et al., 'Lifetime prevalence of mental disorder in Lebanon: first onset, treatment, and exposure to war', *PLoS Medicine* 5 (2008); Lee, S., et al., 'Lifetime prevalence and inter-cohort variation in DSM–IV disorders in metropolitan China', *Psychological Medicine* 37 (2007): 61–71.

10 See Kirk, S. A., and Kutchins, H., *The Selling of DSM: the rhetoric of science in psychiatry*, New York: de Gruyter, 1992.

11 As noted by Cockerham, *Sociology of Mental Disorder*, p. 30.

12 Aneshensel and Phelan, *Handbook of the Sociology of Mental Health*, p. 151.

13 Ibid., p. 128.

14 Ibid., p. 146–50 for bibliography.

15 Scheper-Hughes, N., *Saints, Scholars, and Schizophrenics: mental illness in rural Ireland*, University of California Press, 2001.

16 Cockerham, *Sociology of Mental Disorder*, p. 136.

17 DSM IV, p. xxi.

18 Brown, P., *The Body and Society: men, women, and sexual renunciation in early Christianity*, Faber and Faber, 1990, p. 6.

19 Scheper-Hughes, N., *Death without Weeping: the violence of everyday life in Brazil*, Berkeley, CA: University of California Press, 1992.

20 Paulus *Opinions* 1.21.8–14, quoted in Shelton, *As the Romans Did*, p. 94.

21 Firm. Mat. 6.29.6 *obstinato matris animo nata soboles exponitur*.

22 Sen. *Contr.* 10.4.20.

23 *Life of St Theodore of Sykeon* 25.

24 As noted by van Hooff, A. J. L., *From Autothanasia to Suicide: self-killing in classical antiquity*, Routledge, 1990, p. 155, with this translation, slightly adapted, of *Papiri della Società Italiana* 3.177.

25 *Philogelos* 77.

26 Keay, S., 'Tarraco in late antiquity', in N. Christie and S. T. Loseby (eds), *Towns in Transition: urban evolution in late antiquity and the early Middle Ages*, Aldershot: Scolar, 1996, pp. 18–44, p. 32.

27 Firm. Mat. 3.2.5; cf. 4.15.7.

28 On the differences between peasant and elite bodies, see Volpe, G. (ed.), *San Giusto: la villa, le ecclesiae*, Bari: Edipuglia, 1998, pp. 234–6.

29 See Garnsey, *Food and Society*, p. 2.

30 Synesius *Ep.* 16.

31 Firm. Mat. 4.8.1.

32 Doroth. Sidon. *Carmen Astrolog.* 2.16.21.

33 Firm. Mat. 3.3.16.

34 Doroth. Sidon. *Carmen Astrolog.* 2.15.23 and 2.16.20.

35 Firm. Mat. 8.11.4.

36 Val. Max. 4.4.8 eulogizing the Aelian family of old.

37 Aneshensel and Phelan, *Handbook of the Sociology of Mental Health*, provides an excellent overview and bibliography of all these issues.

38 Hopkins, *Conquerors and Slaves*, p. 30.

39 *CTh* 7.13.4–5.

40   Procop. *History of the Wars* 6.20.18–33.
41   Epict. *Diss*. 4.1.79.
42   *CIL* 8.10570 and 14464.
43   Sen. *Ep*. 14.6.
44   Mark 5:1–13; cf. Luke 8:26–36.
45   My thanks go to Justin Meggitt for pointing this out to me.
46   Liban. *Or*. 1.9 and 1.77.
47   Ibid., 1.118.
48   See van Hooff, *From Autothanasia to Suicide*, p. 28.
49   Quint. *Inst*. 4.2.69 *ingenuum stupravit et stupratus se suspendit*.
50   See van Hooff, *From Autothanasia to Suicide*, p. 118.
51   Art. 5.63.
52   Ovid *Am*. 2.14.
53   Lendon, J. E., 'Social control at Rome', *Classical Journal* 93 (1997): 83–8, p. 86.
54   See Lelis, A. A., Percy, W. A., and Verstraete, B. C., *The Age of Marriage in Ancient Rome*, Lampeter: Edwin Mellen, 2003.
55   *Anthologia Palatina* 9.245; Plut. *Comparison of Lycurgus and Numa* 4.1, quoted in Brown, *Body and Society*, p. 14.
56   Art. 2.53.
57   *Anthologia Palatina* 5.297.
58   Aug. *Conf*. 9.9.
59   Art. 2.48.
60   Firm. Mat. 6.29.17.
61   Art. 1.78.
62   Plut. *Mor*. 140A quoted in Shelton, *As the Romans Did*, p. 44.
63   Aug. *Conf*. 9.9.
64   On women's emotional work, see Richlin, A., 'Emotional work: lamenting the Roman dead', in E. Tylawsky and C. Weiss (eds), *Essays in Honor of Gordon Williams: twenty-five years at Yale*, New Haven, CT: H. R. Schwab, 2001, pp. 229–48; and for a modern comparative analysis of flight attendants and bill collectors, see Hochschild, A. R., *The Managed Heart: commercialization of human feeling*, Berkeley, CA: University of California Press, 2003.
65   Synesius *Ep*. 132.
66   van Hooff, *From Autothanasia to Suicide*, p. 45.
67   *Philogelos* 200.
68   Sen. *Contr*. 10.4.
69   Art. 3.26.
70   *Aesop Romance* 37.
71   Aesop 119.
72   For figures, see Scheidel, 'Demography', who suggests a possible range of 15–25 per cent. Hopkins, *Conquerors and Slaves*, p. 68, gives a higher figure of a third.
73   Bradley, K. R., 'Animalizing the slave: the truth of fiction', *JRS* 90 (2000): 110–25.
74   Varro *de Ag*. 1.17.1 *instrumenti genus vocale*.
75   Diod. Sic. 5.38.1.

76   *AE* 1971, 88, quoted in Bodel, J. (ed.), *Epigraphic Evidence: ancient history from inscriptions*, Routledge, 2001, p. 111.
77   Art. 1.70.
78   Sen. *de Ira* 3.24 and 32.
79   Galen K5.17–18, in Singer, P. N., *Galen: selected works*, Oxford: Oxford University Press, 1997, pp. 107–8.
80   Firm. Mat. 3.11.8.
81   Plin. *Ep.* 3.14 *non enim iudicio domini sed scelere perimuntur.*
82   Plin. *NH* 28.36 *levatur ilico in percusso culpa.*
83   Art. 1.78.
84   Pet. *Sat.* 57 on her what is not quite clear, even if the sense is.
85   Ibid., 75.
86   For example, Juv. 10.216.
87   Galen K8.226.
88   *Philogelos* 122.
89   Pet. *Sat.* 103; see Jones, C. P., 'Stigma: tattooing and branding in Graeco-Roman antiquity', *JRS* 77 (1987): 139–55.
90   Doroth. Sidon. *Carmen Astrolog.* 5.36.
91   Salv. *de Gub. Dei* 4.3.15.
92   Col. *de Ag.* 1.8.19.
93   Aesop 202 moral.
94   Cato *de Ag.* 2.7 *servum senem, servum morbosum, et si quid aliud supersit, vendat.*
95   Suet. *Cl.* 25.
96   Sen. *de Ira* 3.29.
97   Art. 3.28.
98   Varro *de Ag.* 1.17.3–5.
99   Sen. *de Tranq. An.* 8.8 *et flentium detestantiumque ministeriis utendum.*
100   *Dig.* 21.1.23.3; 21.1.1.1.
101   Doroth. Sidon. *Carmen Astrolog.* 5.36.46.
102   Gell. 5.14.7; see Bradley, *Slavery and Society*, p. 108.
103   Art. 2.3.
104   Sen. *Ep. Mor.* 80.4 *peculium suum, quod conparaverunt ventre fraudato, pro capite numerant.*
105   Bodel, *Epigraphic Evidence*, p. 111.
106   Lucian *Timon the Misanthrope* 23.
107   See n.89 above.
108   Galen K8.190.
109   Alexander of Tralles *Twelve Books on Medicine*, ed. T. Puschmann, 2 vols, 1878, vol.1, pp. 605 and 607.
110   Cels. *de Med.* 3.18.10.
111   Hor. *Ep.* 2.2.128–40.
112   Luke 8:26–9.
113   Art. 1.76.
114   Aretaeus *On the Causes and Symptoms of Chronic Diseases* 1.6.
115   Plin. *NH* 28.36; Plaut. *Capt.* 547–55; cf. Apul. *Apol.* 44 where an epileptic slave is spat at, prevented from eating with others, and sent away lest he contaminate the family.

116 Plin. *NH* 28.25.
117 Plaut. *Poen.* 527.
118 Art. 1.76; Hor. *Ars* 455–6; Cic. *Verr.* 2.4.148; Pet. *Sat.* 92.
119 Lib. 1.235.
120 Art. 3.42.
121 Matt. 8:28.
122 Firm. Mat. 8.6.7.
123 See Parkin, T. G., *Old Age in the Roman World: a cultural and social history*, Johns Hopkins University Press, 2002, p. 281, for mortality tables. P. quotes M. I. Finley, 'I can find hardly any reference specific to mental illness in old age, and then only of the most casual kind', p. 228. Some awareness of dementia did exist, e.g., Juv 10.232: 'dementia is worse than all physical ills'; see pp. 228–30. Caelius Aurelianus *On Chronic Diseases* 1.6.181 notes that 'melancholy is more characteristic of middle age', whereas (1.5.146) mania occurs rarely in old men.
124 Chadwick, H., in G. W. Bowersock, P. Brown and O. Grabar (eds), *Interpreting Late Antiquity: essays on the postclassical world*, Belknap, 2001, p. 61.
125 Firm. Mat. 3.4.11.
126 Ibid., 8.17.9–10.
127 Galen K1.325–6.
128 Cael. Aurel. *On Chronic Diseases* 1.5.146.
129 Ibid. 1.4.116–19.
130 Galen K14.632.
131 Cels. *de Med.* 3.18.21 Loeb translation; cf. *Dig.* 1.18.14 which says that someone insane is to be restrained with chains for their own safety.
132 Cael. Aurel. *On Acute Diseases* 1.9.58.
133 Cael. Aurel. *On Chronic Diseases* 4.9.131–7.
134 Aristides *Sacred Tales* 1.65.
135 *Philogelos* 184.
136 Firm. Mat. 4.14.15.
137 Art. 3.42.
138 On the variety of responses to possession in the early Byzantine era, see Horden, P., 'Responses to possession and insanity in the earlier Byzantine world', *Social History of Medicine* 6 (1993): 177–94. Also Grey, C., 'Demoniacs, dissent, and disempowerment in the late Roman West: some case studies from the hagiographical literature', *Journal of Early Christian Studies* 13 (2005): 39–69.
139 *Life of St Theodore of Sykeon* 143.
140 Ibid., 114.
141 See Hansen, *Anthology of Ancient Greek Popular Literature*, pp. 42–3.
142 *Life of St Theodore of Sykeon* 106.
143 Art. 3.8.
144 *Life of St Theodore of Sykeon* 43, 123, 8; Athanasius *Life of St Anthony* 9 and 24.
145 Ibid., 36.

146   *PGM* 4.1227–64.
147   Quoted in Gager, J. G. (ed.), *Curse Tablets and Binding Spells from the Ancient World*, Oxford: Oxford University Press, 1992, pp. 234 and 236, with slight alterations.
148   *PDM* 14.1182–7.
149   Quoted in Gager, *Curse Tablets and Binding Spells*, pp. 203–4.
150   Ibid., p. 116.
151   *TAMV*. 1.460, quoted in Chaniotis, 'Illness and cures', p. 328.
152   Firm. Mat. 3.7.10.
153   Cael. Aurel. *On Acute Diseases* 1.3.35.
154   Cael. Aurel. *On Chronic Diseases* 4.9.131.
155   Art. 3.42.
156   Lucian *Peregrinus* 11–14, 18.
157   See Meggitt, 'The madness of King Jesus'.
158   Plato *Phaedrus* 265, 244.
159   Aretaeus *On the Symptoms of Chronic Diseases* 1.6.
160   *PGM* 7.260–71.
161   Soranus, *Gyn.* 3.26.
162   Galen K8.420.
163   *In Ep.* 1 *ad Cor.* 21.5–6 (= *PG* 61.177–8).
164   Aug. *Serm.* 344.5, in Getty, *The Life of the North Africans*, p. 25.
165   Aretaeus *On the Symptoms of Chronic Diseases* 1.6.
166   Brown, P., *The Making of Late Antiquity*, Cambridge, MA: Harvard University Press, p. 5.
167   Ibid., p. 82.
168   Brown, *The Body and Society*.
169   Brown, *The Making of Late Antiquity*, pp. 94 and 89.
170   *Acts* 19:13–16.
171   See Brown, P., *The Cult of the Saints: its rise and function in Latin Christianity*, SCM Press, 1981.
172   See Ibid. p. 111.

Chapter 3   The World Turned Bottom Up

1   Lucian *Sat.* 2.
2   Sen. *Ep.* 18.3.
3   On carnival, see Bakhtin, M. M., *Rabelais and his World*, trans. H. Iswolsky, Bloomington, IN: Indiana University Press, 1984.
4   Sen. *Ep.* 18.1 *cum maxime civitas sudat*.
5   Aug. *Serm.* 198.1, in Getty, *The Life of the North Africans*, p. 52.
6   Plin. *Ep.* 2.17.24.
7   Mart. 14.1.
8   Art. 1.76.
9   Pet. *Sat.* 44 *nam isti maiores maxillae semper Saturnalia agunt*.
10   Tac. *Ann.* 13.15; Epict. *Diss.* 1.25.8; Lucian *Sat.* 4.

11 Var. *de Ling. Lat.* 6.18; Plut. *Rom.* 29, *Camil.* 33; Macr. *Sat,* 1.11.36–40.
12 Ovid *Fast.* 3.675f.
13 *PG* 48.957, quoted in Gleason, M. W., 'Festive satire: Julian's *Misopogon* and the New Year at Antioch', *JRS* 76 (1986): 106–19, p. 110.
14 Liban. *Or.* 9.5–6.
15 Dion. Halic. 7.72.10–11.
16 *Hom. de Pythonibus et Maleficiis, PL* 65.27, quoted in in Gleason, 'Festive satire', p. 110.
17 Dio 50.10.2.
18 *CIL* 4.575 and 4.576.
19 *CIL* 4.581.
20 See Clarke, J. R., *Looking at Laughter: humor, power, and transgression in Roman visual culture, 100 B.C.–A.D. 250*, Berkeley, CA: University of California Press, 2007, pp. 125–32.
21 Plut. *De San. Praec.* 16.
22 Philostr. *VA* 4.20.1.
23 Aesop 409.
24 Macr. *Sat.* 2.4.8; 2.6.4.
25 Lucian *Demonax* 46.
26 Aesop 358 moral.
27 See Versnel, H. S., 'Punish those who rejoice in our misery: on curse tablets and Schadenfreude', in D. R. Jordan, H. Montgomery and E. Thomassen (eds)., *The World of Ancient Magic*, Bergen: Norwegian Institute at Athens, 1999, pp. 125–62.
28 Aesop 60.
29 John Lydus *On the Magistracies of the Roman State* 3.58, quoted in Kelly, *Ruling the Later Roman Empire*, p. 60.
30 Synesius *Ep.* 4.
31 Gell. 1.5.2–3; cf. Cic. *Brut.* 216; Plin. *NH* 7.55.
32 *Philogelos* 115.
33 Plin. *NH* 8.209 on the popularity of pork.
34 *CTh* 14.4.10.5.
35 Phaedrus *Fab.* 5.5.
36 Jerome *Against Rufinus* 1.17; Champlin, E., 'The testament of the piglet', *Phoenix* 41 (1987): 174–83, p. 174.
37 Dio 56.43.3.
38 An alternative, complete translation with comments on the legal form can be found in Daube, D., *Roman Law: linguistic, social and philosophical aspects*, Edinburgh: Edinburgh University Press, 1969, pp. 77–81.
39 Dio Chrys. *Or.* 32.9, quoted in Parkin, *Poverty in the Early Roman Empire*, p. 126.
40 John Chrys. *In Act. Ap.* 18.4.
41 *Philogelos* 177.
42 Asterius *PG* 40.222A, quoted in Gleason, 'Festive Satire', p. 112.
43 Lib. *Or.* 19.48.
44 Amm. Marc. 16.10.13.

45 Suet. *Tib.* 45.
46 Suet. *Galb.* 13.
47 SHA *Maximin.* 9.3.
48 See Gleason, 'Festive satire'.
49 Suet. *Ner.* 39.
50 Suet. *Dom.* 10.
51 Suet. *Cal.* 27.
52 For example, Gell. 15.4.3; Suet. *Jul.* 20, 80; *Aug.* 70; *Tib.* 59.
53 Aug. *de Opera Monachorum* 20.
54 *CIL* 13.10047.4; see Williams, C. A., *Roman Homosexuality: ideologies of masculinity in classical antiquity*, Oxford: Oxford University Press, 1999, p. 20.
55 *CIL* 11.6721.7, quoted in ibid., p. 21.
56 Apul. *Met.* 4.3.
57 Aesop 109.
58 Suet. *Aug.* 43.
59 Suet. *Jul.* 61.
60 For example, Mart. 3.82; 6.39; 12.93; 14.210; Suet. *Tib.* 61; Quint. *Inst.* 2.5.11.
61 Plut. *Mor.* 520c.
62 Suet. *Tib.* 61.
63 On Roman ideas about sexuality, see Williams, *Roman Homosexuality*.
64 Clarke, *Looking at Laughter*, p. 208.
65 See Bonner, C., 'A Tarsian peculiarity', *Harvard Theological Review* 35 (1942): 1–11; Purcell, 'Literate games', p. 18.
66 *Aesop Romance* 16.
67 See Hopkins, K., 'Novel evidence for Roman slavery', *Past & Present* 138 (1993): 3–27.
68 See appendix L of Beare, W., *The Roman Stage: a short history of Latin drama in the time of the Republic*, Methuen, 1964, pp. 314–19.
69 Cic. *Phil.* 2.65; Sen. *Ep.* 114.6; Suet. *Cal.* 57.
70 Cic. *Att.* 1.16.13; Sen. *Apoc.* 9.3.
71 Ovid *Trist.* 2.497–506.
72 Cic. *Cael.* 27.
73 On mime nudity, Val. Max. 2.10.8; Sen. *Ep. Mor.* 97.8.
74 Proc. *HA* 9.20.
75 SHA *Hel.* 25.4; Minuc. Felix *Oct.* 37; Val. Max. 2.6.7.
76 Quint. *Inst.* 11.3.178–80; 6.3.29.
77 Plut. *de Sollert. Anim.* 973e–f.
78 Gell. 16.7.4 *ex sordidiore vulgi usu.*
79 Macr. *Sat.* 2.7.11.
80 Phil. *Flacc.* 9.72, 10.85.
81 Cic. *Att.* 14.2.1; 14.3.2; Choricius of Gaza *Apologia Mimorum* 14.3.
82 Quint. *Inst.* 6.3.47.
83 Shaw, B., 'Rebels and Outsiders', *Cambridge Ancient History*, vol. 11, Cambridge: Cambridge University Press, 2000, pp. 361–403, p. 397.
84 Choricius *Apol. Mim.* 30.

85 Ibid., 114 and 118, quoted in Roueché, C., *Performers and Partisans at Aphrodisias in the Roman and Late Roman Periods: a study based on inscriptions from the current excavations at Aphrodisias in Caria*, Society for the Promotion of Roman Studies, 1993, p. 28, with n.84.

86 *Ad Fam.* 7.1.1–3.

87 Apul. *Met.* 10.31–2.

88 Plin. *Ep.* 10.34 *sed meminerimus provinciam istam et praecipue eas civitates eius modi factionibus esse vexatas. quodcumque nomen ex quacumque causa dederimus iis, qui in idem contracti fuerint, hetaeriae eaeque brevi fient.*

89 Ibid., 10.93–4.

90 For processions ranked by status, see van Nijf, O. M., *The Civic World of Professional Associations in the Roman East*, Amsterdam: J. C. Gieben, 1997, p. 128; for Aphrodisias, see Roueché, *Performers and Partisans at Aphrodisias*, pp. 131–46.

91 *CIL* 14.2112.

92 Synesius *Ep.* 32.

93 See O'Neill, P. 'Going round in circles: popular speech in ancient Rome', *Classical Antiquity* 22 (2003): 135–65.

94 *Philogelos* 227.

95 See Toner, *Leisure and Ancient Rome*, pp. 65–88.

96 For more, see Purcell, 'Literate games', p. 9.

97 Amm. Marc. 28.4.21.

98 Corbeill, A., *Nature Embodied: gesture in ancient Rome*, Princeton, NJ: Princeton University Press, 2004, pp. 107–39.

99 Cameron, *Circus Factions*, p. 293.

100 Claudian *in Eurtop.* 1.303–7; Phil. *de Animalibus* 28.

101 Mart. 1.6, 14, 22, 48, 51, 104.

102 Aelian 2.11; Plin. *NH* 8.6; Phil. *de Animal.* 24.

103 Stat. *Silv.* 1.6.51–64; Dio 67.8.4.

104 Suet. *Dom.* 4.

105 Tert. *de Spect.* 21.

106 Sen. *Ep.* 74.8.

107 For example, *CIL* 8.6947 and 6948 in North Africa.

108 Suet. *Ner.* 11; cf. Titus in Dio 66.25.

109 *Dig.* 18.1.8.1.

110 SHA *Hel.* 22.

111 Herodian 5.6.9–10.

112 Suet. *Dom.* 4.

113 Marcus Aurelius *Med.* 6.46.

114 Tac. *Ann.* 15.44.

115 Plin. *NH* 29.9.

116 Roueché, *Performers and Partisans at Aphrodisias*, p. 79.

117 Plin. *Ep.* 9.6.

118 K10.478.

119 Quoted in H. A. Harris, *Sport in Greece and Rome*, Thames and Hudson, pp. 235–6.

120 See Cameron, *Circus Factions*, p. 104.

121 Suet. *Ner.* 16.
122 Scott, J. C., *Domination and the Arts of Resistance: hidden transcripts*, New Haven, CT: Yale University Press, 1990, p. 18.
123 Cameron, *Circus Factions*, pp. 271–96.
124 Amm. Marc. 15.7.2.
125 *Dig.* 48.19.28.3 *solent quidam, qui volgo se iuvenes appellant, in quibusdam civitatibus turbulentis se adclamationibus popularium accommodare.*
126 Tac. *Ann.* 14.17.
127 Art. 3.16.
128 Cassiodorus *Var.* 3.51.13.
129 Ibid., 1.27.5, written by the king of the Ostrogoths, Theodoric, *quicquid illic a gaudenti populo dicitur, iniuria non putatur. locus est qui defendit excessum. quorum garrulitas si patienter accipitur, ipsos quoque principes ornare monstratur.*
130 Aesop 150.
131 Eunapius *Vit. Soph.* 462–3.
132 Yavetz, *Plebs and Princeps*, pp. 137–9.
133 Dio Chrys. *Or.* 21.9–10.
134 Tac. *Ann.* 13.25.
135 Suet. *Ner.* 57.
136 Jerome *Comm. in Dan.* 11.29.
137 Tac. *Ann.* 14.42–5.
138 Dio 63.29.1.
139 Clarke, *Art in the Lives of Ordinary Romans*, p. 219.
140 Bücheler, *Carmina Latina Epigraphica*, no. 1500 *es bibe lude veni.*
141 *CTh* 15.6.2 *tristitia.*
142 The phrase is Scott's in *Domination and the Arts of Resistance*, p. 67.

Chapter 4 Common Scents, Common Senses

1 For an introduction to the burgeoning field of sensory history, see Corbin, A., *The Foul and the Fragrant: odor and the French social imagination*, Leamington Spa: Berg, 1986, and *Village Bells: sound and meaning in the 19th-century French countryside*, trans. M. Thom, Papermac, 1999; Classen, C., Howes, D., and Synnott, A., *Aroma: the cultural history of smell*, Routledge, 1994; Smith, M. M., *Sensory History*, Oxford: Berg, 2007.
2 *De Rebus Bellicis* 2.2, in Thompson, E. A., *A Roman Reformer and Inventor*, Oxford: Clarendon Press, 1952.
3 Brown, *Power and Persuasion*.
4 *Collectio Casinensis* 294, quoted in Kelly, *Ruling the Later Roman Empire*, p. 172.
5 Harvey, S. A., *Scenting Salvation; ancient Christianity and the olfactory imagination*, Berkeley, CA: University of California Press, 2006, p. 30.
6 Cael. Aurel. *On Chronic Diseases* 1.5.168.

7   Aretaeus *On the Cure of Chronic Diseases* 1.5.
8   Aretaeus *On the Treatment of Acute Diseases* 1.1.
9   Plin. *NH* 37.44.
10 See Rüpke, *Religion of the Romans*, pp. 86–116.
11 Prudentius *Apotheosis* 456, quoted in ibid., p. 99.
12 See Harvey, *Scenting Salvation*, p. 13; e.g., Philostr. *VA* 1.5.
13 Philostorgius *Eccl. Hist.* 2.2, quoted in MacMullen, R., *Enemies of the Roman Order: treason, unrest, and alienation in the Empire*, Cambridge, MA: Harvard University Press, 1966, p. 109.
14 Luke 8:43–6.
15 *Life of St Daniel the Stylite* 18.
16 Clem. *Strom.* 1.143.
17 Porphyry *Vit. Pythag.* 41.
18 Wallace-Hadrill, A., *Houses and Society in Pompeii and Herculaneum*, Princeton, NJ: Princeton University Press, 1994, p. 31.
19 Euseb. *Praep. Evang.* 4.22.
20 Aretaeus *On the Causes and Symptoms of Chronic Diseases* 1.5.
21 Ibid., 1.6.
22 Amm. Marc. 16.10.10.
23 Suet. *Claud.* 32.
24 Pet. *Sat.* 47.
25 SHA *Hel.* 25.
26 Plin. *NH* 46.11.
27 Art. 2.26.
28 Frontinus *Aqueducts of Rome* 2.88.
29 Hor. *Carm.* 1.2.13.
30 Hopkins, J. N. N., 'The Cloaca Maxima and the monumental manipulation of water in archaic Rome', *The Waters of Rome* 4 (2007): 1–15, p. 1.
31 Col. *de Ag.* 1. pr. 17.
32 Tac. *Hist.* 1.4 *pars populi integra et magnis domibus adnexa ... plebs sordida et circo ac theatris sueta, simul deterrimi servorum.*
33 Juv. 3.277.
34 Ibid., 1.131.
35 *Philogelos* 85.
36 Pet. *Sat.* 47.
37 Tac. *Ann.* 14.44 *conluviem istam non nisi metu coercueris.*
38 Art. 2.26.
39 Ibid., 3.52.
40 Ibid., 2.9.
41 Galen K12.249, 290ff.
42 *CTh* 16.5.21 *servili faece descendens*; 9.42.5 *per egestatem abiecti sunt in faecem vilitatemque plebeiam.*
43 Cic. *Off.* 1.150 *sordidi.*
44 Cic. *Qfr.* 2.4.
45 Cic. *Flacc.* 18 *illam omnem faecem civitatum.*
46 Cic. Att. 1.19.4 *sentinam urbis.*
47 Juv. 3.62–4.

48   Mart. *Ep.* 1.86.
49   Juv. 3.236f; Hor. *Ep.* 2.2.79f; *Carm.* 3.29.12.
50   Fagan, G. G., *Bathing in Public in the Roman World*, Ann Arbor, MI: University of Michigan Press, 1999, pp. 30–1 with examples.
51   Hor. *Ep.* 1.17.6; Sen. *Ep.* 104.6; Virg. *Copa* 1–6.
52   Mart. 6.93.4.
53   Ibid. 10.12.
54   Juv. 3.236ff.
55   Mart. 10.3; 12.57; Stat. *Silv.* 1.6.73; *Dig.* 14.3.5.4.
56   Sen. *Ep.* 56.1–2.
57   Ibid., 47.3.
58   Dio Chrys. *Orat.* 20.9–10 Loeb translation with minor alterations.
59   On perfumed and spiced food, see Apicius *de Re Coquinaria* passim; Plut. *de Esu Carnium* 2.1.
60   Juv. 5.67–75; Cic. *Tusc.* 5.34.97.
61   Firm. Mat. 5.3.49.
62   Sen. *Contr.* 10.4.8.
63   Parkin, *Poverty in the Early Roman Empire*, p. 147.
64   Juv. 6.542; Mart. 12.32.7–8; Firm. Mat. 4.10.2.
65   Ibid., 6.31.28.
66   Art. 2.14.
67   Ibid., 1.27.
68   Suet. *Aug.* 4.
69   Juv. 14.200–5; cf. Suet. *Vesp.* 23 for Vespasian's comments that the money raised from his tax on piss-pots did not smell of urine.
70   See Gowers, E., *The Loaded Table: representations of food in Roman literature*, Oxford: Clarendon Press, 1993, pp. 280–310, esp. 291–4.
71   See Lilja, S., *The Treatment of Odours in the Poetry of Antiquity*, Helsinki: Societas Scientiarum Fennica, 1972, pp. 128–9, with reference to Aristophanes *Wasps* 609 and 790f.
72   *Philogelos* 231, 235; see also 232–4, 236–40, 242.
73   Pet. *Sat.* 43.
74   Mart. 11.30;12.85.
75   Juv. 6.117–8 and 11.172–3; Dio Chrys. *Or.* 7.133.
76   Josephus *BJ* 2.101–10 on a slave imposter for a prince being discovered by his rough, servile body.
77   Val. Max. 7.5.2.
78   Lib. *Or.* 1.228.
79   Ibid., 1.208.
80   In Rawson, B. (ed.), *Marriage, Divorce and Children in Ancient Rome*, Oxford: Clarendon Press, 1991, p. 153.
81   Achilles Tatius *Leucippe and Cleitiphon* 5.17.
82   Lucian *Timon the Misanthrope* 23.
83   Tert. *ad Mart.* 5.
84   Mart. 6.64.26; 10.56.6; Scrib. Larg. *Comp.* 231. See Jones, 'Stigma: tattooing and branding'.
85   Suet. *Tib.* 34.
86   Plin. *NH* 26.3.

87   Tac. *Ann.* 4.57.
88   Epict. *Diss.* 4.1.17.
89   Dio 59.27.
90   Juv. 4.116–7; see Parkin, *Poverty in the Early Roman Empire,* pp. 47–8: 'one wonders whether this was sincere gratitude or irony'.
91   Apul. *Met.* 2.2 and 4.9.
92   Art. 2.3.
93   Ibid.
94   *Life of St John the Almsgiver* 21.
95   Plin. *NH* 9.169 says that inns were full of fleas in the summer.
96   Col. *de Ag.* 1.8.5, quoted in Shelton, *As the Romans Did,* p. 169.
97   *Aesop Romance* 21.
98   Ovid *Am.* 1.14.45–6.
99   Mart. 4.61; 8.6; 9.59; 10.87; 12.69.
100 Plin. *NH* 37.83, 197–200; Sen. *Ep.* 90.33.
101 *PGM* 7.167–86.
102 Amm. Marc. 14.6.25.
103 Sidon. Ap. *Ep.* 2.9.
104 Suet. *Vit. Hor.* 1–3.
105 See Bonner, 'A Tarsian peculiarity'.
106 Tatian *adv. Gr.* 22.
107 *Philogelos* 141.
108 Pet. *Sat.* 117.
109 Hor. *Ep.* 1.19.37 *ventosa* has the primary meaning of 'fickle' in this context.
110 Art. 4.44.
111 *CIL* 4.1527, 4.9987, 4.4401,quoted in Horsfall, N., '"The Uses of Literacy" and the *Cena Trimalchionis*', *Greece & Rome* 36 (1989): 74–89 and 194–209, p. 79.
112 *PL* 26.357 *et ipsa latinitas et regionibus quotidie mutetur et tempore.*
113 Mart. 7.30.
114 Pet. *Sat.* 46 *non es nostrae fasciae, et ideo pauperorum verba derides.*
115 Ibid., 57; see Marchesi, I., 'Traces of a freed language: Horace, Petronius, and the rhetoric of fable', *Classical Antiquity* 24 (2005): 307–30.
116 *P. Oxy.* 51.3617.
117 Quint. *Inst.* 11.3.83, quoted in George, M., 'Slave disguise in ancient Rome', *Slavery & Abolition* 23 (2002): 41–54, n.29 to p. 48.
118 Lucian *Hist. Conscr.* 22, in Parkin, *Poverty in the Early Roman Empire,* p. 36.
119 See, for example, Pet. *Sat.* 57.
120 On popular Latin, see Abbott, F. F., *The Common People of Ancient Rome: studies of Roman life and literature,* Routledge, 1912, pp. 32–78; Palmer, L. R., *The Latin Language,* Faber and Faber, 1954; Herman, J., *Vulgar Latin,* trans. R. Wright, University Park, PA: Pennsylvania State University Press, 2000. The stylistic examples given are taken from these sources.
121 Pet. *Sat.* 42 *neminem nihil boni facere oportet.*

122   Plaut. *Mil.* 131–2 *dedi mercatori cuidam, qui ad illum deferat meum erum, qui Athenis fuerat, qui hanc amaverat.*
123   Liban. *Or.* 15.77.
124   Quint. *Inst.* 2.12.10 *iam collidere manus, terrae pedem incutere, femur pectus frontem caedere, mire ad pullatum circulum facit.*
125   *PGM* 7.203–5; 1.247–62; 4.88–93.
126   *PGM* 7.727–39; 1.222–31.
127   *PGM* 3.612–32; 7.201–2; 4.26–51.
128   Apul. *Met.* 10.31–2.
129   Art. 1.75.
130   Sen. *Ep.* 86.12.
131   Pet. *Sat.* 28.
132   Ibid., 38 and 54.
133   Plin. *NH* 19.55; Sen. *Ep.* 78.23. Snow was easily available in Rome, according to Galen, K7.508, which was good for providing cooling medications. On cushions, Plin. *NH* 10.53.
134   Ibid., 34.160.
135   Suet. *Ner.* 30.
136   Quint. *Inst.* 1.10.31.
137   Plut. *de Esu Carnium* 2.2.
138   Mart. 14.59; 3.63.4.
139   Olson, K., *Dress and the Roman Woman: self-presentation and society*, Routledge, 2008, p. 113.
140   Suet. *Ner.* 51.
141   Suet. *Cal.* 52.
142   SHA *Hel.* 23.
143   Corbeill, A., *Nature Embodied: gesture in ancient Rome*, Princeton, NJ: Princeton University Press, 2004, pp. 133–7.
144   Cic. *de Leg. Ag.* 2.13 *alio vultu, alio vocis sono, alio incessu esse meditabatur, vestitu obsoletiore.*
145   Suet. *Jul.* 67.
146   See MacMullen, *Roman Social Relations*, p. 63.
147   Plin. *NH* 14.11.
148   Kellum, B.A., 'What we see and what we don't see. Narrative structure and the Ara Pacis Augustae', *Art History* 17 (1994): 26–45, p. 31.
149   Plin. *NH* 15.47.
150   Ibid., 36.123.
151   Purcell, N., 'Rome and its development under Augustus and his successors', *Cambridge Ancient History*, vol. 10, Cambridge: Cambridge University Press, 1996, pp. 782–811, p. 796.
152   Wallace-Hadrill, *Rome's Cultural Revolution*, p. 275.
153   See Mac Mahon, A., 'The taberna counters of Pompeii and Herculaneum', in A. Mac Mahon and J. Price (eds), *Roman Working Lives and Urban Living*, Oxford: Oxbow, 2005, pp. 70–87.
154   The surviving parts are Severan from the early third century, but this may have replaced an earlier model of unknown date.
155   Pseudo-Orpheus *Lithika* 410–11, quoted with the next example in Gager, *Curse Tablets and Binding Spells*, p. 239.

156 Pseudo-Orpheus, *lithika kerugmata* 20.14ff; on texts relating to stones, see Halleux, R., and Schamp, J. (eds), *Les lapidaires grecs*, Paris: Belles Lettres, 1985.

157 Plin. *NH* 36.121.

158 Sozomon *HE* 8.20, quoted in Roueché, *Performers and Partisans at Aphrodisias*, pp. 146–7.

159 Plin. *NH* 34.34.

160 Sen. *Ep.* 86.6.

161 Suet. *Aug.* 28.

162 Juv. 3.35.

163 On the place of smell in Roman religion, see the excellent Harvey, *Scenting Salvation.*

164 Herodian 4.8.8.

165 Cic. *Verr.* 2.158 and 141 for decoration in the forum during the Roman games.

166 SHA *Car.* 19.

167 Stat. *Silv.* 1.6.85ff.

168 Suet. *Cal.* 18; Tac. *Ann.* 14.20–1; cf. Suet. *Dom.* 4.

169 Dio 58.19.2.

170 Plin. *NH* 19.25.

171 Aug. *In Psalm* 128.5, in Getty, *The Life of the North Africans*, p. 123.

172 For example, *CIL* 4.1189.

173 Pet. *Sat.* 45.

174 See André, J., *Étude sur les termes de couleur dans la langue latine*, Paris: C. Klincksieck, 1949.

175 Plin. *NH* 35.50.

176 Ibid., 35.49 on the colourful effect of gladiators.

177 Herodian 4.2.2.

178 Sen. *Ep.* 41.6; SHA *Gord.* 3.

179 Plut. *de Sera Num. Vind.* 9; *Passio Perpetua* 18.

180 SHA *Gord.* 3, *Prob.* 19; Dio 74.1.4; Calpurnius *Ecl.* 7.69ff.

181 SHA *Car.* 19.

182 Cic. *Tusc.* 2.20.46.

183 SHA *Prob.* 19.

184 Ps.-Quint. *Decl.* 9.6.

185 Solinus *de Mirab. Mundi* 45.12.

186 See Roueché, C., 'Acclamations in the later Roman Empire: new evidence from Aphrodisias', *JRS* 74 (1984): 181–99.

187 For example, Dio 76.4.4.

188 Sil. Ital. 16.315ff; Lact. *Div. Inst.* 6.20.

189 Mart. 14.160.

190 Juv. 11.8; Pet. *Sat.* 117.

191 SHA *Comm.* 16.

192 Dio 59.7.8.

193 Ovid *Am.* 3.2.73–4.

194 Suet. *Dom.* 4; Stat. *Silv.* 1.6.28ff.

195 Josephus *BJ* 7.5.

196   Cic. *Sest.* 93; Hor. *Ars* 20, or perhaps these images were to be used as votive offerings in gratitude for their survival.

197   Ter. *Hecyra* 28–57; Ovid *Am.* 3.2.23–4.

198   Wallace-Hadrill, *Houses and Society*, p. 17.

199   Cic. *Att.* 2.19 on the different receptions for Pompey, Caesar and Cicero.

200   See Kelly, *The Roman Empire*, pp. 55–7.

201   About 70 per cent of the time according to Vanderbroeck, P. J. J., *Popular Leadership and Collective Behavior in the Late Roman Republic (ca. 80–50 B.C.)*, Amsterdam: J. C. Gieben, 1987, pp. 152–3.

202   Dio 59.27.2.

203   See Gowers, *The Loaded Table*, pp. 280–310.

204   Plin. *Pan.* 26.

205   *P. Lond.* 1912.

206   For example, Tac. *Hist.* 3.85; Dio 58.11.3.

207   Fiske, J., *Understanding Popular Culture*, Unwin Hyman, 1989, p. 140.

208   Procop. *HA* 7.8–14; cf. Agathias 5.14.4.

209   *CTh* 14.10.4 (416 CE).

210   See Reinhold, M., 'History of purple as a status symbol in antiquity', *Collection Latomus* 116 (1970): 48–73.

211   Suet. *Dom.* 8; Mart. 5.23; cf. 4.2; 5.8; 14.131, 137.

212   Roueché, *Performers and Partisans at Aphrodisias*, p. 102.

213   Ovid *Ars* 1.135–63.

214   Plut. *Pomp.* 48; Suet. *Vit.* 17.

215   Lact. *Div. Inst.* 6.20.

216   Lent, F., 'The Life of St Simeon Stylites', *Journal of the American Oriental Society* 35 (1915): 103–98, p. 156.

217   *Life of St Theodore of Sykeon* 20.

218   Clem. Alex. *Strom.* 7.7.36, quoted in Harvey, *Scenting Salvation*, p. 43 with minor changes.

219   Basil *Regula fusius tractacta* 22 quoted in Brown, *Poverty and Leadership*, p. 53.

220   *Acts* 19:12.

221   *Sibylline Oracles* 5.386–433; 5.155–78; 3.356–80, in Bate, H. N., *The Sibylline Oracles, Books III–V*, SPCK, 1918; Commodian *Instr.* 1.41.

Chapter 5   Popular Resistance

1   Firm. Mat. 1.7.7.

2   Kelly, *Ruling the Later Roman Empire*, p. 130.

3   Tac. *Ag.* 29–31.

4   Babrius 102.

5   See esp. Scott, *Domination and the Arts of Resistance*, and *Weapons of the Weak: everyday forms of peasant resistance*, New Haven, CT: Yale University Press, 1990 and 1985 respectively.

6   Hopkins, 'Novel evidence for Roman slavery', p. 5.

7   Col. *de Ag.* 1.7.6–7; 1.8.1–2; see also Bradley, *Slavery and Society*, p. 110.

8 Sen. *de Tranq. An.* 8.8.
9 *Querolus* 74.
10 *Aesop Romance* 25.
11 Pub. Syr. 596 *qui docte servit partem dominatus tenet.*
12 Sen. *de Tranq. An.* 8.8.
13 Bradley, K. R., 'Animalizing the slave: the truth of fiction', *JRS* 90 (2000): 110–125.
14 See Bradley, *Slavery and Society*, pp. 177–8.
15 Hopkins, *Conquerors and Slaves*, p. 121
16 *Dig.* 21.1.18 pr. which adds that 'all these qualities should be expected within reason'.
17 *Ephesians* 6:5.
18 *Querolus* 74, in Mathisen, *People, Personal Expression, and Social Relations*, vol. 1, p. 63.
19 *Aesop Romance* 26.
20 *Comm. Pet.* 17; Mart. 7.62.4.
21 Art. 1.24.
22 Amm. Marc. 16.8.9.
23 Art. 1.32.
24 Phaedrus *Fab.* 3. prol. 33–40.
25 Diod. Sic. 34.2 frag.
26 Quint. *Inst.* 5.11.19.
27 Aesop 227.
28 Ibid., 131, 179 moral.
29 Ibid., 1, 238.
30 Ibid., 394 moral, 144 moral, 70, 98.
31 *Dig.* 11.4.2, runaways that have pretended to be free are usually punished more severely.
32 See MacMullen, *Roman Social Relations*, n.102 to p. 119, for various references to the poor hating the rich.
33 Reymond, E. A. E., and Barns, J. W. B. (eds), *Four Martyrdoms from the Pierpont Morgan Coptic Codices*, Oxford: Clarendon Press, 1973, p. 6.
34 Epict. *Diss.* 4.1.79.
35 Simeon ben Lakish, B Sanhedrin 98b, quoted in de Lange, N. R. M., 'Jewish attitudes to the Roman Empire', in P. Garnsey and C. R. Whittaker (eds), *Imperialism in the Ancient World*, Cambridge: Cambridge University Press, 1978, pp. 255–81, p. 274.
36 Quint. *Inst.* 6.3.47.
37 Suet. *Jul.* 49; for other political jokes, see Macr. *Sat.* 2.1.8–15; 2.4.20.
38 Suet. *Vesp.* 23; Dio 65.14.5.
39 Suet. *Ner.* 41.
40 Firm. Mat. 6.29.18.
41 K5.40–1 in Singer, *Galen*, p. 119.
42 Firm. Mat. 6.30.11; 3.6.25; 3.4.10.
43 *P. Ryl.* 1.28, quoted in Parsons, P., *City of the Sharp-nosed Fish: Greek lives in Roman Egypt*, Weidenfeld and Nicolson, 2007, p. 189.
44 *Philogelos* 247.

45   Sall. *Cat.* 25.
46   Dio Chrys. *Orat.* 32.32.
47   Col. *de Ag.* 1.8.2.
48   Dyson, S. L., *Community and Society in Roman Italy*, Baltimore, MD: Johns Hopkins University Press, 1992, p. 176.
49   Firm. Mat. 3.5.23; 3.6.15; 3.6.9; 8.7.2.
50   Williams, *Roman Homosexuality*, p. 183.
51   Ibid.
52   Amm. Marc. 21.12.24 *querelae plebis . . . solitae.*
53   For example, ibid., 14.7.5–6.
54   Ibid., 27.3.4.
55   Symm. *Ep.* 6.18.
56   For example, Amm. Marc. 14.7.2–8.
57   Dio 76.4.4–5.
58   Josephus *BJ* 2.425–7.
59   See Wallace, R., and Williams, W., *The Acts of the Apostles: a companion*, Bristol: Bristol Classical Press, 1993.
60   *Acts* 4:13; 4:21.
61   Ibid., 19:21; 19:24–9.
62   Ibid., 16:16–22.
63   Ibid., 17:6–7.
64   Ibid., 18:14–15.
65   *P. Oxy.* 2661.
66   *CIL* 8.10570.
67   Dio 77.10.7.
68   Apul. *Met.* 7.4.
69   Oros. *Hist.* 7.41 *Romani, qui malint inter barbaros pauperem libertatem, quam inter Romanos tributariam sollicitudinem sustinere.*
70   Priscus 11.2.407–510.
71   *De Rebus Bellicis* 4.1 and 2.3.
72   Grünewald, T., *Bandits in the Roman Empire: myth and reality*, trans. J. Drinkwater, Routledge, 2004, p. 12.
73   Tac. *Ann.* 3.40 *igitur per conciliabula et coetus seditiosa disserebant de continuatione tributorum, gravitate faenoris, saevitia ac superbia praesidentium.*
74   Dyson, S. L., 'Native revolt patterns in the Roman Empire', *ANRW* 2/3 (1975): 138–75, pp. 139 and 140.
75   SHA *Alex. Sev.* 60 on the doom predicted by a Druid woman in the local language in 235 CE; cf. Tac. *Hist.* 4.54.
76   See Elsner, J., *Roman Eyes: visuality and subjectivity in art and text*, Princeton, NJ: Princeton University Press, 2007, ch. 10, 'Viewing and resistance', pp. 253–88.
77   On Christian attitudes to property, see Garnsey, P., *Thinking about Property: from Antiquity to the age of revolution*, Cambridge: Cambridge University Press, 2007, pp. 59–83.
78   Hopkins, K., *A World Full of Gods: pagans, Jews and Christians in the Roman Empire*, Weidenfeld & Nicolson, 1999, pp. 78 and 98; on WUD, see, for example, 1 Timothy 6:17.

79 *Acts* 4:32–5.
80 Tert. *Apol.* 39 *oramus etiam pro imperatoribus, pro ministris eorum et potestatibus, pro statu saeculi, pro rerum quiete, pro mora finis.*
81 Justin *Apol.* 1.11.1.
82 Lucian *Peregrinus* 14 in Costa, *Lucian.*
83 Brown, *The Making of Late Antiquity*, p. 86.
84 Quoted in Brown, P., 'Holy men', *Cambridge Ancient History*, vol. 14, Cambridge: Cambridge University Press, 1998, pp. 781–810, p. 785.
85 Whitby, M., 'Maro the Dendrite: an anti-social holy man?', in M. Whitby, P. Hardie and M. Whitby (eds), *Homo Viator: classical essays for John Bramble*, Bristol: Bristol Classical Press, 1987, pp. 309–17.
86 On resistance literature, see de Ste. Croix, G. E. M., *The Class Struggle in the Ancient Greek World: from the archaic age to the Arab conquests*, Duckworth, 1981, pp. 441–52.
87 For prophesies about the doom of Rome, see 3.45–62, 350–5, 356–80; 5.155–78, 386–433, in Bate, *The Sibylline Oracles*, with minor alterations.
88 For example, *Revelation* 2:13; 6:9–10; 12–17; 19:2.
89 *P. Oxy.* 2554, quoted in MacMullen, R., *Changes in the Roman Empire: essays in the ordinary*, Princeton, NJ: Princeton University Press, 1990, p. 221.
90 *P. Oxy.* 2332; see Koenen, L., 'The prophecies of a potter: a prophecy of world renewal becomes an apocalypse', *American Studies in Papyrology* 7 (1970): 249–54.
91 *Sib. Or.* 4.117–24, 137–9; 5.27–34, 137–54, 214–24, 361–85; Commodian *Instruct.* 1.41; *Carm. Apol.* 791–1060.
92 As the editor comments on *P. Oxy.* 2332 vol. 22, p. 89.
93 Dio 57.18.4–5.
94 Veyne, P., *Bread and Circuses: historical sociology and political pluralism*, trans. B. Pearce, Harmondsworth: Penguin, 1992, pp. 295 and 296.
95 Stat. *Silv.* 1.6.81–3 *tollunt innumeras ad astra voces Saturnalia principis sonantes et dulci dominum favore clamant.*
96 See Garland, R., *Celebrity in Antiquity: from media tarts to tabloid queens*, Duckworth, 2006, pp. 57–8; Fronto *Ep. ad Caes.* 4.12; cf. Severian *Sermons on the Creation of the World* 6.5 (= *PG* 56.489), quoted in Hopkins, *Conquerors and Slaves*, p. 224.
97 *CTh* 15.4.1.
98 Aelius Aristides *Panegyric on Rome, Or.* 26.65–7.
99 Millar, F., *The Emperor in the Roman World (31 BC–AD 337)*, Duckworth, 1977, p. xi.
100 Scott, *Weapons of the Weak.*
101 Dio 69.6.3; see Kelly, *Ruling the Later Roman Empire*, n.1 to p. 114, for various references to this story.
102 Tac. *Ann.* 3.36.
103 Lib. *Or.* 22.7; Soz. *HE* 7.23, quoted in Hopkins, *Conquerors and Slaves*, pp. 225–6.
104 See ibid. for various examples.
105 Dio 59.30.1; Plin. *Pan.* 52; cf. Sejanus's statues in Juv. 10.56–64.

106   SHA *Carac.* 5.7.
107   *Acta Appiani* (*P. Oxy.* 33), in Musurillo, H. A. (ed.), *The Acts of the Pagan Martyrs*, Oxford: Clarendon Press, 1954.
108   *CTh* 9.4.1 *unde integris omnibus ad nostram scientiam referatur*.
109   Amm. Marc. 14.1.9, which states that the emperor Gallienus had also acted in this way.
110   Epict. *Diss.* 4.13.5.
111   Tac. *Ann.* 1.15 after Tiberius ends popular elections in 14 CE: *neque populus ademptum ius questus est nisi inani rumore*.
112   *CIL* 4.8075 *cicuta ab rationibus Neronis Augusti*; an alternative reading has *Cucuta* as a name. See also Suet. *Aug.* 55 for anonymous critical posters in the Senate House.
113   O'Neill, 'Going round in circles', p. 162.
114   Purcell, 'Rome and its development under Augustus', p. 801.
115   For an excellent analysis of how a modern totalitarian regime generates compliance and cynicism in equal measure, see Wedeen, L., *Ambiguities of Domination: politics, rhetoric, and symbols in contemporary Syria*, Chicago, IL: University of Chicago Press, 1999.
116   Harries, J., *Law and Empire in Late Antiquity*, Cambridge: Cambridge University Press, 1999, pp. 163–4.
117   Hor. *Sat.* 2.7.80–2, quoted in Oliensis, E. '*Ut arte emendaturus fortunam*: Horace, Nasidienus, and the art of satire,' in T. Habinek and A. Schiesaro (eds), *The Roman Cultural Revolution*, Cambridge: Cambridge University Press, 1997, pp. 90–104, p. 94.
118   See de Certeau, M., *The Practice of Everyday Life,* trans. S. Rendall, Berkeley, CA: University of California Press, 1984, p. xvii.
119   Aesop 569.

Conclusion: Towards a Christian Popular Culture

1   Plin. *NH* 15.120f.
2   Hopkins, *Conquerors and Slaves*, p. 68, estimates 315,000 adult Italian male citizens leaving by 28 BCE.
3   Woolf, G., *Becoming Roman: the origins of provincial civilization in Gaul*, Cambridge: Cambridge University Press, 1998, p. 241.
4   *Querolus* 74, in Mathisen, *People, Personal Expression, and Social Relations*, vol. 1, p. 64.
5   Purcell, 'Rome and its development under Augustus', p. 805.
6   See de Lange, 'Jewish attitudes to the Roman Empire', p. 269.
7   Woolf, *Becoming Roman*, p. 170.
8   Scott, *Domination and the Arts of Resistance*, p. 67.
9   Tert. *de Idol.* 15; Herodian 4.2.
10   Phaedrus 1.15.
11   Sall. *Hist.* 4.69.18 *pauci libertatem, pars magna iustos dominos*.
12   Scott, *Domination and the Arts of Resistance*, p. xii.
13   Ibid., p. xiii.

14 See Garnsey, P., and Humfress, C., *The Evolution of the Late Antique World*, Cambridge: Orchard Academic, 2001, pp. 83ff.

15 Kelly, *Ruling the Later Roman Empire*.

16 Brown, *Poverty and Leadership*, p. 51.

17 Ibid., p. 81.

18 Ibid., p. 74. On almsgiving, see Finn, R. D., *Almsgiving in the Later Roman Empire: Christian promotion and practice (313–450)*, Oxford: Oxford University Press, 2006.

19 Eusebius *HE* 6.43.11.

20 See Miller, T. S., *The Birth of the Hospital in the Byzantine Empire*, Baltimore, MD: Johns Hopkins University Press, 1985, pp. 21–9.

21 Greg. Nyss. *PG* 46.557.

22 Brown, *Poverty and Leadership*, p. 20.

23 For example, Gregory of Tours *VJ* 36.129.

24 Prudentius *Peristephanon* 11.191–2; 199–202, quoted in Brown, *Cult of the Saints*, p. 42.

25 Ibid., p. 48.

26 Baynes, *Three Byzantine Saints*, p. 197.

27 For example, Gregory of Tours *Life of the Fathers* 13.3, on a fight for the relics of St Lupicinus.

28 Tert. *adv. Val.* 20.

29 Philostorgius *HE* 2.2.

30 Aug. *Civ. Dei* 22.8.20.

31 Bede *Eccl. Hist.* 1.30, quoted in Burke, *Popular Culture in Early Modern Europe*, p. 229.

32 Gregory of Tours *Book of Miracles* 1.64, quoted in Gurevich, A., *Medieval Popular Culture: problems of belief and perception*, trans. J. M. Bak and P. A. Hollingsworth, Cambridge: Cambridge University Press, 1988, p. 49.

33 Brown, *Poverty and Leadership*, p. 50.

34 *CJ* 1.1.4.

35 Greg. Nyss. *PG* 46.557.

36 *Life of St John the Almsgiver* 26.

37 *Life of St Theodore of Sykeon* 143.

38 Aug. *In Ps.* 70.17, in Getty, *The Life of the North Africans*, p. 143.

39 Caesarius of Arles *Serm.* 44.7.

40 SHA *Firm., Sat., Proc. & Bon.* 8 Loeb translation with minor changes.

Select Bibliography

Place of publication is London unless otherwise stated.

Abbott, F. F., *The Common People of Ancient Rome: studies of Roman life and literature*, Routledge, 1912.

Abercrombie, N., Hill, S., and Turner B. S., *The Dominant Ideology Thesis*, Allen & Unwin, 1980.

Adams, J. N., *The Latin Sexual Vocabulary*, Duckworth, 1982.

Aldrete, G. S., *Gestures and Acclamations in Ancient Rome*, Baltimore, MD: Johns Hopkins University Press, 1999.

Alföldy, G., *The Social History of Rome*, Croom Helm, 1985.

Allen, R. C., 'How prosperous were the Romans? Evidence from Diocletian's Price Edict (301 AD)', Oxford University Department of Economics, *Working Paper Number 363*, 2007.

Amundsen, D. W., 'Images of physicians in classical times', *Journal of Popular Culture* 11 (1977): 642–55.

Anderson, G., *Fairytale in the Ancient World*, Routledge, 2000.

Anderson, G., *Greek and Roman Folklore: a handbook*, Greenwood Press, 2006.

Ando, C., *Imperial Ideology and Provincial Loyalty in the Roman Empire*, Berkeley, CA: University of California Press, 2000.

André, J., *Étude sur les termes de couleur dans la langue latine*, Paris: C. Klincksieck, 1949.

Aneshensel, C. S., and Phelan, J. C. (eds), *Handbook of the Sociology of Mental Health*, Kluwer Academic, 1999.

Ashley, L. R. N., *Elizabethan Popular Culture*, Bowling Green, OH: Bowling Green State University Popular Press, 1988.

Atherton, C., (ed.), *Monsters and Monstrosity in Greek and Roman Culture*, Bari: Levante, 1998.

Atkins, M., and Osborne, R. (eds), *Poverty in the Roman World*, Cambridge: Cambridge University Press, 2006.

Babcock, B. A. (ed.), *The Reversible World: symbolic inversion in art and society*, Ithaca, NY: Cornell University Press, 1978.

Bailey, P., *Popular Culture and Performance in the Victorian City*, Cambridge: Cambridge University Press, 1998.

Bakhtin, M. M., *Rabelais and His World*, trans. H. Iswolsky, Bloomington, IN: Indiana University Press, 1984.

Baldwin, B., *The Philogelos or Laughter-lover*, Amsterdam: J. C. Gieben, 1983.

Barnish, S. J. B., 'Pigs, Plebeians and *Potentes*: Rome's economic hinterland, *c*.350–600 AD', *PSBR* 55 (1987): 157–85.

Barns, J., 'Shenute as a historical source', in J. Wolski (ed.), *Actes du Xe Congrès International de Papyrologues, Varsovie, Cracovie, 3–9 Septembre, 1961*, Wrocław: Wydawnictwo Polskiej Akademii Nauk, 1964, 151–9.

Barton, C. A., *Roman Honor: the fire in the bones*, Berkeley, CA: University of California Press, 2001.

Barton, T. S., *Power and Knowledge: astrology, physiognomics, and medicine under the Roman Empire*, Ann Arbor, MI: University of Michigan Press, 1994.

Barton, T. S., *Ancient Astrology*, Routledge, 1994.

Bate, H. N., *The Sibylline Oracles, Books III–V*, SPCK, 1918.

Baynes, N. H., and Dawes, E., *Three Byzantine Saints: contemporary biographies*, Oxford: Blackwell, 1948.

Beacham, R. C., *The Roman Theatre and its Audience*, Routledge, 1991.

Beard, M., *The Roman Triumph*, Belknap, 2007.

Beard, M., *Pompeii: the life of a Roman town*, Profile, 2008.

Beare, W., *The Roman Stage: a short history of Latin drama in the time of the Republic*, Methuen, 1964.

Bendle, M. F., 'The apocalyptic imagination and popular culture', *Journal of Religion and Popular Culture* 11 (2005).

Berger, A. A., *Narratives in Popular Culture, Media, and Everyday Life*, Sage, 1997.

Betz, H. D. (ed.), *The Greek Magical Papyri in Translation, including the Demotic Spells*, Chicago, IL: University of Chicago Press, 1992.

Bigsby, C. W. E, *Approaches to Popular Culture*, Edward Arnold, 1976.

Billeter, G., *Geschichte des Zinsfusses im griechisch-römischen Altertum bis auf Justinian*, Leipzig: Teubner, 1898.

Blümner, H., *Fahrendes Volk im Altertum*, Munich: Koniglich Bayerischen Akademie der Wissenschaften, 1918.

Bodel, J. (ed.), *Epigraphic Evidence: ancient history from inscriptions*, Routledge, 2001.

Bonner, C., 'A Tarsian peculiarity', *Harvard Theological Review* 35 (1942): 1–11.

Boswell, J., '*Expositio* and *Oblatio*: the abandonment of children and the ancient and medieval family', *American Historical Review* 89 (1984): 10–33.

Boswell, J., *The Kindness of Strangers: the abandonment of children in Western Europe from late antiquity to the Renaissance*, Allen Lane, 1989.

Bourdieu, P., *Distinction: a social critique of the judgement of taste*, trans. R. Nice, Routledge & Kegan Paul, 1984.

Bowersock, G. W., Brown, P., and Grabar, O. (eds), *Interpreting Late Antiquity: essays on the postclassical world*, Belknap, 2001.

Bradley, K. R., *Discovering the Roman Family: studies in Roman social history*, Oxford: Oxford University Press, 1991.

Bradley, K. R., *Slavery and Society at Rome*, Cambridge: Cambridge University Press, 1994.

Bradley, K. R., 'Animalizing the slave: the truth of fiction', *JRS* 90 (2000): 110–125.

Bram, J. R., *Ancient Astrology, Theory and Practice: Matheseos Libri VIII by Firmicus Maternus*, Park Ridge, NJ: Noyes Press, 1975.

Branham, R. B., *Bakhtin and the Classics*, Evanston, IL: Northwestern University Press, 2002.

Brenner, M. H., *Mental Illness and the Economy*, Cambridge, MA: Harvard University Press, 1973.

Brown, P., *Religion and Society in the Age of Saint Augustine*, Faber and Faber, 1972.

Brown, P., *The Making of Late Antiquity*, Cambridge, MA: Harvard University Press, 1978.

Brown, P., *The Cult of the Saints: its rise and function in Latin Christianity*, SCM Press, 1981.

Brown, P., 'Dalla *"Plebs Romana"* alla *"Plebs Dei"*: aspetti della cristianizzazione di Roma', in P. Brown, L. Cracco Ruggini, and M. Mazza (eds), *Governanti e intelletuali: populo di Roma e populo di Dio (I–VI secolo)*, Turin: Giappichelli, 1982, pp. 123–45.

Brown, P., *The Body and Society: men, women, and sexual renunciation in early Christianity*, Faber and Faber, 1990.

Brown, P., *Power and Persuasion in Late Antiquity: towards a Christian empire*, Madison, WI: University of Wisconsin Press, 1992.

Brown, P., 'Holy men', *Cambridge Ancient History*, vol. 14, Cambridge: Cambridge University Press, 1998, pp. 781–810.

Brown, P., *Poverty and Leadership in the Later Roman Empire*, Hanover, NH: University Press of New England, 2002.

Brunt, P. A., 'Charges of provincial maladministration under the early principate', *Historia* 10 (1961): 189–227.

Brunt, P. A., 'The Roman Mob', *Past & Present* 35 (1966): 3–27.

Brunt, P. A., *Social Conflicts in the Roman Republic*, Chatto and Windus, 1971.

Brunt, P. A., *Italian Manpower, 225 B.C.–A.D. 14*, Oxford: Clarendon Press, 1971.

Bücheler, F. (ed.), *Carmina Latina Epigraphica*, Leipzig: Teubner, 1895–7.

Budde, M. L., and Brimlow, R. W. (eds), *The Church as Counterculture*, Albany, NY: State University of New York Press, 2000.

Bull, M., and Back, L. (eds), *The Auditory Culture Reader*, Oxford: Berg, 2003.

Burke, P., *Popular Culture in Early Modern Europe*, Temple Smith, 1978.

Burke, P., and Porter, R. (eds), *The Social History of Language*, Cambridge: Cambridge University Press, 1987.

Burkert, W., *Ancient Mystery Cults*, Cambridge, MA: Harvard University Press, 1987.

Bynum, W. F., and Porter, R. (eds), *Medicine and the Five Senses*, Cambridge: Cambridge University Press, 1993.

Cameron, A., *Porphyrius the Charioteer*, Oxford: Clarendon Press, 1973.

Cameron, A., *Circus Factions: blues and greens at Rome and Byzantium*, Oxford: Clarendon Press, 1976.

Cantor, N. F., and Werthman, M. S., *The History of Popular Culture*, New York: Macmillan, 1968.

Carroll, M. T., and Tafoya, E., *Phenomenological Approaches to Popular Culture*, Bowling Green, OH: Bowling Green State University Popular Press, 2000.

Caseau, B., 'Euodia: the use and meaning of fragrances in the ancient world and their Christianization (100–900 A.D.)', unpublished PhD dissertation, Princeton University, 1994.

Castriota, D., *The Ara Pacis Augustae and the Imagery of Abundance in Later Greek and Early Roman Imperial Art*, Princeton, NJ: Princeton University Press, 1995.

Champlin, E., 'The testament of the piglet', *Phoenix* 41 (1987): 174–83.

Chaniotis, A., 'Illness and cures in the Greek propitiatory inscriptions and dedications of Lydia and Phrygia', in P. J. van der Eijk, H. F. J. Horstmanshoff and P. H. Schrijvers (eds), *Ancient Medicine in its Sociocultural Context*, 2 vols, Amsterdam: Rodopi, 1995, pp. 323–44.

Charlesworth, S. J., *A Phenomenology of Working Class Experience*, Cambridge: Cambridge University Press, 2000.

Chitty, D. J., *The Desert a City: an introduction to the study of Egyptian and Palestinian monasticism under the Christian Empire*, Oxford: Blackwell, 1966.

Clarke, J. R., *Art in the Lives of Ordinary Romans: visual representation and non-elite viewers in Italy, 100 B.C.–A.D. 315*, Berkeley, CA: University of California Press, 2003.

Clarke, J. R., *Looking at Laughter: humor, power, and transgression in Roman visual culture, 100 B.C.–A.D. 250*, Berkeley, CA: University of California Press, 2007.

Classen, C., *Worlds of Sense: exploring the senses in history and across cultures*, Routledge, 1993.

Classen, C., Howes, D., and Synnott, A., *Aroma: the cultural history of smell*, Routledge, 1994.

Cockayne, E., *Hubbub: filth, noise & stench in England 1600–1770*, New Haven, CT: Yale University Press, 2007.

Cockerham, W. C., *Sociology of Mental Disorder*, Prentice Hall, 2000.

Collins, J., *Uncommon Cultures: popular culture and post-modernism*, Routledge, 1989.

Combet-Farnoux, B., *Mercure romain: le culte public de Mercure et la fonction mercantile à Rome, de la République archaïque à l'époque augustéenne*, Rome: École française de Rome, 1980.

Cooper, F. T., *Word Formation in the Roman Sermo Plebeius: an historical study of the development of vocabulary in vulgar and late Latin, with special reference to the Romance languages*, New York: Trow, 1895.

Corbeill, A., *Controlling Laughter: political humor in the late Roman Republic*, Princeton, NJ: Princeton University Press, 1996.

Corbeill, A., *Nature Embodied: gesture in ancient Rome*, Princeton, NJ: Princeton University Press, 2004.

Corbett, P., *The Scurra*, Edinburgh: Scottish Academic, 1986.

Corbin, A., *The Foul and the Fragrant: odor and the French social imagination*, Leamington Spa: Berg, 1986.

Corbin, A., *Time, Desire, and Horror: towards a history of the senses*, trans. J. Birrell, Cambridge: Polity, 1995.

Corbin, A., *Village Bells: sound and meaning in the 19th-century French countryside*, trans. M. Thom, Papermac, 1999.

Corsten, T., 'Ein neues Buchstabenorakel aus Kibyra', *Epigraphica Anatolica* 28 (1997): 41–9.

Costa, C. D. N., *Lucian: selected dialogues*, Oxford: Oxford University Press, 2005.

Cotter, W., *Miracles in Greco-Roman Antiquity: a sourcebook*, Routledge, 1999.

Cowan, A., and Steward, J. (eds), *The City and the Senses: urban culture since 1500*, Aldershot: Ashgate, 2007.

Daly, L. W. (ed.), *Aesop without Morals: the famous fables and a life of Aesop*, New York: T. Yoseloff, 1961.

Darnton, R., *The Great Cat Massacre: and other episodes in French cultural history*, Allen Lane, 1984.

D'Arms, J. H., *Commerce and Social Standing in Ancient Rome*, Cambridge, MA: Harvard University Press, 1981.

Daube, D., *Roman Law: linguistic, social and philosophical aspects*, Edinburgh: Edinburgh University Press, 1969.

Davis, N. Z., *Society and Culture in Early Modern France: eight essays*, Cambridge: Polity, 1987.

Davis, R. C., *The War of the Fists: popular culture and public violence in late Renaissance Venice*, Oxford: Oxford University Press, 1994.

de Certeau, M., *The Practice of Everyday Life*, trans. S. Rendall, Berkeley, CA: University of California Press, 1984.

de Lange, N. R. M., 'Jewish attitudes to the Roman Empire', in P. Garnsey and C. R. Whittaker (eds), *Imperialism in the Ancient World*, Cambridge: Cambridge University Press, 1978, pp. 255–81.

de Ligt, L., *Fairs and Markets in the Roman Empire: economic and social aspects of periodic trade in a pre-industrial society*, Amsterdam: J. C. Gieben, 1993.

de Ste. Croix, G. E. M., 'Why were the early Christians persecuted', *Past & Present* 26 (1963): 6–38.

de Ste. Croix, G. E. M., *The Class Struggle in the Ancient Greek World: from the archaic age to the Arab conquests*, Duckworth, 1981.

Deacy, S., and Pierce, K. F. (eds), *Rape in Antiquity*, Duckworth, 1997.

Diagnostic and Statistical Manual of Mental Disorders, 4th edn, Washington, DC: American Psychiatric Association, 1994.

Dickey, E., *Latin Forms of Address: from Plautus to Apuleius*, Oxford: Oxford University Press, 2002.

Dietz, M., *Wandering Monks, Virgins, and Pilgrims: ascetic travel in the Mediterranean world, A.D. 300/800*, University Park, PA: Pennsylvania State University Press, 2005.

Dionisotti, A. C., 'From Ausonius' schooldays? A schoolbook and its relatives', *JRS* 72 (1982): 83–125.

Docker, J., *Postmodernism and Popular Culture: a cultural history*, Cambridge: Cambridge University Press, 1994.

Dodds, E. R., *The Greeks and the Irrational*, Berkeley, CA: University of California Press, 1951.

Dodds, E. R., *Pagan and Christian in an Age of Anxiety: some aspects of religious experience from Marcus Aurelius to Constantine*, Cambridge: Cambridge University Press, 1965.

Donnelly, J. S., and Miller, K. A. (eds), *Irish Popular Culture 1650–1850*, Dublin: Irish Academic Press, 1998.

Dover, K. J., *Greek Popular Morality in the time of Plato and Aristotle*, Oxford: Blackwell, 1974.

Drobnick, J., *The Smell Culture Reader*, Oxford: Berg, 2006.

Duckworth, G. E., *The Nature of Roman Comedy: a study in popular entertainment*, Princeton, NJ: Princeton University Press, 1952.

Dufallo, B., *The Ghosts of the Past: Latin literature, the dead, and Rome's transition to a principate*, Columbus, OH: Ohio State University Press, 2007.

Duncan-Jones, R., *The Economy of the Roman Empire: quantitative studies*, Cambridge: Cambridge University Press, 1982.

Duncan-Jones, R., *Money and Government in the Roman Empire*, Cambridge: Cambridge University Press, 1994.

Dupont, F., *L'acteur-roi: le théâtre dans la Rome antique*, Paris: Belles Lettres, 1985.

Dyson, S. L., 'Native revolts in the Roman Empire', *Historia* 20 (1971): 239–74.

Dyson, S. L., 'Native revolt patterns in the Roman Empire', *ANRW* 2/3 (1975): 138–75.

Dyson, S. L., *Community and Society in Roman Italy*, Baltimore, MD: Johns Hopkins University Press, 1992.

Easterlin, R. A., 'Does economic growth improve the human lot?', in P. A. David and M. W. Reder (eds), *Nations and Households in Economic Growth: essays in honor of Moses Abramovitz*, New York: Academic Press, 1974, pp. 89–125.

Easton, S., et al., *Disorder and Discipline: popular culture from 1550 to the present*, Aldershot: Temple Smith, 1988.

Eaton, W. W., *The Sociology of Mental Disorders*, Praeger, 2000.

Edelstein, E. J. and Edelstein, L. E., *Asclepius: a collection and interpretation of the testimonies*, New York: Arno Press, 1975.

Edmondson, J., and Keith, A. (eds), *Roman Dress and the Fabrics of Roman Culture*, University of Toronto Press, 2008.

Edwards, C., and Woolf, G. (eds), *Rome the Cosmopolis*, Cambridge: Cambridge University Press, 2003.

Eidinow, E., *Oracles, Curses, and Risk among the Ancient Greeks*, Oxford: Oxford University Press, 2007.

Ellis, S. P., *Roman Housing*, Duckworth, 2000.

Elsner, J., *Roman Eyes: visuality and subjectivity in art and text*, Princeton, NJ: Princeton University Press, 2007.

Entralgo, P. L., *The Therapy of the Word in Classical Antiquity*, trans. L. J. Rather and J. M. Sharp, New Haven, CT: Yale University Press, 1970.

Evans, J. K., 'Plebs Rustica. The peasantry of classical Italy', *AJAH* 5 (1980): 19–47 and 134–73.

Eyben, E., 'Family planning in Graeco-Roman antiquity', *Ancient Society* 11/12 (1980–81): 5–82.

Eyben, E., *Restless Youth in Ancient Rome*, Routledge, 1993.

Fabian, J., *Moments of Freedom: anthropology and popular culture*, Charlottesville, VA: University Press of Virginia, 1998.

Fagan, G. G., *Bathing in Public in the Roman World*, Ann Arbor, MI: University of Michigan Press, 1999.

Favro, D., *The Urban Image of Augustan Rome*, Cambridge: Cambridge University Press, 1996.

Fentress, J., and Wickham, C., *Social Memory*, Oxford: Blackwell, 1992.

Finn, R. D., *Almsgiving in the Later Roman Empire: Christian promotion and practice (313–450)*, Oxford: Oxford University Press, 2006.

Fishburn, K., *Women in Popular Culture: a reference guide*, Greenwood, 1982.

Fiske, J., *Understanding Popular Culture*, Unwin Hyman, 1989.

Fitzgerald, W., *Slavery and the Roman Literary Imagination*, Cambridge: Cambridge University Press, 2000.

Flemming, R., *Medicine and the Making of Roman Women: gender, nature, and authority from Celsus to Galen*, Oxford: Oxford University Press, 2000.

Foster, G. M., 'Peasant society and the image of limited good', *American Anthropologist* 67 (1965): 293–315.

Foucault, M., *Madness and Civilization: a history of insanity in the Age of Reason*, trans. R. Howard, Routledge, 1971.

Frayn, J. M., *Markets and Fairs in Roman Italy: their social and economic importance from the second century BC to the third century AD*, Oxford: Clarendon Press, 1993.

Frazer, J. G., 'Some popular superstitions of the ancients', *Folklore* 1 (1890): 145–71.

Frazer, J. G., *The Golden Bough: a study in magic and religion*, 3rd edn, Macmillan, 1911–15.

Freccero, C., *Popular Culture: an introduction*, New York: New York University Press, 1999.

Fredrick, D. (ed.), *The Roman Gaze: vision, power, and the body*, Baltimore, MD: Johns Hopkins University Press, 2002.

Freeman, H. (ed.), *Mental Health and the Environment*, Churchill Livingstone, 1984.

Funari, P. P. A., 'Graphic caricature and the ethos of ordinary people at Pompeii', *Journal of European Archaeology* 1 (1993): 133–50.

Gage, J., *Colour and Culture: practice and meaning from antiquity to abstraction*, Thames and Hudson, 1993.

Gager, J. G. (ed.), *Curse Tablets and Binding Spells from the Ancient World*, Oxford: Oxford University Press, 1992.

Gallant, T. W., *Risk and Survival in Ancient Greece: reconstructing the rural domestic economy*, Cambridge: Polity, 1991.

Gans, H. J., *Popular Culture and High Culture: an analysis and evaluation of taste*, New York: Basic Books, 1999.

Gardner, J. F., *Being a Roman Citizen*, Routledge, 1993.

Gardner, J. F., and Wiedemann, T. (eds), *The Roman Household: a sourcebook*, Routledge, 1991.

Garland, R., *The Eye of the Beholder: deformity and disability in the Graeco-Roman world*, Duckworth, 1995.

Garland, R., *Celebrity in Antiquity: from media tarts to tabloid queens*, Duckworth, 2006.

Garnsey, P., *Famine and Food Supply in the Graeco-Roman world: responses to risk and crisis*, Cambridge: Cambridge University Press, 1988.

Garnsey, P., *Food and Society in Classical Antiquity*, Cambridge: Cambridge University Press, 1999.

Garnsey, P., *Thinking about Property: from antiquity to the age of revolution*, Cambridge: Cambridge University Press, 2007.

Garnsey, P., and Humfress, C., *The Evolution of the Late Antique World*, Cambridge: Orchard Academic, 2001.

Garnsey, P., and Scheidel, W. (eds), *Cities, Peasants and Food in Classical Antiquity: essays in social and economic history*, Cambridge: Cambridge University Press, 1998.

Garnsey, P., and Whittaker C. R. (eds), *Imperialism in the Ancient World*, Cambridge: Cambridge University Press, 1978.

George, M., 'Slave disguise in ancient Rome', *Slavery & Abolition* 23 (2002): 41–54.

Getty, M. M., *The Life of the North Africans as Revealed in the Sermons of Saint Augustine*, Washington, DC: Catholic University of America, 1931.

Ginzburg, C., *The Cheese and the Worms: the cosmos of a sixteenth-century miller*, trans. J. and A. Tedeschi, Routledge & Kegan Paul, 1980.

Gleason, M. W., 'Festive satire: Julian's *Misopogon* and the New Year at Antioch', *JRS* 76 (1986): 106–19.

Godsland, S., and White, A. M. (eds), *Cultura Popular: studies in Spanish and Latin American popular culture*, Oxford: Peter Lang, 2002.

Golby, J. M., and Purdue, A. W., *The Civilization of the Crowd: popular culture in England, 1750–1900*, Stroud: Sutton, 1999.

Goldberg, D., and Huxley, P., *Common Mental Disorders: a bio-social model*, Routledge, 1992.

Golden, M., 'Did the ancients care when their children died?', *Greece & Rome* 35 (1988): 152–63.

Goodall, P., *High Culture, Popular Culture*, Allen & Unwin, 1995.

Goodman, M., 'Opponents of Rome: Jews and others', in L. Alexander (ed.), *Images of Empire*, Sheffield: JSOT Press, 1991, pp. 222–38.

Gowers, E., *The Loaded Table: representations of food in Roman literature*, Oxford: Clarendon Press, 1993.

Graf, F., 'Rolling the dice for an answer', in S. I. Johnston and P. T. Struck (eds), *Mantikê: studies in ancient divination*, Leiden: Brill, 2005, pp. 51–97.

Graham, T. F., *Medieval Minds: mental health in the Middle Ages*, Allen & Unwin, 1967.

Green, C. M. C., *Roman Religion and the Cult of Diana at Aricia*, Cambridge: Cambridge University Press, 2007.

Gregory, T. E., *Vox Populi: popular opinion and violence in the religious controversies of the fifth century A.D.*, Columbus, OH: Ohio State University Press, 1979.

Grey, C., 'Demoniacs, dissent, and disempowerment in the late Roman West: some case studies from the hagiographical literature', *Journal of Early Christian Studies* 13 (2005): 39–69.

Grottanelli, C., 'Tricksters, scapegoats, champions, saviors', *History of Religion* 23 (1983): 117–39.

Grünewald, T., *Bandits in the Roman Empire: myth and reality*, trans. J. Drinkwater, Routledge, 2004.

Gunderson, E., 'The ideology of the arena', *Classical Antiquity* 15 (1996): 113–51.

Gurevich, A., *Medieval Popular Culture: problems of belief and perception*, trans. J. M. Bak and P. A. Hollingsworth, Cambridge: Cambridge University Press, 1988.

Habinek, T., *The World of Roman Song: from ritualized speech to social order*, Baltimore, MD: Johns Hopkins University Press, 2005.

Habinek, T., 'Slavery and class', in Harrison, S. (ed.), *A Companion to Latin Literature*, Oxford: Blackwell, 2005. pp. 385–93.

Habinek, T., and Schiesaro, A. (eds), *The Roman Cultural Revolution*, Cambridge: Cambridge University Press, 1997.

Hahn, R. A., *Sickness and Healing: an anthropological perspective*, New Haven, CT: Yale University Press, 1995.

Halleux, R., and Schamp, J. (eds), *Les lapidaires grecs*, Paris: Belles Lettres, 1985.

Halliday, W. R., *Greek and Roman Folklore*, Harrap, 1927.

Hands, A. R., *Charities and Social Aid in Greece and Rome*, Thames and Hudson, 1968.

Hansen, W., *Phlegon of Tralles' Book of Marvels*, Exeter: University of Exeter Press, 1996.

Hansen, W. (ed.), *Anthology of Ancient Greek Popular Literature*, Bloomington, IN: Indiana University Press, 1998.

Harrington, C. L., and Bielby, D. D. (eds), *Popular Culture: production and consumption*, Oxford: Blackwell, 2001.

Harries, J., *Law and Empire in Late Antiquity*, Cambridge: Cambridge University Press, 1999.

Harris, H. A., *Sport in Greece and Rome*, Thames and Hudson, 1972.

Harris, W. V., *Ancient Literacy*, Cambridge, MA: Harvard University Press, 1989.

Harvey, S. A., *Scenting Salvation; ancient Christianity and the olfactory imagination*, Berkeley, CA: University of California Press, 2006.

Hauken, T., *Petition and Response: an epigraphic study of petitions to Roman emperors, 181–249*, Bergen: Norwegian Institute at Athens, 1998.

Herman, J., *Vulgar Latin*, trans. R. Wright, University Park, PA: Pennsylvania State University Press, 2000.

Hingley, R., *Globalizing Roman Culture: unity, diversity and empire*, Routledge, 2005.

Hobsbawm, E., 'Peasants and politics', *Journal of Peasant Studies* 1 (1973): 3–22.

Hobsbawm, E., *On History*, Weidenfeld & Nicolson, 1997.

Hochschild, A. R., *The Managed Heart: commercialization of human feeling*, Berkeley, CA: University of California Press, 2003.

Hoggart, R., *The Uses of Literacy: aspects of working class life*, Chatto and Windus, 1957.

Holman, S. R., '"You speculate on the misery of the poor": usury as civic injustice in Basil of Caesarea's second homily on Psalm 14', in Hopwood, K. (ed.), *Organised Crime in Antiquity*, Duckworth, 1999, pp. 207–28.

Homer, S., and Sylla, R., *A History of Interest Rates*, New Brunswick, NJ: Rutgers University Press, 1991.

Hoogendijk, F. A. J., and Clarysse, W., 'De Sortes van Astrampsychus: een orakelboek uit de oudheid bewerkt voor het middelbaar onderwijs', *Kleio* 11 (1981): 53–99.

Hopkins, J. N. N., 'The Cloaca Maxima and the monumental manipulation of water in archaic Rome', *The Waters of Rome* 4 (2007): 1–15.

Hopkins, K., *Conquerors and Slaves*, Cambridge: Cambridge University Press, 1978.

Hopkins, K., *Death and Renewal*, Cambridge: Cambridge University Press, 1983.

Hopkins, K., 'Novel evidence for Roman slavery', *Past & Present* 138 (1993): 3–27.

Hopkins, K., 'Christian number and its implications', *Journal of Early Christian Studies* 6 (1998): 185–226.

Hopkins, K., *A World Full of Gods: Pagans, Jews and Christians in the Roman Empire*, Weidenfeld & Nicolson, 1999.

Hopkins, K., and Beard, M., *The Colosseum*, Profile, 2005.

Hopwood, K. (ed.), *Organised Crime in Antiquity*, Duckworth, 1999.

Horden, P., 'Responses to possession and insanity in the earlier Byzantine world', *Social History of Medicine* 6 (1993): 177–94.

Horden, P., and Purcell, N., *The Corrupting Sea: a study of Mediterranean history*, Oxford: Blackwell, 2000.

Horsfall, N., '"The Uses of Literacy" and the *Cena Trimalchionis*', *Greece & Rome* 36 (1989): 74–89 and 194–209.

Horsfall, N., *The Culture of the Roman Plebs*, Duckworth, 2003.

Horsley, G. H. R., and Mitchell, S. (eds), *The Inscriptions of Central Pisidia*, Bonn: Habelt, 2000.

Hoskins, J., *Biographical Objects: how things tell the stories of people's lives*, Routledge, 1998.

Hotchkiss, V. R., *Clothes Make the Man: female cross dressing in medieval Europe*, Garland, 1996.

Howes, D. (ed.), *Empire of the Senses: the sensual culture reader*, Oxford: Berg, 2005.

Huskinson, J. (ed.), *Experiencing Rome: culture, identity and power in the Roman Empire*, Routledge, 2000.

Inglis, F., *Popular Culture and Political Power*, New York: Harvester/ Wheatsheaf, 1988.

International Statistical Classification of Diseases and Related Health Problems: ICD 10, 3 vols, Geneva: World Health Organisation, 1992–4.

Jackson, S. W., 'Galen on mental disorders', *Journal of the History of the Behavioral Sciences*, 5 (1969): 365–84.

Jenkins, H., McPherson, T., and Shattuc, J. (eds), *Hop on Pop: the politics and pleasures of popular culture*, Durham, NC: Duke University Press, 2002.

Johnston, S. I., and Struck, P. T. (eds), *Mantikê: studies in ancient divination*, Leiden: Brill, 2005.

Jones, C. P., 'Stigma: tattooing and branding in Graeco-Roman antiquity', *JRS* 77 (1987): 139–55.

Jordan, D. R., Montgomery, H., and Thomassen, E. (eds)., *The World of Ancient Magic*, Bergen: Norwegian Institute at Athens, 1999.

Joshel, S. R., *Work, Identity, and Legal Status at Rome: a study of the occupational inscriptions*, Norman, OK: University of Oklahoma Press, 1992.

Joshel, S. R., Malamud, M., and McGuire, D. T. (eds), *Imperial Projections: ancient Rome in modern popular culture*, Baltimore, MD: Johns Hopkins University Press, 2001.

Joyce, P., *Visions of the People: industrial England and the question of class 1848–1914*, Cambridge: Cambridge University Press, 1991.

Jütte, R., *Poverty and Deviance in Early Modern Europe*, Cambridge: Cambridge University Press, 1994.

Kaplan, S. L., *Understanding Popular Culture: Europe from the Middle Ages to the nineteenth century*, New York: Mouton, 1984.

Karem. E. G., et al., 'Lifetime prevalence of mental disorder in Lebanon: first onset, treatment, and exposre to war, *PLoS Medicine* 5 (2008).

Kaster, R. A., *Emotion, Restraint, and Community in Ancient Rome*, Oxford: Oxford University Press, 2005.

Keay, S., 'Tarraco in late antiquity', in N. Christie and S. T. Loseby (eds), *Towns in Transition: urban evolution in late antiquity and the early Middle Ages*, Aldershot: Scolar, 1996, pp. 18–44.

Kellum, B. A., 'What we see and what we don't see. Narrative structure and the Ara Pacis Augustae', *Art History* 17 (1994): 26–45.

Kelly, C., *Ruling the Later Roman Empire*, Belknap, 2004.

Kelly, C., *The Roman Empire: a very short introduction*, Oxford: Oxford University Press, 2006.

Kenner, H., *Das Phänomen der verkehrten Welt in der griechisch–römischen Antike*, Klagenfurt: Geschichtsverein f. Kärnten, 1970.

Kirk, S. A., and Kutchins, H., *The Selling of DSM: the rhetoric of science in psychiatry*, New York: de Gruyter, 1992.

Klingshirn, W., 'The *Sortes Sangallenses*', in S. I. Johnston and P. T. Struck (eds), *Mantikê: studies in ancient divination*, Leiden: Brill, 2005, pp. 99–128.

Kloppenborg, J. S., and Wilson, S. G. (eds), *Voluntary Associations in the Graeco-Roman World*, Routledge, 1996.

Koenen, L., 'The prophecies of a potter: a prophecy of world renewal becomes an apocalypse', *American Studies in Papyrology* 7 (1970): 249–54.

Koenig, H. G. (ed.), *Handbook of Religion and Mental Health*, Academic Press, 1998.

Kraemer, R. S. (ed.), *Maenads, Martyrs, Matrons, Monastics: a sourcebook on women's religions in the Greco-Roman world*, Philadelphia, PA: Fortress, 1988.

Kraemer, R. S., *Her Share of the Blessings: women's religions among pagans, Jews, and Christians in the Greco-Roman world*, Oxford: Oxford University Press, 1992.

Krantz, F. (ed.), *History from Below: studies in popular protest and popular ideology*, Oxford: Blackwell, 1988.

Kudlien, F., 'Schaustellerei und Heilmittelvertrieb in der Antike', *Gesnerus* 40 (1983): 91–8.

Kurke, L., 'Plato, Aesop, and the beginnings of mimetic prose', *Representations* 94 (2006): 6–52.

Lançon, B., *Rome in Late Antiquity: everyday life and urban change*, AD 312–609, trans. A. Nevill, Edinburgh: Edinburgh University Press, 2000.

Laing, R. D., *The Divided Self: an existential study in sanity and madness*, Harmondsworth: Penguin, 1977.

Laing, R. D. and Esterson, A., *Sanity, Madness and the Family*, Tavistock, 1964.

Langlands, R., *Sexual Morality in Ancient Rome*, Cambridge: Cambridge University Press, 2006.

Larner, C., *The Thinking Peasant: popular and educated belief in pre-industrial culture*, Glasgow: Pressgang, 1982.

Laurence, R., and Berry, J. (eds), *Cultural Identity in the Roman Empire*, Routledge, 1998.

Laurence, R., and Wallace-Hadrill, A. (eds), *Domestic Space in the Roman World: Pompeii and beyond*, Portsmouth, RI: JRA, 1997.

Le Roy Ladurie, E., *The Peasants of Languedoc*, trans. J. Day, Champaign, IL: University of Illinois Press, 1974.

Le Roy Ladurie, E., *Carnival: a people's uprising at Romans 1579–1580*, trans. M. Feeney, Scolar, 1980.

Lee, S., et al., 'Lifetime prevalence and inter-cohort variation in DSM-IV disorders in metropolitan China', *Psychological Medicine* 37 (2007): 61–71.

Leighton, A. H., et al., *Psychiatric Disorder among the Yoruba*, Ithaca, NY: Cornell University Press, 1963.

Lelis, A. A., Percy, W. A., and Verstraete, B. C., *The Age of Marriage in Ancient Rome*, Lampeter: Edwin Mellen, 2003.

Lendon, J. E., *Empire of Honour: the art of government in the Roman world*, Oxford: Clarendon Press, 1997.

Lendon, J. E., 'Social control at Rome', *Classical Journal* 93 (1997): 83–8.

Lent, F., 'The Life of St Simeon Stylites', *Journal of the American Oriental Society* 35 (1915): 103–98.

Levick, B., *The Government of the Roman Empire: a sourcebook*, Routledge, 2000.

Levinson, S. C., and Brown, P., *Politeness: some universals in language usage*, Cambridge: Cambridge University Press, 1987.

Lewis, L. A., *The Adoring Audience: fan culture and popular media*, Routledge, 1992.

Lieu, S. N. C., *Manichaeism in the Later Roman Empire and Medieval China*, Tübingen: Mohr, 1992.

Lieu, S. N. C., *Manichaeism in Mesopotamia and the Roman East*, Leiden: Brill, 1994.

Lilja, S., *Terms of Abuse in Roman Comedy*, Helsinki: Suomalainen Tiedeakatemia, 1965.

Lilja, S., *The Treatment of Odours in the Poetry of Antiquity*, Helsinki: Societas Scientiarum Fennica, 1972.

Lott, J. B., *The Neighborhoods of Augustan Rome*, Cambridge: Cambridge University Press, 2004.

Luck, G., *Arcana Mundi: magic and the occult in the Greek and Roman worlds*, Baltimore, MD: Johns Hopkins University Press, 1985.

Lull, J., and Hinerman, S. (eds), *Media Scandals: morality and desire in the popular culture marketplace*, Cambridge: Polity, 1997.

McCambley, C., 'Against those who practice usury by Gregory of Nyssa', *Greek Orthodox Theological Review* 36 (1991): 287–302.

MacDonald, M., *Mystical Bedlam: madness, anxiety and healing in seventeenth-century England*, Cambridge: Cambridge University Press, 1981.

Mac Mahon, A., 'The taberna counters of Pompeii and Herculaneum', in A. Mac Mahon and J. Price (eds), *Roman Working Lives and Urban Living*, Oxford: Oxbow, 2005, pp. 70–87.

MacMullen, R., 'A note on *Sermo Humilis*', *Journal of Theological Studies* 17 (1966): 108–12.

MacMullen, R., *Enemies of the Roman Order: treason, unrest, and alienation in the Empire*, Cambridge, MA: Harvard University Press, 1966.

MacMullen, R., 'Market days in the Roman Empire', *Phoenix* 24 (1970): 333–41.

MacMullen, R., *Roman Social Relations, 50 B.C. to A.D. 284*, New Haven, CT: Yale University Press, 1974.

MacMullen, R., *Changes in the Roman Empire: essays in the ordinary*, Princeton, NJ: Princeton University Press, 1990.

McRobbie, A., *Postmodernism and Popular Culture*, Routledge, 1994.

Maier, H. O., 'The topography of heresy and dissent in late fourth-century Rome', *Historia* 44 (1995): 232–49.

Marchesi, I., 'Traces of a freed language: Horace, Petronius, and the rhetoric of fable', *Classical Antiquity* 24 (2005): 307–30.

Markowitz, H. M., 'Portfolio selection', *Journal of Finance* 7 (1952): 77–91.

Mathisen, R. W., *People, Personal Expression, and Social Relations in Late Antiquity*, 2 vols, Ann Arbor, MI: University of Michigan Press, 2003.

Mattingly, D. J. (ed.), *Dialogues in Roman Imperialism: power, discourse, and discrepant experience in the Roman empire*, Portsmouth, RI: JRA, 1997.

Meggitt, J. J., *Paul, Poverty and Survival*, Edinburgh: T&T Clark, 1998.

Meggitt, J. J., 'Sources: use, abuse, neglect. The importance of ancient popular culture', in E. Adam and D. G. Horrell (eds), *Christianity at Corinth: The Quest for the Pauline Church*, John Knox, 2004, pp. 241–53.

Meggitt, J. J., 'The madness of King Jesus: why was Jesus put to death, but his followers were not?', *Journal for the Study of the New Testament* 29 (2007): 379–413.

Meslin, M., *La fête des kalendes de janvier dans l'empire romaine: étude d'un rituel de Nouvel An*, Bruxelles: Latomus, 1970.

Midelfort, H. C. E., 'Madness and civilization in early modern Europe: a reappraisal of Michel Foucault', in B. C. Malament (ed.), *After the Reformation: essays in honor of J. H. Hexter*, Manchester: Manchester University Press, 1980, pp. 247–65.

Midelfort, H. C. E., *A History of Madness in Sixteenth-century Germany*, Stanford, CA: Stanford University Press, 1999.

Millar, F., 'Emperors at work', *JRS* 57 (1967): 9–19.

Millar, F., *The Emperor in the Roman World (31 BC–AD 337)*, Duckworth, 1977.

Millar, F., 'The world of the Golden Ass', *JRS* 71 (1981): 63–75.

Millar, F., *The Crowd in Rome in the Late Republic*, Ann Arbor, MI: University of Michigan Press, 1998.

Miller, T. S., *The Birth of the Hospital in the Byzantine Empire*, Baltimore, MD: Johns Hopkins University Press, 1985.

Momigliano, A., *Essays in Ancient and Modern Historiography*, Oxford: Blackwell, 1977.

Moore, B., *Injustice: the social bases of obedience and revolt*, Macmillan, 1978.

Morgan, J., O'Neill, C., and Harré, R., *Nicknames: their origins and social consequences*, Routledge & Kegan Paul, 1979.

Morgan, T., *Popular Morality in the Early Roman Empire*, Cambridge: Cambridge University Press, 2007.

Mouritsen, H., *Plebs and Politics in the Late Roman Republic*, Cambridge: Cambridge University Press, 2001.

Muchembled, R., *Popular Culture and Elite Culture in France, 1400–1750*, trans. L. Cochrane, Baton Rouge, LA: Louisiana State University Press, 1985.

Mullett, M., *Popular Culture and Popular Protest in Late Medieval and Early Modern Europe*, Croom Helm, 1987.

Musurillo, H. A. (ed.), *The Acts of the Pagan Martyrs*, Oxford: Clarendon Press, 1954.

Nichols, S. G., Kablitz, A., and Calhoun, A. (eds), *Rethinking the Medieval Senses: heritage, fascinations, frames*, Baltimore, MD: Johns Hopkins University Press, 2008.

Nippel, W., *Public Order in Ancient Rome*, Cambridge: Cambridge University Press, 1995.

Noy, D., *Foreigners at Rome: citizens and strangers*, Duckworth, 2000.

Nutton, V., 'Murders and miracles: lay attitudes towards medicine in classical antiquity', in R. Porter (ed.), *Patients and Practitioners: lay perceptions of medicine in pre-industrial society*, Cambridge: Cambridge University Press, 1985, pp. 23–53.

Obelkevich, J., 'Proverbs and social history', in P. Burke and R. Porter (eds), *The Social History of Language*, Cambridge: Cambridge University Press, 1987, pp. 43–72.

O'brien-Moore, A., *Madness in Ancient Literature*, Weimar: Wagner Sohn, 1924.

Oliensis, E., '*Ut arte emendaturus fortunam*: Horace, Nasidienus, and the art of satire,' in T. Habinek and A. Schiesaro (eds), *The Roman Cultural Revolution*, Cambridge: Cambridge University Press, 1997, pp. 90–104.

Oliensis, E., *Horace and the Rhetoric of Authority*, Cambridge: Cambridge University Press, 1998.

Olson, K., *Dress and the Roman Woman: self-presentation and society*, Routledge, 2008.

O'Neill, P., 'Going round in circles: popular speech in ancient Rome', *Classical Antiquity* 22 (2003): 135–65.

O'Rourke, D. K., *Demons by Definition: social idealism, religious nationalism, and the demonizing of dissent*, New York: Peter Lang, 1998.

Palmer, L. R., *The Latin Language*, Faber and Faber, 1954.

Parkin, A. R., 'Poverty in the early Roman Empire: ancient and modern conceptions and constructs', unpublished PhD dissertation, Cambridge University, 2001.

Parkin, A. R., '"You do him no service": an exploration of pagan almsgiving', in M. Atkins and R. Osborne, *Poverty in the Roman World*, Cambridge: Cambridge University Press, 2006, pp. 60–82.

Parkin, T. G., *Demography and Roman Society*, Baltimore, MD: Johns Hopkins University Press, 1992.

Parkin, T. G., *Old Age in the Roman World: a cultural and social history*, Baltimore, MD: Johns Hopkins University Press, 2002.

Parsons, P., *City of the Sharp-nosed Fish: Greek lives in Roman Egypt*, Weidenfeld and Nicolson, 2007.

Patlagean, E., 'Ancient Byzantine hagiography and social history', in S. Wilson (ed.), *Saints and their Cults: studies in religious sociology, folklore and history*, Cambridge: Cambridge University Press, 1983, pp. 101–22.

Patlagean, E., 'The poor', in G. Cavallo (ed.), *The Byzantines*, Chicago, IL: University of Chicago Press, 1997, pp. 15–42.

Patterson, O., *Slavery and Social Death: a comparative study*, Cambridge, MA: Harvard University Press, 1982.

Perkins, J., *The Suffering Self: pain and narrative representation in the early Christian era*, Routledge, 1995.

Pigeaud, J., *Folie et cures de la folie chez les médecins de l'antiquité gréco–romaine: la manie*, Paris: Belles Lettres, 1987.

Pingree, D. (ed.), *Dorothei Sidonii Carmen Astrologicum: interpretationem Arabicam in linguam Anglicam versam una cum Dorothei fragmentis et Graecis et Latinis*, Leipzig: Teubner, 1976.

Porter, R., *A Social History of Madness: stories of the insane*, Weidenfeld & Nicolson, 1987.

Potter, D. S., 'Odor and power in the Roman Empire', in J. I. Porter (ed.), *Constructions of the Classical Body*, Ann Arbor, MI: University of Michigan Press, 1999, pp. 169–89.

Purcell, N., 'The city of Rome and the plebs urbana in the late Republic', *Cambridge Ancient History*, vol. 9, Cambridge: Cambridge University Press, 1994, pp. 644–88.

Purcell, N., 'Literate games: Roman urban society and the game of alea', *Past & Present* 147 (1995): 3–37.

Purcell, N., 'Rome and its development under Augustus and his successors', *Cambridge Ancient History*, vol. 10, Cambridge: Cambridge University Press, 1996, pp. 782–811.

Purcell, N., 'The populace of Rome in late antiquity: problems of classification and historical description', in W. V. Harris (ed.), *The Transformations of Urbs Roma in Late Antiquity*, Portsmouth, RI: JRA, 1999, pp. 135–61.

Raaflaub, K. A., et al., *Opposition et résistances à L'Empire d'Auguste à Trajan*, Geneva: Fondation Hardt, 1987.

Randall, A., and Charlesworth, A. (eds), *Markets, Market Culture and Popular Protest in Eighteenth-century Britain and Ireland*, Liverpool: Liverpool University Press, 1996.

Rawson, B, 'Family life among the lower classes at Rome in the first two centuries of the empire', *Classical Philology* 61 (1966): 71–83.

Rawson, B. (ed.), *The Family in Ancient Rome: new perspectives*, Croom Helm, 1986.

Rawson, B. (ed.), *Marriage, Divorce and Children in Ancient Rome*, Oxford: Clarendon Press, 1991.

Rawson, B., and Weaver, P. (eds), *The Roman Family in Italy: status, sentiment, space*, Oxford: Clarendon Press, 1997.

Reay, B. (ed.), *Popular Culture in Seventeenth-century England*, Croom Helm, 1985.

Redhead, S., *Unpopular Cultures: the birth of law and popular culture*, Manchester: Manchester University Press, 1995.

Reinhold, M., 'History of purple as a status symbol in antiquity', *Collection Latomus* 116 (1970): 48–73.

Reinhold, M., 'Usurpation of status and status symbols in the Roman Empire', *Historia* 20 (1971): 275–302.

Reymond, E. A. E., and Barns, J. W. B. (eds), *Four Martyrdoms from the Pierpont Morgan Coptic Codices*, Oxford: Clarendon Press, 1973.

Reynolds, R. W., 'The adultery mime', *CQ* 40 (1946): 77–84.

Rich, J., and Wallace-Hadrill, A. (eds), *City and Country in the Ancient World*, Routledge, 1991.

Richlin, A., 'Emotional work: lamenting the Roman dead', in E. Tylawsky and C. Weiss (eds), *Essays in Honor of Gordon Williams: twenty-five years at Yale*, New Haven, CT: H. R. Schwab, 2001, pp. 229–48.

Roberts, R., *The Classic Slum: Salford life in the first quarter of the century*, Manchester: Manchester University Press, 1971.

Rogler, L. H., 'Making sense of historical changes in the Diagnostic and Statistical Manual of Mental Disorders: five propositions', *Journal of Health and Social Behavior* 38 (1997): 9–20.

Rosen, G., *Madness in Society: chapters in the historical sociology of mental illness*, Routledge & Kegan Paul, 1968.

Rosen, G., *From Medical Police to Social Medicine: essays of the history of health care*, New York: Science History, 1974.

Rosenberg, B. A., 'Was there a popular culture in the Middle Ages?', *Journal of Popular Culture* 14 (1980): 149–54.

Ross, A., *No Respect: intellectuals and popular culture*, Routledge, 1989.

Roth, M., and Kroll, J., *The Reality of Mental Illness*, Cambridge: Cambridge University Press, 1986.

Roth, R., and Keller, J. (eds), *Roman by Integration: dimensions of group identity in material culture and text*, Portsmouth, RI: JRA, 2007.

Roueché, C., 'Acclamations in the later Roman Empire: new evidence from Aphrodisias', *JRS* 74 (1984): 181–99.

Roueché, C., *Performers and Partisans at Aphrodisias in the Roman and Late Roman Periods: a study based on inscriptions from the current excavations at Aphrodisias in Caria*, Society for the Promotion of Roman Studies, 1993.

Rowe, G., *Princes and Political Cultures: the new Tiberian senatorial decrees*, Ann Arbor, MI: University of Michigan Press, 2002.

Rüpke, R., *Religion of the Romans*, trans. R. Gordon, Cambridge: Polity, 2007.

Scheidel, W. (ed.), *Debating Roman Demography*, Leiden: Brill, 2001.

Scheidel, W., 'Demography', in W. Scheidel, I. Morris, and R. Saller (eds), *The Cambridge Economic History of the Greco-Roman World*, Cambridge: Cambridge University Press, 2007, pp. 38–86.

Scheidel, W., 'Real wages in Roman Egypt: a contribution to recent work on pre-modern living standards', *Princeton/Stanford Working Papers in Classics*, 2008.

Scheper-Hughes, N., *Death without Weeping: the violence of everyday life in Brazil*, Berkeley, CA: University of California Press, 1992.

Scheper-Hughes, N., *Saints, Scholars, and Schizophrenics: mental illness in rural Ireland*, University of California Press, 2001.

Schumaker, J. F. (ed.), *Religion and Mental Health*, Oxford: Oxford University Press, 1992.

Scobie, A., *Apuleius and Folklore*, Folklore Society, 1983.

Scobie, A., 'Slums, sanitation, and mortality in the Roman world', *Klio* 68 (1986): 399–433.

Scott, J. C., *The Moral Economy of the Peasant: rebellion and subsistence in Southeast Asia*, New Haven, CT: Yale University Press, 1976.

Scott, J. C., *Weapons of the Weak: everyday forms of peasant resistance*, New Haven, CT: Yale University Press, 1985.

Scott, J. C., *Domination and the Arts of Resistance: hidden transcripts*, New Haven, CT: Yale University Press, 1990.

Scott, J. C., and Bhatt, N. (eds), *Agrarian Studies: synthetic work at the cutting edge*, New Haven, CT: Yale University Press, 2001.

Scullard, H. H., *Festivals and Ceremonies of the Roman Republic*, Thames and Hudson, 1981.

Shaw, B., 'Bandits in the Roman Empire', *Past & Present* 105 (1984): 3–52.

Shaw, B., 'The family in late antiquity: the experience of Augustine', *Past & Present* 115 (1987): 3–51.

Shaw, B., 'Our daily bread', *Social History of Medicine* 2 (1989): 205–13.

Shaw, B., 'The Passion of Perpetua', *Past & Present* 139 (1993): 3–45.

Shaw, B., 'Rebels and Outsiders', *Cambridge Ancient History*, vol. 11, Cambridge: Cambridge University Press, 2000, pp. 361–403.

Shelton, J., *As the Romans Did: a sourcebook in Roman social history*, Oxford: Oxford University Press, 1998.

Shershow, S. C., *Puppets and 'Popular' Culture*, Ithaca, NY: Cornell University Press, 1995.

Siegel, R. E., *Galen on Psychology, Psychopathology, and Function and Diseases of the Nervous System: an analysis of his doctrines, observations and experiments*, New York: Karger, 1973.

Simon, B., *Mind and Madness in Ancient Greece: the classical roots of modern psychiatry*, Ithaca, NY: Cornell University Press, 1978.

Singer, P. N., *Galen: selected works*, Oxford: Oxford University Press, 1997.

Sinnigen, W. G., 'Two branches of the late Roman secret service', *American Journal of Philology* 80 (1959): 238–54.

Slater, W. J., 'Pantomime riots', *Classical Antiquity* 13 (1994): 120–44.

Slater, W. J. (ed.), *Roman Theater and Society*, Ann Arbor, MI: University of Michigan Press, 1996.

Smith, J. Z., 'Towards interpreting demonic powers in Hellenistic and Roman antiquity', *ANRW* 2.16.1 (1978): 425–39.

Smith, M. M., *Sensory History*, Oxford: Berg, 2007.

Smith, R. C., and Lounibos, J. (eds), *Pagan and Christian Anxiety: a response to E. R. Dodds*, Lanham, MD: University Press of America, 1984.

Sopp, E., 'The gluttony of Garnsey', *Journal of Overnight Studies* 3 (2006): 189–90.

Stallybrass, P., and White, A., *The Politics and Poetics of Transgression*, Methuen, 1986.

Storch, R. D. (ed.), *Popular Culture and Custom in Nineteenth-century England*, Croom Helm, 1982.

Storey, J., *An Introduction to Cultural Theory and Popular Culture*, Prentice Hall, 1997.

Street, J., *Politics and Popular Culture*, Cambridge: Polity, 1997.

Szasz, T. S., *The Myth of Mental Illness: foundations of a theory of personal conduct*, Paladin, 1972.

Tanzer, H. H., *The Common People of Pompeii: a study of the graffiti*, Baltimore, MD.: Johns Hopkins Press, 1939.

Temkin, O., *Galenism: rise and decline of a medical philosophy*, Ithaca, NY: Cornell University Press, 1973.

Thomas, R., *Oral Tradition and Written Record in Classical Athens*, Cambridge: Cambridge University Press, 1989.

Thompson, E. A., *A Roman Reformer and Inventor: being a new text of the treatise De rebus bellicis*, Oxford: Clarendon Press, 1952.

Thompson, E. P., 'The moral economy of the English crowd in the eighteenth century', *Past & Present* 50 (1971): 76–136.

Toner, J. P., *Leisure and Ancient Rome*, Cambridge: Polity, 1995.

Townsend, M. L., *Forbidden Laughter: popular humor and the limits of repression in nineteenth-century Prussia*, Ann Arbor, MI: University of Michigan Press, 1992.

Treggiari, S., 'Lower class women in the Roman economy', *Florilegium* 1 (1979): 65–86.

van de Horst, P. W., 'Is wittiness unchristian? A note on *eutrapelia* in Eph. V 4', in T. Baarda, A. F. J. Klijn, and W. C. van Unnik (eds), *Miscellanea Neotestamentica*, Leiden: Brill, 1978, pp. 163–77.

van Hooff, A. J. L., *From Autothanasia to Suicide: self-killing in classical antiquity*, Routledge, 1990.

van Hooff, A. J. L., 'Female suicide: between ancient fiction and fact', *Laverna* 3 (1992): 142–72.

van Nijf, O. M., *The Civic World of Professional Associations in the Roman East*, Amsterdam: J. C. Gieben, 1997.

van Zoonen, L., *Entertaining the Citizen: when politics and popular culture converge*, New York: Rowman and Littlefield, 2005.

Vanderbroeck, P. J. J., *Popular Leadership and Collective Behavior in the Late Roman Republic (ca. 80–50 B.C.)*, Amsterdam: J. C. Gieben, 1987.

Versnel, H. S., 'Punish those who rejoice in our misery: on curse tablets and Schadenfreude', in D. R. Jordan, H. Montgomery and E. Thomassen (eds), *The World of Ancient Magic*, Bergen: Norwegian Institute at Athens, 1999, pp. 125–62.

Veyne, P., *Bread and Circuses: historical sociology and political pluralism*, trans. B. Pearce, Harmondsworth: Penguin, 1992.

Veyne, P., 'La "plèbe moyenne" sous le Haut-Empire romain', *Annales* (ESC) 6 (2000): 1169–99.

Volpe, G. (ed.), *San Giusto: la villa, le ecclesiae*, Bari: Edipuglia, 1998.

Wallace, R., and Williams, W., *The Acts of the Apostles: a companion*, Bristol: Bristol Classical Press, 1993.

Wallace-Hadrill, A., 'The social spread of Roman luxury: sampling Pompeii and Herculaneum', *PBSR* 58 (1990): 145–92.

Wallace-Hadrill, A., *Houses and Society in Pompeii and Herculaneum*, Princeton, NJ: Princeton University Press, 1994.

Wallace-Hadrill, A., *Rome's Cultural Revolution*, Cambridge: Cambridge University Press, 2008.

Webster, J., 'Creolizing the Roman provinces', *American Journal of Archaeology* 105 (2001): 209–25.

Wedeen, L., *Ambiguities of Domination: politics, rhetoric, and symbols in contemporary Syria*, Chicago, IL: University of Chicago Press, 1999.

Wegert, K., *Popular Culture, Crime, and Social Control in 18th-century Württemberg*, Stuttgart: F. Steiner, 1994.

Welsford, E., *The Fool: his social and literary history*, Faber and Faber, 1935.

Westermeyer, J. (ed.), *Anthropology and Mental Health*, The Hague: Mouton, 1976.

Wheelock, A. K., and Seeff, A., *The Public and Private in Dutch Culture of the Golden Age*, Associated University Presses, 2000.

Whitby, M., 'Maro the Dendrite: an anti-social holy man?', in M. Whitby, P. Hardie and M. Whitby (eds), *Homo Viator: classical essays for John Bramble*, Bristol: Bristol Classical Press, 1987, pp. 309–17.

Wiedemann, T., *Greek and Roman Slavery*, Croom Helm, 1981.

Williams, C. A., *Roman Homosexuality: ideologies of masculinity in classical antiquity*, Oxford: Oxford University Press, 1999.

Williams, S. C., *Religious Belief and Popular Culture in Southwark c.1880–1939*, Oxford: Oxford University Press, 1999.

Willis, P. E., *Learning to Labour: how working class kids get working class jobs*, Farnborough: Saxon House, 1977.

Wilson, L. M., *The Clothing of the Ancient Romans*, Baltimore, MD: Johns Hopkins Press, 1938.

Wirszubski, C., '*Audaces*: a study in political phraseology', *JRS* 51 (1961): 12–22.

Woolf, G., *Becoming Roman: the origins of provincial civilization in Gaul*, Cambridge: Cambridge University Press, 1998.

Woolgar, C. M., *The Senses in Late Medieval England*, New Haven, CT: Yale University Press, 2006.

Wright, D., and Digby, A., *From Idiocy to Mental Deficiency: historical perspectives on people with learning disabilities*, Routledge, 1996.

Wyke, M., 'Women in the mirror: the rhetoric of adornment in the Roman world', in L. Archer, S. Fischler and M. Wyke (eds), *Women in Ancient Societies: an illusion of the night*, Macmillan, 1994, pp. 134–51.

Yavetz, Z., 'The living conditions of the urban plebs in republican Rome', *Latomus* 17 (1958): 500–17.

Yavetz, Z., 'Plebs sordida', *Athenaeum* 43 (1965): 295–311.

Yavetz, Z., *Plebs and Princeps*, Oxford: Clarendon Press, 1969.

Yavetz, Z., 'Caligula, imperial madness and modern historiography', *Klio* 78 (1996): 105–29.

Yeo, E., and Yeo, S. (eds), *Popular Culture and Class Conflict 1590–1914: explorations in the history of labour and leisure*, Brighton: Harvester Press, 1981.

Index

Lightning Source UK Ltd.
Milton Keynes UK
UKOW03f1504140714

235090UK00006B/113/P